# *Contextual Authority and Aesthetic Truth*

*SUNY Series in Aesthetics and the Philosophy of Art*
*Mary C. Rawlinson*

*SUNY Series, The Margins of Literature*
*Mihai I. Spariosu*

# *Contextual Authority and Aesthetic Truth*

*James S. Hans*

*State University of New York Press*

Published by
State University of New York Press, Albany



Printed in the United States of America



For information, address State University of New York
Press, State University Plaza, Albany, N.Y., 12246

Library of Congress Cataloging in Publication Data

Hans, James S., 1950–
Contextual authority and aesthetic truth / James S. Hans.
p. cm.
Includes bibliographical references.
ISBN 0-7914-0917-1 (alk. paper) : $49.50. — ISBN
0-7914-0918-X
(pbk. : alk. paper) : $16.95
1. Authority. 2. Aesthetics. 3. Truth. I. Title
801'.9—dc20 91-12724
CIP

10 9 8 7 6 5 4 3 2 1

For Carola

# Contents

# Acknowledgments

This book is dedicated to Carola Sautter, my editor at SUNY Press, who has been more instrumental than anyone else over the past few years in encouraging my work and in relieving me of many of the onerous burdens that begin once one has completed a manuscript. I am most grateful for her help and friendship.

Permission has been granted from the following publishers for reprinting the works I make use of in the text:

Quotations from "What Is an Author?" are reprinted from Michel Foucault, *Language, Counter-Memory, Practice: Selected Essays and Interviews,* translated by Donald F. Bouchard and Sherry Simon, and edited by Donald F. Bouchard. Copyright © 1977 by Cornell University. Used by permission of the publisher, Cornell University Press.

References to the work of Max Weber are reprinted with permission of The Free Press, a Division of Macmillan, Inc. from Max Weber, *The Theory of Social and Economic Organization,* translated by A. M. Henderson and Talcott Parsons. Edited by Talcott Parsons. Copyright 1947, renewed 1975 by Talcott Parsons.

Selections from *Ecce Homo,* by Friedrich Nietzsche, translated by Walter Kaufmann, copyright © 1967 by Random House Inc, are reprinted by permission of Random House Inc.

Quotations from *The Wisdom of Confucius,* edited and translated by Lin Yutang, copyright 1938 and renewed 1966 by Random House Inc, are reprinted by permission of Random House Inc.

Lines from *The Odyssey of Homer* by Allen Mandelbaum, translation copyright © 1990 by Allen Mandelbaum, are used by permission of Bantam Books, a division of Bantam Doubleday Dell Publishing Group, Inc.

# Introduction:

## "What Matter Who's Speaking?"

In one of his most famous essays, Michel Foucault asks "What Is an Author?" and he proceeds to articulate a good number of the questions through which we have come to constitute our current ways of thinking. If the author is a function through which certain social forces have circulated, what purpose did the author serve, and what has changed now that we no longer grant a sacred status to such a figure? The question of the function of the author arises only in a world in which the gods have been declared dead, so Foucault's article would not have been possible without Nietzsche's original speculations on the self and its relation to the gods, and in some respects the question of the author is really only a subset of the larger question of the authority of God: what function did God's authority serve in our civilization, and what changes when He is no longer granted that authority? If one were to investigate only the modes of social circulation that were invested in God and the author, there would clearly be different functions that would apply to the two, for even if the investments are similar, the kinds of property rights that are linked to the function of God are considerably different from those to which the author lays claim. Similarly, the discourse of the book is of a different, if related, order to the discourse of the Book, and the distinction between the two would have to be elaborated with considerable care.

Our own critical efforts of late, however, have been chiefly devoted to an exposition of the ways in which power has circulated through the author and a demonstration of the various ways the author-function has filled out certain spaces within the social network. That many literature departments have come to devote more time to "cultural studies" than to "literary studies" reflects the influence of Foucault's work on power, and the questions Foucault raises in his essay on the author remain as compelling today as they were twenty years ago. So is his cautionary statement: "It is obviously insufficient to repeat empty slogans: the author has disappeared; God and man died a common death. Rather, we should reexamine the empty space left by the author's disappearance; we should attentively observe, along its gaps and fault lines, its new demarcations, and the reapportionment of this void; we should await the fluid functions released by this disappearance."[1] Within the matrix that was once occupied by the author, we have come to imagine any number of things, most of them having to do with power of one sort or another and with the uneven distribution of forces over the social field, but we have yet thoroughly to delineate precisely all the functions that the author took up. We know of the author-function as a repository of property rights; we understand the ways in which texts were turned into works with greater authority through the establishment of the author's special terrain; and we recognize the ways in which the decline in the authority of the church was in some respects connected to the increase in the authority of authors. But even if we have worked through these issues with great zeal, we have yet to address fully the most important question of all, the one of authority.

God is dead, the author is dead, and therefore there is no longer a location within the social space through which our discourse can be conveniently authorized. When the author disappears, so does his authority. When books become texts, they no longer carry the weight they had when the author's name on the title page conferred a special status upon them. So we have cultural studies, a mode of textual production that is devoted more or less to the endless articulation of the ruses of authorial discourse, the means through which prior writers have employed fictional strategies of one sort or another to confer a kind of authority on their work that was intrinsically unmerited. The need for such studies has been great, for our disciplines have been constructed on the basis of the authority of God and the author (and more recently the scientist as well) and thus need careful scrutiny into their origins and into the ways in which they dispose of their power.

If Foucault was concerned about the ways in which the death of God and the absence of the author had become empty slogans, though, our own sloganeering these days about the artificial ways in which various groups have blatantly abused power-relations in order to establish positions of unmerited authority equally threatens to get out of hand. It has certainly been necessary to perform the critique on our culture that we have been working on for a century now, and it will continue to be necessary to undertake this task. But at present it is still an inquiry that insufficiently questions its own authority even as it argues for the lack of grounds for authority in those authors it seeks to overwhelm with its discourse. We have found ourselves in the midst of an increasingly diffuse interregnum of sorts in which we know full well the ways in which the rules of the older order were flawed, yet we have nontheless been unable to work without them.

For there can be no mistaking the fact that those whose voices can be heard loudest today are at one and the same time those who celebrate the end of the old vision of authority—authority that is based on a ground, be it God or the sacred author or whatever—and yet assume that their own discourse should nevertheless have a recognizable authority. We need to understand clearly what the issues are here, for this kind of contradiction has been a grave problem ever since Nietzsche declared everything to be interpretation, and what is at stake is not simply the traditional problem of a violation of the law of non-contradiction or the potential hypocrisy of those whose discourse operates under the burden of this contradiction. It is easy enough to find in virtually any writer's work moments that are based on an authority that doesn't exist, just as it is the task of fools to point out that anyone who declares everything to be interpretation has therefore undermined the truth-value of his own utterance. If all statements are declared "false" in some sense, then how can the statement that all statements are false be true? These facile arguments fail to get at the larger question, which is under what kind of authority are the statements of a given writer made? The work that has issued from Nietzsche and Heidegger, from Derrida and Foucault, from the cultural critics of various stripes from feminists to anti-ethnocentrists, is all caught in the bind that it is based on a dissolution of the traditional concepts of authority at the same time that it fully expects its statements to have authority.

Inasmuch as I see the problem of authority in current discourse as the paramount one, I would like to return to one of its seminal sites, Foucault's essay, and I would do so by focussing on the question Foucault steals from Beckett: "'What matter who's speaking?'" (p. 138). Foucault suggests that it shouldn't matter who is speaking, that we ought to look forward to a day when such questions of authority no longer come up in the tedious way they do today: "We can easily imagine a culture where discourse would circulate without any need for an author. Discourses, whatever their status, form, or value, and regardless of our manner of handling them, would unfold in a pervasive anonymity. No longer the tiresome repetitions:

> 'Who is the real author?'
> 'Have we proof of his authenticity and originality?'
> 'What has he revealed of his most profound self in his language?'" (p. 138).

The writer clearly has grown weary of hearing all the banal questions about the author that our society is so eager to formulate, and Foucault is no doubt right to hope for a day when one will no longer be greatly concerned with the question of who the *real* author is, or the question of the writer's authenticity, or the issue of how the writer's central self was presented to us through the language of the text. These are not the kinds of problems we should be working on in an era when the author has disappeared, when the self upon which the author was constituted has long been declared dead. Foucault, we could say, is once again expressing his exasperation at the ways in which Western cultures have fetishized both self and author, reflecting his own sense that the fetishized self/author has so long been dead that we shouldn't be wasting our time on such matters. And I personally would agree wholeheartedly with him.

But the question of the author, the question of who is speaking, isn't only related to the tedious queries Foucault mentions in the above quotation; if that were so, his assertions would have less force than they do. The problem is today what it always was, that even when the author disappears the question of authority does not. If texts are not authorized by the author, then they must be authorized in some other way. If the self is dead and the author is dead, and we no longer resemble those fetishized products of an earlier age, the problem of authority has not gone away simply because we declared the self and the author to be dead. So Foucault is really making his task too easy here. It is one thing to say "What matter who's speaking?" when the question reflects on the issues of the fetishization of self and authority; it is another thing to say "What matter who's speaking?" when the question concerns how our discourse could conceivably circulate in a society in which no one fetishized authors anymore.

The most obvious manifestation of this problem is once again localized in the kind of contradiction that those who are opposed to writers like Foucault and Derrida love to point out: the writers who have done most in the past generation to argue against the fetishization of self and author (and thus have worked most strenuously against the standard modes of authorized discourse) have been most fetishized and relied upon for authorization by those within the intellectual community. Surely the speaker's fees for the most important of the cultural critics are considerably higher than those for the less well-known figures; surely a writer like Derrida could make a comfortable living by touring the United States and giving talks on the dissolution of authority and the end of the ontotheological world of discourse; surely a writer like Derrida (and Foucault while he was still alive) has become a major source of authority.

It is worth emphasizing that, at least in his earlier work, Derrida in particular went out of his way to seek to overcome this problem: one of the most important reasons for not remaining steadfast to any particular terminology is to avoid its reification into a form of grounded authority, and Derrida was well aware of this problem. If the word *deconstruction* today is used by everyone from the most serious of cultural critics down to the writers on gourmet food and the mass-magazine essayists who expound on international politics, Derrida can hardly be blamed for the misuse of the term. And no one could fault him for giving lectures throughout the world in order to provide his work with the largest possible audience. What else would one expect him to do? Nevertheless, it seems an unavoidable part of such an exercise that one inevitably gets fetishized; one becomes the ground of authorization for other people's utterances even if one seeks to put the problem of authorization out of play.

Given these circumstances, one could say that the problem inheres in a local context: the people of the United States have a great desire for fetishized figures, be they movie stars or deconstructionists, and they will have them, even if they embrace figures whose work is devoted to bringing an end to the fetishization of self and author. And there is enough of the herd mentality in the academic community to explain the ways in which writers like Derrida get fetishized even as their work argues against such a use of them. One could also say that the problem of the fetishization of figures like Derrida is a local one that comes about precisely because we have yet to get past our desire for authority, our need for an authorized discourse. It is possible, as Foucault says, to imagine a culture with different needs and expectations: we can indeed "easily imagine a culture where discourse would circulate without any need for an author." The question is whether we can imagine *ourselves* inhabiting such a culture.

We know that there were centuries when the question of authorship was framed differently than it is now, and it is worth remembering this: "the 'author-function' is not universal or constant in all discourse. Even within our civilization, the same types of texts have not always required authors; there was a time when those texts which we now call 'literary' (stories, folk tales, epics, and tragedies) were accepted, circulated, and valorized without any question about the identity of their author. Their anonymity was ignored because their real or supposed age was a sufficient guarantee of their authenticity" (p. 125). Important works can clearly exist outside of the author-function, as current scientific discourse makes most plain to us. But Foucault again slides past the real problem here by framing the issue in this way, for it is not a question of whether or not we can exist without authors or the author-function—we can clearly do that, and we may even want to; it is a question of how things get authorized once we dispense with the author.

The work of the last hundred years has done much to establish our difference from a number of the presuppositions upon which our culture was originally based. We could say that our difference is marked by the statement that God is dead, or by the assertion that everything is interpretation, or by the fact that the self (or the author) has dissolved into a multiplicity. Each of these statements is related to the others; each is in some senses no more than a restatement of the others. Yet we have failed to see that there are different problems inherent in each formulation, or rather, we have been unwilling to explore in any detail the problem intrinsic to each of them: how is authority conferred once God is dead, once everything is interpretation, once there is no self or author to ground and authenticate an utterance? We have devoted enormous amounts of energy to the question of discourse and the ways in which it circulates. We have killed off entire forests in our efforts to show the ways in which our forebears misappropriated the circulations of discourse for their own fundamentally unauthorized activities. We have even every now and then had something useful to say about the changed condition of the self in a groundless, unauthorized world, though far less attention has been paid to this problem than to the question of discourse. But we have not asked ourselves how humans authorize some forms of discourse and not others.

❦

To return to Foucault's formulation of the problem, we could say that if it is indeed possible for us to imagine a culture in which discourse would circulate without the legitimizing function of the author—and we may well end up concluding that that is precisely what we need to do, though the matter is far from determined at the moment—we would still have to deal with the question of how one form of discourse, or one manifestation of one form of discourse, is legitimized over another. If there are no grounds of authority, still some statements will become authorized in some fashion and others will not. Derrida will have an audience, let's say, and the question is *why?* If it is not "Derrida" who authorizes the work, and if its authority inheres in no particular self or author-function, as it doubtless does not, still people pay more attention, positive *and* negative, to Derrida's words than those of a great many others. Is this fact an accident of history? A reflection of the human (or the American) need to fetishize, to localize, to insist on authority? Or is there something in Derrida's work that *deserves* more authority than the work of many others? And if there is something in that work that deserves more authority, then obviously our facile discussions of modes of circulation of discourse and the fetishization of authors and the unfair disposition of various figures of authority are precisely that: facile. We have yet to discuss the serious matter that emanates from Nietzsche's work: how to determine what statements shall have authority from those that shall not in a cultural context in which the tacit assumption is that there is no ground for *any* authority.

If we ask ourselves why this question hasn't even been seriously asked for the most part, we could turn to the simpleminded way in which it has played itself out in the academic world, where the issue has quickly become little more than a litmus test for one's relative conservatism or liberality.

The conservatives assert that the horrible vacuum that "God is dead" brings about is simply not something that a culture can live with; the only possible vision to emanate from "God is dead" is a nihilistic one. There *must* be grounds for authority, or the will to power is all. Or so the conservatives have it. The liberals in turn would argue for the utter hopelessness of the conservative position in the late twentieth century, and they would do so with equal *moral* fervor: first, the conservative position is obviously thoroughly discredited by everything the West has learned in the past four hundred years; second, as a result, no one in good conscience could declare that there is any real mode of authorization to be had anymore. One can *repress* one's knowledge of the death of God, or one can acknowledge it even as one concedes the necessity for a ground of authorization, but neither position is the least bit tenable at this point in our history.

Even worse, inasmuch as we know that the former modes of authorization were used to usurp the power of others, we must recognize that *any* attempt to ground the forms of authorization will end up in the unfair oppression of the other in terms of which the ground will inevitably be defined. Inasmuch as grounds, like God, can only be determined on the basis of what they are not, that which is *not* the ground gets "marginalized" at the expense of those who come to occupy the holy center. Given the inevitable ways in which these forms of marginalization come about in *any* attempt to ground a form of discourse, the conservative position can be little more in the end than a continuing defense of the totally indefensible, the brutalizing dehumanizing that we have seen occur within all cultures, but most specifically within the West. Or so the "liberals" would have it.

Even if the lines of this debate are not quite as clearly drawn as these remarks suggest, there is more truth to the description than one might wish. And it is worth emphasizing that both sides of this polemic do indeed argue with the greatest of *moral* fervors. When I employ a term like "inter regnum," I do so deliberately, for both the conservatives and the liberals demonstrate through their rhetoric that what is at stake is the entire disposition of the culture, both in terms of the ways in which it conceives of itself and in terms of the ways in which the circulations of discourse—and thus the disposition of power—take place. The mutual revulsion of the groups further reflects the deep needs at the center of the debate and prompts us to ask what has been left out in the endless proselytizing on both sides.

If we look at the strengths and weaknesses of the conservative and liberal positions, we can begin to get an idea of what must still be considered as we reformulate our attitudes toward authority. One of the virtues of the conservative position is its relative clarity. In general, such critics are insistent that there are only two positions available when it comes to questions of authority: either it is grounded in some kind of absolute structure, or relativism and nihilism are the result. The standards that serve as ground are not always the same, at times specifically deriving from a Judeo-Christian structure of absolutes, at other times more generally humanistic in nature; but regardless of the nature of the absolutes, a belief in their necessity is paramount. There is both a strong and a weak position in this context, the strong one asserting that such values do indeed exist and are demonstrable, the weak one maintaining that societies cannot exist without a belief in absolutes, even if the disseminators of them do not necessarily grant them the credence they expect from others. The latter, more clearly elitist viewpoint, as manifested in one context by Leo Strauss, for example, bears certain similarities to Nietzsche's argument that the herd cannot bear very much reality and that it is therefore the goal of the strong to keep from them the knowledge that would devastate their lives. If Nietzsche was inclined to embrace this perspective himself, though, his goals in the end were directed elsewhere, for such an elitism is in its own way only another form of the decadence he decried throughout his work.

What both conservative viewpoints recognize is that humans have a limited tolerance for uncertainty and therefore desire the stability they perceive to exist within absolute frameworks. An ordered life of tradition and ritual serves to orient the individual to the world in a meaningful way and allows the individual to take up his or her space within the socius in a useful context. Given this, it would seem at a certain level that the question of whether or not absolutes exist is beside the point. What matters is that the general belief in them allows a society to dispose of itself in significant ways through an order that is based on such a belief.

The absolutes that tend to be upheld, naturally enough, are the ones that have formed the basis of Western societies for centuries, and the fact that those absolutes are therefore also attached to some of the more pernicious aspects of the civilization—from genocide to slavery to racism and sexism—is perceived to be merely an unfortunate side-effect of our long history. From a conservative perspective, there is nothing inherent in the nature of the absolutes upon which we base our societies that would inevitably lead to inhuman treatment of others, and so there is no reason why they should be discredited just because abuses have occurred under such regimes. And the conservatives would point out that even if the attacks on the basic values of the West seek to undermine the very nature of its practice, it by no means follows that it is deserving of such treatment. They would assert that whereas it is true that genocide, slavery, and other forms of abuse have been present in the West, they have existed elsewhere as well, and indeed they have been eliminated, or at least confronted, more conscientiously in the West than in other places on the globe. Our human rights record might not be exemplary, the conservatives would argue, but it is certainly superior to the performances of most other cultures and thus ought not to be a badge of shame. The very fact that we have worked more assiduously than other cultures to eliminate the abuses of our societies should demonstrate our greater nobility.

Instead of acceding to the notion that our values are deeply flawed because they are based on untenable absolutes, then, the conservative would be inclined to assert the great value of the absolutes and the societies that are based upon them. Instead of conceding the ethnocentrism inherent in the traditional Western perspective and acknowledging the inevitable relativism to be found in all modes of discourse, the conservative would argue that if there is no definitive evidence for absolutes, there is no compelling case against absolutes either, while there is a good deal of historical data to suggest that societies without strict beliefs and values are doomed to chaos and decline. Given the very real prospect of nihilism, of a world driven solely by the will to power, the conservative would argue that our only hope for the future would be a reestablishment of the fundamental values upon which our culture was originally based.

Of course, the conservative would have some difficulty establishing just what values our culture was originally based on, for one of the more obvious problems of a lack of grounds for authority comes in locating any beginning to a system of values. Once one steps into an historical awareness of existence, once one acknowledges the degree to which values are shaped by particular circumstances as they measure themselves out over large periods of time, it becomes impossible to locate the origin of *any* system of values. One must concede that the Judeo-Christian and the Greek elements of the West have their origins in the East, and given that, the purity of origins is as much a lost concept as is the search for the Holy Grail. No origins are forthcoming that would meet the needs of those who both believe in absolutes *and* seek to maintain intellectual integrity. In the most basic of ways this point has been driven home repeatedly over the past century and more as historical investigations into the composition of the Bible have demonstrated what a motley production it was. If one assumes that the Bible's origin must be pure and clean, research demonstrates the impossibility of such an origin. If one then shifts the terms of the argument to a more symbolic level, arguing that even if the particular composition of the various chapters is heterogeneous, the general text itself has a symbolic coherence and authenticity nonetheless, there is nothing left but belief to argue so. And if there is no arguing about beliefs, there is no further discourse that can take place either.

The liberal would assert that it is precisely this obvious lack of grounds that finally undermines the entire value system of the West. If the origin is not to be located—if the very *idea* of the, or even *an*, origin—has been discredited, then it is intellectually dishonest to adhere to the absolutes that are based on the (non-existent) origin. If everything is interpretation, then we can only lead ourselves into delusion by continuing to act as though definitive statements about the nature of our world will eventually be forthcoming. The only honorable course from this perspective would be to address seriously the lack of grounds—and the consequent lack of authority—to be found in the world that the West has engendered. And this investigation has led, for one reason or another, to a continuing and savage critique of the basic values of the West. It has itself engendered a seemingly endless flogging of the previously sacrosanct structure of the social system. And indeed, quite often the intellectual problem of interpretation slides so quickly into a cultural critique of the unfair disposition of the differences in the West that it is difficult to discern how (or if) the one is connected to the other.

In general it could be said that the liberal perspective is based on the fact that everything is interpretation, and that as a result all discourse is controlled by power mechanisms that seek to institute series of differences that maintain the status quo, that uphold the positions of those already in power. And there is no doubt that the one who controls the discourse also controls the disposition of power relations in the system. The problems that arise once one accepts the interpretive nature of existence—once, that is, one concedes the death of God and the dissolution of the self/author—can be established quite concisely in Foucault's list of new questions to ask now that we have had done with the older notions of author and authority:

> 'What are the modes of existence of this discourse?'
> 'Where does it come from; how is it circulated; who controls it?'
> 'What placements are determined for possible subjects?'
> 'Who can fulfill these diverse functions of the subject?' (p. 138)

The informed and up-to-date academic of the late twentieth century should be dealing with these questions in order to redress the flaws that have been found in traditional culture. If we used to *assume* the privileged mode of existence of various forms of discourse, now we are presumably compelled to investigate their different modes of existence in order to locate the power relations within them. In asking "Where does it come from; how is it circulated; who controls it?" we can begin to discern where the advantages lie in the disposition of differences in the overall circulation of discourse. In determining the various possible placements for subjects within the discourse, we can establish which modes of the subject are privileged and why, thereby laying bare the inherent bias that originally determined these placements and the powers that are upheld by them. And once we determine who can fulfill the requirements for the ideal subject posited in the discourse, we can locate in turn the power within the network of circulation.

Whether one is looking at various models of feminism, marxism, or new historicism, Foucault's questions have become the operative mechanism of our day, providing the orientation toward the circulations of discourse that posits the eventual overturning of the system of values upon which the older, absolutist view was based. And again, one needs to emphasize that much important and necessary work has been done as a result of these questions and their orientation. After the death of the author, this was one of the regions of discourse that was opened up that most needed to be addressed because of the inherent problems of the socius at large. Foucault's questions may be about the nature of interpretation, after all, but they are obviously and deliberately *engaged* questions as well, designed to redress the imbalances in the modes of circulation in the West.

Nevertheless, it is also worth emphasizing that in all too many respects the work of the cultural critics who have followed in Foucault's wake has been imbued with a kind of shrill narrowness that was at times to be found in Foucault's writings as well. If the conservative critics can be faulted for the ways in which they refuse to admit to any problems in their absolutist viewpoint, they are also right in arguing that turning everything that was previously good in the West into the evil demon that has destroyed the planet will not do either. It is not sufficient to address one kind of facile response to the world with another facile response, and all too often the critics of the left have assumed that the West can be responsible for only the evil in the world. All of the repression and unfair disposition of differences on the planet somehow seems to have its origin in the Western desire for hegemony, as if other societies—Islamic cultures, for example—don't have their own zealous desires for hegemony. A careful sifting of the relations within the modes of discourse has not really been seriously forthcoming as yet. We have many studies on how, say, the *feminine*—that is, the *good*—within this or that writer has previously been ignored, just as we have many studies on how the *male*—that is, the *bad*—within a writer reflects the distortions of the West; and we have a good number of studies that show how the West has distorted the third world and Islamic culture and Eastern cultures and Irish culture; but we don't have many serious appraisals of the very rich mixture Western culture is. There are glorifications, and there are denunciations, but not very much in the middle way at all.

A complex assessment of the strengths and weaknesses of the Western system of values need not solely be the province of the left, to be sure, though it is more likely to come from that arena simply because the tools of these critics seem to be more finely honed at the moment. But even such a critique fails to get at the other, more serious, problem of the criticism of the left, and that is that it can no more provide a justification for its own agenda than can the critics of the right. We have a fairly secure sense of some of the crucial limitations and biases of the West, and we have taken at least some serious steps to address them, but these two facts don't lead to the next one, which seems from the vantage point of the left to be that only its implementations of power are virtuous. The left has its own problem of legitimation, and inasmuch as it has for the most part refused to address it, it leaves itself vulnerable to its own logic. If, after all, there is nothing but interpretation, and if that leads to a world in which the endless exertions of the will to power are the sole dynamics for the circulations within our modes of discourse, then there is no good reason why a conservative critic ought to accede to the power dynamics of the left. Why *willingly* give up one's relative power within the system if that is all that is at stake in any case? One should defend one's turf as long as possible, until, that is, it becomes clear that it is strategically preferable to accede to the values of the prevailing dynamic.

The issue is not that this is the level to which the debate has been reduced, for it is not. It is rather that without a comprehensive articulation of modes of legitimation *beyond* the traditional forms of authorization, there are some serious flaws in the critique of the left, particularly because it has itself been so righteous in tone. If the traditional model of authority has been discredited, and if the existential vision of heroically-made subjective choices has likewise been rejected, what is to fill the void? Endless culture critique? Is that sufficient? I would argue to the contrary precisely because it lacks truly positive goals. It may *appear* to have a positive agenda, described in terms of the need to redress the shortcomings of the former system, but that very way of phrasing the issue suggests the essentially retrospective nature of the program of action. Under the banners of "openness" and "tolerance" and "non-difference" and the like, one tends to find only a different kind of closedness, intolerance, and redifferentiation. At the very least it is not obvious that the goal of the left is to redress the unfair implementation of differences. Instead of eliminating exclusionary structures, it seems more often than not devoted to imposing a different set of exclusionary differences at the expense of those currently in the authorized positions. This in itself might be one position to occupy, but it ought to be honestly taken up in the brutal terms of will to power instead of the more devious route of turning the guilt of the paternalistic West back on those who profited most from making the structure a function of the guilt one feels in the face of the authority.

One is led back to the question "What matter who's speaking?" If neither the right- nor the left-wing perspective has adequately addressed the question of who is speaking—the one because it refuses to concede the ways in which it doesn't finally matter who's speaking, the other because it cannot acknowledge that at some level it *always* matters who is speaking—we must seek for the ways in which this question has meaning. If the speaker cannot be considered the repository of authority, and that is the gist of our inquiries over the past century, does it follow that there is no repository to be found? If one takes the word *repository* seriously, one would have to conclude that indeed there can be no such location, for, as Derrida would have it, any such site would inevitably be another mark in the displaced chain of essences to be found from the very beginning in the West. It does no good to declare that the subject no longer has authority if one is inclined in turn to find another location for authority, for the crucial point is always the same: there can be no location—there can be no *ground*—for authority, unless one wishes to deny the place where our inquiries have taken us. A location or ground is not to be found outside of one's desire for it, and there would seem to be no way of overcoming this obstacle.

It is worth noting in this context that those who employ one of the more popular words today—the word *process*—are equally guilty of establishing grounds, even if they seek to temporalize the problem by suggesting that the authority doesn't inhere in any specific location or ground but rather in the process itself. This sounds very good indeed, but it fails to recognize that the process itself is totally meaningless until some location within it provides an interpretation of it, until, that is, some creature, usually human, seeks to authorize a particular way of looking at the process in which the various locations are involved. There can no more be an authority, or a mode of authorization, in process—in *any* process—than there can be such an authority from any particular location within any such process.

We are left, then, with a general reassessment of the relations between three interconnected alterations in our way of thinking: the assertion that everything is interpretation; the dissolution of the grounds of authority previously found in God, the self, or the author; and the cultural critique that has emanated from the recognition of the first two points. If the most important work of the past century has developed through these ideas, what has been left out of the linkages in this network that would better help us to address the question of authority that remains the fundamental issue of our time? If the fact that God is dead means that everything is interpretation, that there is no authority for our discourse, and if these facts have prompted us to realize the ways in which our modes of discourse have unfairly disposed of the differences of the system, what more is there to be said? What is left out of these connections? I would suggest that what remains to be articulated is the fact that these statements are not direct translations of the same problem but rather are crucially different manifestations of the same problem of authority, each expressing something useful that the other cannot, each suggesting in turn a different way of understanding the circulation of discourse that would prompt us toward a larger view of authority.

If we think first of the circulations surrounding the notion that God is dead, we can see how this was the opening assertion that our discourse was no longer authorized because it was God who was said to legitimize certain ways of being and condemn others. Likewise, the Bible was the repository of authorized wisdom and was thought to contain that which was necessary for the proper disposition of every human life. If one denies the central place of authority to God, then in a sense everything in the past hundred years follows: the self dissolves, the authority of the author disappears, everything becomes interpretation, and the culture as a whole comes to be seen as a defensive structure in which certain behavior is arbitrarily authorized in order to preserve the domain of those who control the circulations of discourse. If God is the ground of our authority, then we have truly stripped ourselves of authorization.

"What matter who's speaking?" is an utterance that follows directly from this, for the slogans about the death of God and the death of the self and the author are but links in the same chain. If that centralizing vision embodied by God no longer holds together, neither does the central vision of self that was molded in the image of God, nor does the self's authority hold any more legitimacy than the now-dead God; for the self gained its power from its ability to assert a knowledge of the authority of God, to claim mastery over the sacred Word. Likewise, if the self is no inherent repository for any legitimating authority because there is no essential ground to its activities, the author of the book, the locus of secular authority in various universes of discourse, can no longer possess the near-sacred powers of genius, the one who has been inspired and who therefore brings back from the gods the most profound knowledge. The author becomes the author-function, a locus of property rights, a neutralizing function in a system of discourse that disposes of the available benefits within the socius.

It is worth remembering, however, what Foucault points out in his essay: discourse did indeed at one time have a privileged, albeit dangerous, role in the circulations of society. If it is true that the invention of the author is a relatively recent phenomenon in the course of human history, it is also true that the space this function came to occupy was at one time a risky location of uncertain consequences: "In our culture—undoubtedly in others as well—discourse was not originally a thing, a product, or a possession, but an action situated in a bipolar field of sacred and profane, lawful and unlawful, religious and blasphemous. It was a gesture charged with risks long before it became a possession caught in a circuit of property values. But it was at the moment when a system of ownership and strict copyright rules were established (toward the end of the eighteenth and beginning of the nineteenth century) that the transgressive properties always intrinsic to the act of writing became the forceful imperative of literature" (p. 124, 25). Once the author transforms this space into a location of property values, into a place that establishes certain rules of consumption, the danger of the transgressive properties of authorial discourse begins to disappear, even as over time the author loses force.

We might ask, though, what happens to the transgressive properties intrinsic to writing once the author dies? What becomes of that bipolar field of sacred and profane and its uncertain circulations? Because we have acknowledged the death of God and the author, we think we have eliminated the riskiness of this field. After all, once the sacred itself disappears, there is no longer a bipolar field of action, and it was the play between the two fields that engendered the risk of transgression. This is the region of discourse that Foucault himself cannot get at because he assumes that the death of the author and the full implementation of capitalist circulations eliminate the transgressive properties of both the author and of discourse itself.

In terms of the self that has dissolved upon the death of God, the issue remains the same. If there is no essential self to guarantee or authenticate the circulation of discourse, still there is a location that bears some responsibility for its participation in the flows of language. It may be shorn of its religious authority, and it may therefore have no grounds for its utterances, but somewhere within that location that the self is there must reside authority of some sort. Foucault and the cultural critics would be inclined to assert that the authority of such a self comes from its participation within the circulation of certain flows of discourse, or, to put it more conventionally, the authority of the self in fact resides in the class or social unit that authorizes the discourse that any particular self might speak.

Authorization becomes dispersed into the interstices of the discourse itself, though again Foucault is careful not to fetishize language either:

> In granting a primordial status to writing, do we not, in effect, simply reinscribe in transcendental terms

> the theological affirmation of its sacred origin or a critical belief in its creative nature? To say that writing, in terms of the particular history it made possible, is subjected to forgetfulness and repression, is this not to reintroduce in transcendental terms the religious principle of hidden meanings (which require interpretation) and the critical assumption of implicit significations, silent purposes, and obscure contents (which give rise to commentary)? Finally, is not the conception of writing as absence a transposition into transcendental terms of the religious belief in a fixed and continuous tradition or the aesthetic principle that proclaims the survival of the work as a kind of enigmatic supplement of the author beyond his own death? (p. 120).

As a response to Derrida's work, this argument against the foundational status of language would appear to be more misreading than cogent attack, but it does demonstrate that the authority of discourse for Foucault resides not in some otherworldly enigma—as in Heidegger's statement that "Language speaks man"—but rather in the simple social circulation of interest. The language of the bourgeoisie, if you will, authorizes the actions of the bourgeoisie. It is as simple as that, and this is the central premise of most current cultural criticism. With the death of the self and the author, discourse becomes nothing more than the circulation of class interest, and thus the goal is to articulate the ways in which those interests shape the flows of language.

At the same time, there remains the nagging thought that somehow it *does* matter who is speaking, even if that is not precisely the way we might wish to formulate the matter. Again, it does make a difference if it is someone like Derrida who speaks to us or someone with no reputation at all. Is Derrida's reputation exclusively a function of the interests of the classes who control the flows of academic discourse? Perhaps so, but I am inclined to think otherwise, and the easiest way to get at what is not accounted for by such interests is to review the basic facets of the author-function as Foucault conceives them. He tells us that "A name can group together a number of texts and thus differentiate them from others. A name also establishes different forms of relationships among texts" (p. 123). In this way the inscription "Derrida" marks out the location of a series of texts for easy identification. We can recognize *L'écriture et la différence* as a text of a particular sort because the words "Jacques Derrida" are listed above the title, marking it as a different space from that occupied by, say, the works of Sartre or Nietzsche. And if we include *De la grammatologie, Marges* and the other texts upon which "Derrida" is inscribed, we have clearly differentiated these texts from others on the basis of Derrida's name. Foucault doesn't tell us why we should want to do this and seems to suggest that this is no better a way of naming texts than the Library of Congress system, that it is simply one way of grouping texts. And this is true enough in its own way, but even given the death of the author, we might be inclined to think that this grouping of texts under the rubric of "Derrida" has something useful to offer. It may not be the kind of coherence and essentializing authority we used to confer upon authors, but still there is something important in this way of collocating texts that Foucault fails to discuss. At the very least, what is left out is the fact that some people are likely to find the grouping highly attractive precisely because of the name attached to it, or highly revolting as a result of the same name.

Foucault also tells us that "Discourse that possesses an author's name is not to be immediately consumed and forgotten; neither is it accorded the momentary attention given to ordinary, fleeting words. Rather, its status and its manner of reception are regulated by the culture in which it circulates" (p. 123). "Derrida," we might say, marks out certain texts as more than ephemeral discourse and suggests that they should not simply be consumed and forgotten but rather should be put on the shelf for further reading and consideration. Perhaps most tellingly, we are informed that the status and manner of reception of such a text is "regulated by the culture in which it circulates." As always, Foucault doesn't tell us precisely how or why a culture would declare a text like *La dissémination* to be significant and therefore would choose to govern its manner of reception in order to disseminate it in particular ways, but we can assume once again that this is a question of *interest*. If the culture stands to gain from the authority of Derrida, it will regulate the reception of his texts in such a way that they receive cultural valorization. If it perceives Derrida's work to be threatening to its ways of disposing of the discourse, then it will regulate the texts in a way that will deauthorize them, at least theoretically.

One might ask, though, why a culture like ours wouldn't simply try to ignore Derrida's work, since it clearly is not in the best interests of those with the major interests, and one might argue that his work has indeed been more or less ignored, most tellingly in the way that its vital forces have been contained by a kind of narrow academic discourse on "him" that has stripped the writing of any potential threat. Instead of an indictment of culture, "Derrida," we might say, has become yet another version of "How to do things with words," and this is the way in which the culture chooses to regulate the circulation of his texts. Still, the same question remains in play: why not strip him of his author-function altogether? Why is it that a culture with the power to regulate discourse, as Foucault suggests it can, would even allow Derrida the kind of neutralized authority he has received in the United States? There is something in Foucault's formulation of the circulations of discourse that ignores this problem, ignores even more the ways in which totalitarian countries have truly tried to erase their authors by refusing to publish their works. In such contexts, one might think, the author-function has indeed been regulated by the culture and its interests, and yet we know that in some respects such banishment of authors gives them greater authority than if they simply had been ignored. If this too is true, it is not enough to say that the name of the author gives the culture a way of regulating the flows of discourse, for if it does that, it is also a way of grouping phenomena that are not completely in the control of those with the primary interests. The transgressive properties of discourse remain operative even after the death of the author, and this is something that Foucault's essay ignores.

In addition, Foucault explains how the author-function is different from the name of an individual: "Derrida" as author does not point to that living, breathing creature who lives in France, the United States, and elsewhere in the late twentieth century, but rather reflects on the disposition of the discourse of the culture in general: "The author's name is not a function of a man's civil status, nor is it fictional; it is situated in the breach, among the discontinuities, which gives rise to new groups of discourse and their singular mode of existence" (p. 123). Here Foucault seems to be taking the author most seriously, perhaps conferring on the title more than it always suggests. But what he says certainly applies to a name like "Derrida," for one can unquestionably discern the ways in which this name is "situated in the breach" between civil status, fictional construct, and regulatory device. The name "Derrida" does indeed give rise to new groups of discourse and thus has altered the circulations of the culture. The very way in which Derrida's texts are disseminated all over the library by the Library of Congress's system of classification suggests that "Derrida" exists in the breach between the traditional modes of bibliographical classification. His texts don't fit the ordinary categories and thus demonstrate their singular mode of existence. So we could say that the author's name is a mark of a change in the flows of cultural discourse. Those whose writing fails to alter the flows are by definition purveyors of that which is to be consumed and forgotten; those whose writing bears a name worth remembering (because of the interests of the culture? of whom?) manifest this worth by the ways in which they have changed the discourse.

To say as much, however, is to suggest that authors deserve the authority they have received. If they have changed the flows of discourse, then their names are not arbitrary markers in the circulation of cultural self-interest but rather are signs of alterations within that mode of circulation. The author is legitimate in a way that the ephemeral writer is not, or so it would seem. And if this is so, then there is an authority to the author that is not accounted for in Foucault's essay. The author Derrida, we might say, has legitimately acquired a certain kind of authority, even if in another sense it doesn't really matter who is speaking. If the authority that Derrida's work asserts could just as easily be covered by another name, if it doesn't inhere in some essential self that Derrida possesses, still there is something more than an author-function at work here. The name of the author may in some respects be little more than the culture's way of marking the shifts in the flows of its own discourse, and those shifts may in some respects be a reflection of the culture's own self-interests (though this is questionable in my view, for it seems equally plausible to assume that a great many changes in the flows of a given culture's discourse are resisted by the culture rather than simply regulated by it), but there is still something more there, the mark of a change, the reflection of authority that exclaims that *this* work has more legitimacy than *that* work.

"Derrida" is a marker of a certain kind of authority, an authority not necessarily to be regulated by the culture and its interests. The culture may seek to neutralize the authority of "Derrida," and it may be fairly successful at this. In this way it is possible to argue that the author's name is a mark in the same way a scar is: it denotes a breach in the flow of a culture's discourse, a threat to the system that was contained by the neutralizing functions that also go with the name, the tendencies toward categorization and reduction. Instead of a transgression that has effects, "Derrida" turns the texts into objects of consumption and becomes the equivalent of a cut in the tissue that was quickly healed. In this way authors become the hidden history of the wounds of a culture, the ways of establishing the sites of formerly toxic flows. Even in this scenario, though, which I would characterize as the most cynical formulation possible, the scar of the author contains authority, remains a repository for authentic discourse. Once all authors are declared to be the scars of a culture's history, one has an opening to a different history of the culture, a new approach to the circulations of discourse that revises the lines of authority in all sorts of compelling ways. Foucault's essay minimizes the value of this kind of authority, yet it can be the locus of great power in a society.

If Foucault is inclined to ignore the very real effects authors have through their authority, and if he is disposed to see their marks simply as means through which a culture regulates itself, there are good reasons why he thinks in these terms. He clearly believes that "the function of an author is to characterize the existence, circulation, and operation of certain discourses within a society" (p. 124), and once he is committed to this viewpoint, he has difficulty seeing much else. This is not to deny that authors do indeed "characterize the existence, circulation, and operation of certain discourses within a society," for they unquestionably do that. But they are also instrumental in changing the flows of those discourses, something considerably more powerful than a mode of characterization. If they are the means through which we come to think of our cultural history, the ways in which we locate the signal achievements within the circulations of society, so much the better. But to see them only in those terms is to ignore the ways they have changed those circulations and to hide from the ways in which their work was a response to certain compelling phenomena, positive or negative, within their own flows.

The leveling language of "certain discourses within a society" is such that it deprives the author of a serious context out of which to write; the author is seen only as something that is placed within a flow of language, a mode of discourse that is taken up and explored through the writing. If this is what an author does, it is conceivable that an author also does much more. If it is possible for an author to gain his or her authority on the exclusive basis of the ways in which the flows of discourse are regulated from the author's location within them, it is also possible to think of that author as gaining authority from the experiences that are lived in the midst of the flows of discourse. Admittedly, "experience" is a word with its own essentializing history, and it is certainly not sufficient to hang an entire theory of authority on, but Foucault's language is so insistently two-dimensional that one wishes at times for something with a little more life in it.

One way or the other, though, authors are part of the economic system that so greatly determines the flows of cultural discourse in the twentieth century, and this is worth emphasizing. The books that authors write "are objects of appropriation; the form of property they have become is of a particular type whose legal codification was accomplished some years ago" (p. 124). This is perhaps the most important way in which the authority of authors is finally regulated and neutralized, for once something becomes an object of appropriation, it runs the risk of being perceived as nothing more than an object, a marker of certain property rights within the social distribution of such rights. And once a book is perceived in this light, any authority it might have is at least dissipated, if not almost completely eliminated. If the author is dead, that is because his work has become nothing more than a marker of property, a sign of possession rather than a transgressive action that actively works to alter the flows of discourse.

The strength of Foucault's analysis comes from his ability to see the ways in which culture puts to use what he characterizes as the author-function. If the intent of the essay is a complete demystification of authorial status in our age, then Foucault has done a good job of showing the ways in which the author-function is contaminated by cultural flows that might appear to be unrelated to its presumed august status. Most specifically, he clearly demonstrates that "the 'author-function' is tied to the legal and institutional systems that circumscribe, determine, and articulate the realm of discourses; it does not operate in a uniform manner in all discourses, at all times, and in any given culture; it is not defined by the spontaneous attribution of a text to its creator, but through a series of precise and complex procedures; it does not refer, purely and simply, to an actual individual insofar as it simultaneously gives rise to a variety of egos and to a series of subjective positions that individuals of any class may come to occupy" (p. 130, 31). One cannot help but come away from "What Is an Author?" with an enriched sense of the cultural dynamics that were (and are) involved in the creation of such a creature, just as one cannot help but recognize Foucault's contribution to the ongoing debate about the problem of authority in an unauthorized culture such as ours. But whereas Foucault is a brilliant expositor of those ways in which a given culture regulates the flows of discourse for its own purposes, he is not as strong on the ways in which that culture confronts more positive kinds of changes. The tacit assumption of Foucault's work has generally been that culture is an exclusively conservative medium dominated by the death instinct: its sole goal is the eternal return of the same, the perpetuation of the status quo, and yet at the same time Foucault suggests that culture is also determined to extend the interests of those who control the circulations of discourse into still other areas of play.

And it may be true that in the modern era in particular cultures have devoted most of their time to reacting to changes that were always emerging faster than their ability to control them or deal with them meaningfully. The very idea of an author as scar tissue suggests precisely this vision of culture, an organism whose role has become little more than a practice of immunology, trying to keep the foreign substances out of the body politic in order to perpetuate the interests of those currently in power. There is far more truth to this vision of culture than many would like to admit, and the delineation of the ways in which these forces of culture mobilize themselves over the entire range of discourses is an endless and necessary task, but one must also finally ask about potentially positive contributions a culture in general might make, just as one might ask what is left of value in the concept of the author. If the author is in some senses little more than an author-function today, and if the authority of the author has thereby been absorbed into the circulations of property rights and appropriation, the author is nevertheless capable of authority, and we know no more about how this authority accrues today than we did at the beginning of our era. What we have learned in a sense has been little more than an extrapolation of Machiavelli and his discussion of the ways in which those in authority should mobilize their resources according to the threat and the audience.

Our investigations into culture still have not adequately addressed the fact that it *does* matter who's speaking. "Where does Derrida get his authority?" and "Why are some books read more than others?" are questions whose answers are not finally exhausted by cultural critique, by the argument from interest, by the claims of those who seek to regulate the flows of discourse within a social system. So where does Derrida get his authority? There is nothing inherent in his self that compels our assent when we read his work, nor are his credentials such that they would necessarily legitimate him in our eyes, though they do not work against his arguments. The language of the texts themselves, often opaque and elliptical, occasionally brilliant pieces of rhetoric, is not sufficient in itself to demand authority, tacitly or otherwise. The arguments of the texts work against the general interests of the culture and the particular interests of many individuals as well, so the legitimacy does not spring from the easy acceptance of facile truths or half-truths. There would seem to be no clear reason why Derrida's work should carry any authority at all; at the least the reasons remain obscure within cultural criticism.

One could argue that Derrida's work garnered the assent it did in the United States because its appeal was such that it fit the spirit of the times. Given the increasingly consumer-oriented nature of the intellectual climate in the United States—a place where the need for a new rage often seems more important than what that new rage might be—Derrida could be seen to have profited from the desire for a different fashion. Likewise, people schooled in the rebelliousness of the '60s might find Derrida's work appealing because it calls into question virtually all of the values of the status quo—Derrida as continuation of the problems of the generation gap manifesting themselves in new ways in the 1980s. Or Derrida's appeal could be seen to derive from the cynicism that also emanated from some circles as a result of the '60s, even if Derrida could hardly be construed as a cynic himself. Although he is excruciatingly careful in his arguments to avoid a simplistic kind of nihilism, it is easy enough to imagine others finding such an appeal within texts that are devoted constantly to erasing the traces that never cover an origin to begin with. The absence of origin, again, can easily enough be construed as an argument for the will to power, a position that has considerable appeal to those who think—erroneously in my view—that the "failures" of the '60s leave one with no alternative but to embrace one's own will to power.

There are other possible explanations for Derrida's authority, and no doubt most of them would be at least partially applicable. Surely Derrida *was* something of a trendy figure for a while, selling the flashiest goods on a fairly decadent intellectual market, and this must have attracted some readers. Surely his work *can* easily enough be construed as being based on a fundamental nihilism, even if it is not, and so the appeal of such a viewpoint doubtless attracted others. And surely the need for a new generation to assert its views in contrast to the prevailing powers of the academy also had something to do with the spread of his reputation. In the midst of these reasons for the relative success of Derrida's work, one must add a collateral one as well: his work was so threatening to some that it created a great furor, and the "negative" publicity of the debates in the journals in the '70s did much to add to the cachet of the work. Add to this the American love of the Gallic sensibility, and there are more than enough cultural reasons to account for the authority Derrida achieved in the United States.

The wave of Derridamania has somewhat abated by now, though, and his texts are still being read, so it may be that there is something more to them that that which an accounting via the assessment of the flows of discourse and power-relations would suggest. Maybe Derrida's work has *merit;* maybe there is something in it that engenders authority on its own, outside of the subject of Derrida himself, outside of the authorizations of intellectual communities and academic fetishes. The authority does not reside in Derrida, nor in the traditions he works out of, nor in the particular language he uses or the orientation he takes toward the past; whatever it is, it cannot be found in the logical places, cannot, in some respects, be found at all. For the authority of Derrida's work exists for the same reasons that some books are read more than others: there is something in the work itself that compels our attention.

Derrida's writing, it should be said, went out of its way to break down the borders between texts and disciplines. This, after all, is what the death of the author is all about: no more fetishizing of individual authors or their autotelic texts. No more assumptions about the autonomy of a book—from now on we are to exist in an intertextuality of signs that defies the very notion of authority inhering in the work of a particular text. And indeed, Derrida himself would seem to have a problem in dissolving the possibility of authority even as he must just as clearly hope that his own writing carries some legitimizing tendencies of its own. He may be conscientious enough not to want to try to start a Derrida industry, just as he was intent on avoiding as much as possible the reification of his deconstructive enterprise. But one would assume that Derrida hoped his work would have effects, and for it to have effects, it must command authority. It may point to relations in other texts; it may in its own way simply be part of the endless play of signs; and it certainly is careful to demonstrate its own lack of closure; but the texts are meant to have effects, and to the extent that this is true, they must be at least generally localizable.

If "Derrida" is a marker of the property rights of a series of texts, it is also a marker of certain interests that are not understood in the same way in any other regions of the modes of discourse currently available to us: in this sense, Derrida is indeed an "author," even if he lives after the death of the author. If "Derrida" is a corporate entity that serves the purposes of the regulators of discourse, whoever those people might be, there can still be no denying the transgressive aspects of his texts and the fact that we can locate those transgressions in particular places, however much they are dependent on what came before them and what will come after them. If "Derrida" is a function of a fetishization process that turned both him and his work into consumer commodities or into symbolic demons for certain cultural conservatives, it is also a locus of authority. The point is so obvious that it shouldn't even need to be made: if "Derrida" were not at this juncture a mark of *some* kind of authority, his name would not be as well known as it is, and his language would not have percolated down to the broadest of cultural contexts. So how is Derrida going to deal with the authority to be found somewhere in his work? *Can* he deal with this? Can Foucault? I think not. And therein lies the rub, for the mastery of their arguments compels a certain kind of assent from the conscientious reader even as the authority of the texts undermines a good bit of the rhetoric. It *matters* that it is Derrida or Foucault who is speaking. It matters a great deal. The imitators are easily recognized as imitators.

So whence comes the authority of a Derrida or a Foucault? Or for that matter, where does the authority of *any* text come from? The conservative plea for absolutes is inevitably a response to our situation that seems wholly inappropriate given our understanding of human language and human communities, and the nihilism of the will to power can offer no arguments whatsoever for authority of the kind that Derrida or Foucault have—its only arguments for authority would have to be of the totalitarian variety and would have to be imposed from the top down simply because by definition those who wield greater will to power command greater authority. The religious absolutism no longer works, yet nihilism cannot even account for its own relative success in the world. What is left?

In a way, perhaps nothing that is nameable, nothing that would satisfy either the absolutist or the nihilist. That is part of the problem of authority, for in the end both the nihilist *and* the absolutist are absolutists; the one is simply a frustrated absolutist, the other a nostalgic one. Beyond those mirror images, there is the muddle of the middle. There are ways of speaking about authority that, as with all other arguments, prompt assent only from those who are inclined to see things that way from the beginning. One could, for example, speak in fairly traditional terms about authority and say that there are some texts that seem to articulate a series of responses to the human world that strike some members of some communities in important ways, either because the way in which the questions of the text are formulated manage to address the needs of the time in useful ways or because the text has found a way of addressing the basic factors of being human in a way that would be useful to anyone who shared some basic assumptions about what it means to be human. We know that some rhetorical contexts are more powerful than others, and we know that some visions of existence seem more compelling, more comprehensive, more *right,* than others. And if our sense of these things is always conditioned by our cultural expectations and our placement within the flows of discourse, regardless of the degree to which we are among the regulators of cultural discourse, it still doesn't follow that all writing is of equal value. One could argue that value is always solely determined by interest, and those texts which finally come to carry authority are the ones that most clearly reflected and directed the interests of those who regulate the discourse—that is certainly a popular argument these days—but it doesn't account for all the facts, even if it does bring to the fore some interesting problems that need constantly to be dealt with.

Again, the basic argument is age-old: does the authority of Sophocles stem from his placement within the sociocultural flows that continue to be regulated in part by his work? Does the authority of Shakespeare derive from the way we have fetishized his texts over the past couple of hundred years? Are some texts more worth reading than others? Yes, unquestionably so, as any honest human being would have to admit. Are the value judgments that are involved in determining what is and is not worth reading contingent on a whole series of "subjective" or ethnocentric features that have nothing in particular to do with authority in the older sense of the term? Yes, again unquestionably so. Even as each reader has his or her own particular proclivities, interests, preoccupations and the like, so too is each reader prompted to seek out texts that unknowingly reinforce biases and prejudgments about the nature of things that form the very basis of the reader's vantage point on the world. As a result of these contingent circumstances, is it the case that there are inevitably texts that should command authority but don't because they don't properly reflect the interests of those who play key roles in regulating the discourse of the socius? Undeniably. But it *still* matters who's speaking, even if the particular name is no more than a marker of a certain region within a larger field of discourse.

❦

For a long time this question of authority was addressed through the cliché of the "test of time." Over the centuries, "time" would tell if, say, Shakespeare's authority was a function of local circumstances and contingent issues or rather a reflection of recurrent—and important—human situations. We all know that time cannot tell anything, and that this expression was only another way of conceding the very real limitations inherent in any one reader's viewpoint—or any one *group* of readers', or any given *epoch's* for that matter. Yet we are more likely to point out the absurdity of saying that "time will tell" when we know that time tells nothing than we are inclined to recognize the virtue of that humility in the face of the authority that some texts maintain over large stretches of cultural territory. In its own way, "time will tell" acknowledges that there are no absolute structures to be revealed by the texts that have authority, for by definition if they revealed those absolute structures, there would be nothing left for time to tell: we would all be able at once to recognize the inherent authority of the text. It is also true that many who would use the test of time as a marker of authority assume that their own values are indeed absolute and above bias and interest, and they are clearly misguided in thinking so. Nevertheless, there remains the residue of authority that cannot be wished away, even by those who find it to be the most inconvenient fact of all.

Foucault demonstrates his own clear awareness of authority in his essay when he seeks to nominate a new category of "transdiscursive practices," and when he tries to account for the effect of writers like Marx and Freud:

> But I believe that the nineteenth century in Europe produced a singular type of author who should not be confused with "great" literary authors, or the authors of canonical religious texts, and the founders of sciences. Somewhat arbitrarily, we might call them "initiators of discursive practices."
>
> The distinctive contribution of these authors is that they produced not only their own work, but the possibility and the rules of formation of other texts. (p. 131)

Whether or not the distinctive feature of the work of Freud and Marx is that it produced the possibility and the rules of formation of other texts is something that remains to be seen. One might say that the notion has potential value, but one might also argue that it is an oblique way of getting around the problem of *authority.* Freud and Marx, we might say, were *major* figures, were writers whose texts commanded great authority. But how is a writer like Foucault to deal with this authority? How can he even talk about it given the death of the author, the self, and God? He can invent a phrase like "initiators of discursive practices," which, among other things, is a way of saying that the work of Freud and Marx had an enormous effect on those who followed after. It may be worth pointing out that its effects were different from those of the great scientists, for it could not be built on in the way that science develops from earlier stages; that the works were not like the canonical religious texts because they did not demand the same kind of absolutist authority (or at least they didn't *receive* such unquestioned authority), nor did they seek to institute a transcendental regime; that they were not finally like literary texts either, for their writings had effects that transcended any particular discursive context (of course "great" novelists, poets and dramatists can also transcend their particular context, but they cannot inaugurate the rules of formation of other discursive contexts, and so they clearly are different in kind from the likes of Freud and Marx). Beyond these useful details, though, is the fact that the effects of these writers need to be noted and the authority accounted for.

Can Foucault account for an authority he acknowledges but still seems to slide past? He doesn't seem to do so in "What Is an Author?" He further explains his own useful distinction, but it doesn't help us to get at the question of authority: ". . . Marx and Freud, as 'initiators of discursive practices,' not only made possible a certain number of analogies that could be adopted by future texts, but, as importantly, they also made possible a certain number of differences. They cleared a space for the introduction of elements other than their own, which, nevertheless, remain within the field of discourse they initiated" (p. 132). I would argue that in some respects this is saying little more than that Marx and Freud have stood the test of time. True, we know, thanks to Foucault's remarks, that one way of characterizing this process as it applies to these two figures in particular has to do with the way they—in contrast to the major figures of earlier centuries—initiated transdiscursive practices and therefore had heterogeneous effects both on the themata of other modes of discourse and on the formation of their rules. But this speculation is only one way among others of accounting for the fact that the work carried great authority and stood the test of time.

It is worth emphasizing that, unlike many of those who have followed in his wake, Foucault knows that he doesn't quite understand how the effects of Freud and Marx are to be charted. He takes a stab at it with his discussion of them as initiators of discursive practices, and he explains how these writers' works bear constant returns that differ from those to be found among the great writers of other eras. But he also asserts that "A last feature of these returns is that they tend to reinforce the enigmatic link between an author and his works. A text has an inaugurative value precisely because it is the work of a particular author, and our returns to it are conditioned by this knowledge" (p. 136). Far from declaring the utter pointlessness—or the utter cynicism—of the author-function, Foucault here admits that one way of speaking about the great authority of the works of Freud and Marx is to acknowledge the ways in which we see again and again that there is an "enigmatic link between an author and his works." Indeed, Foucault maintains that only works that compel our regular reassessment of the enigmatic relationship between writer and text can conceivably have any inaugurative value. It is the very particularity of the author, somehow, in his mysterious link to his writing, that engenders the authority that we find in this class of texts.

Foucault, then, has not denied that some texts have authority and others don't any more than he has argued that all writing is of equal value. On the contrary, he himself works within his essay to establish his own canons of value and authority, for clearly there is something preeminent in the inaugurative status of the work of Freud and Marx, something that confers greater value on their writing precisely because it has constituted the rules of formation for so many other writers. Just as clearly, these are writers whose work has had a great effect on Foucault himself, registering their authority over his own discourse. But "the enigmatic link between an author and his works" remains a recessive marker in "What Is an Author?" One might even say that it represents the uncharacteristic moment when Foucault seems almost ready to concede that actual humans write the texts we read. And if this is truly something of a lapse within the overall rhetoric of the essay, it is worth pointing out because it marks such a vivid contrast to the returning point of the essay near the end:

> Is it not possible to reexamine, as a legitimate extension of this kind of analysis, the privileges of the subject? Clearly, in undertaking an internal and architectonic analysis of a work (whether it be a literary text, a philosophical system, or a scientific work) and in delimiting psychological and biographical references, suspicions arise concerning the absolute nature and creative role of the subject. But the subject

> should not be entirely abandoned. It should be reconsidered, not to restore the theme of an originating subject, but to seize its functions, its intervention in discourse, and its system of dependencies. We should suspend the typical questions: how does a free subject penetrate the density of things and endow them with meaning; how does it accomplish its design by animating the rules of discourse from within? Rather, we should ask: under what conditions and through what forms can an entity like the subject appear in the order of discourse; what position does it occupy; what functions does it exhibit; and what rules does it follow in each type of discourse? In short, the subject (and its substitutes) must be stripped of its creative role and analysed as a complex and variable function of discourse. (p. 137,38)

Foucault is more insistent on demystifying once and for all the creative subject and its phantom the author than he is in questioning seriously the nature of his own—or his mentors'—authority. His interests take him away from a question that is as crucial to his final argument as is his dismantling of the essentialized structure that does indeed need to be abandoned.

To understand a bit more fully why Foucault's interests take him so far from the question at the center of his text, we need to investigate the nature of his language in the passage above. What is at issue here has nothing at all to do with "the absolute nature and creative role of the subject," for that is clearly a notion that ought to be abandoned. Whatever the nature of the authority of the text, it does *not* derive from such a subjective essence. Such queries as "how does a free subject penetrate the density of things and endow them with meaning" thus have no serious meaning anymore simply because there are no free subjects, no autonomous creators; there are no densities for such creatures to penetrate, and there is no possibility for them to endow such densities with meaning. The authority of the text cannot be located in the special endowment of meaning by an individual creator. Nor does it make sense to ask how the subject accomplishes "its design by animating the rules of discourse from within." The very notion of an inside that is animated by a special essence, to be distinguished from an inanimate outside, is again part of the older regime of ideas that has been abandoned. In these respects the subject—and the author—has truly died.

The privileges of the subject are not what is at stake here. If anything is of concern in the question of authority, it has rather to do with the difficulties inherent in understanding the circulations of discourse once the ground of authority has dissolved. Psychological and biographical investigations are not relevant to the question of authority in this context, nor are attempts to locate the essential genius of the writer. Foucault's interests, however, swerve away from the question of authority and return once again to the question of who profits from the investments in the subject we have come until recently to take for granted. In suggesting that "the subject should not entirely be abandoned," and in declaring his wish "to seize its functions, its intervention in discourse, and its system of dependencies," Foucault establishes the itinerary he wishes to pursue given the death of the author, and it leads directly to a cultural critique of the powers that are invested in the autonomous subject and the ways in which the illusions of authority inherent in such a subject allow the regulation of the flows of discourse for the benefit of those who already control the nature of social circulations. As is the case with Derrida, Foucault wishes to deconstruct the self, the image of the essential ground of authorizations that seemingly, but falsely, legitimizes the text. In asking "under what conditions and through what forms can an entity like the subject appear in the order of discourse," Foucault undertakes a political history of the subject and seeks to locate its placement within the power-dynamics of discourse. In inquiring into the position it occupies within the flow of discourse, what functions it exhibits within that flow, what rules it follows, he has reduced the essential self to a political marker in a game devoted to the expression of force within the flows of cultural fields.

And Foucault's work is usually at its best when it undertakes such investigations.

Once the subject is "stripped of its creative role and analysed as a complex and variable function of discourse," we have a richer understanding of the ways in which the flows of language are regulated through such markers, but we are also perilously close to one of the reductions Foucault sought to avoid: the subject has become a fiction, an arbitrary sign in a two-dimensional game. I would argue that it is one thing to strip the subject of its creative role and yet another to dissolve the sign of the self into a mere marker of power within the ongoing dynamic of a culture's discourse. It is true that the mark of the self, the sign of the author, is an instrument for the disposition of relations within a society; that is one of the inevitable functions that accrues to any mark that forces the flows of discourse around it. But it doesn't follow that it is *only* such a political marker, only an arbitrary regulator of the flows for the interests of those who have an investment in the way those flows are measured. Because Foucault ends up restricting the subject or the author to this two-dimensional role, he can indeed ask with all seriousness "What matter who's speaking?" for in this case the only reason we want to know who is speaking is so that we can determine how that "who" contributes to the regulation of the discourse. The subject as political marker does indeed have an importance to be uncovered, and it is laid bare when the self is stripped of its creative role in the disposition of cultural discourse.

The enigma of the relationship between author and text that we found a matter of interest when it came to Foucault's own interests, Freud and Marx, has disappeared from the text forever. Now we have only the question "What matter who's speaking?" Now we have the questions of interest: who controls the modes of existence of the discourses in which we participate? Given the relative opacity of the questions on the last two pages of the essay, one has to wonder if the remarks about the enigmatic relationship between author and text—at least when we are thinking about the initiators of discursive practices—were a mistake, a lapse back into an older way of speaking about writing that Foucault inadvertently slipped into out of his own personal admiration for the work of Freud and Marx.

The enigma itself is clearly out of place in an essay that ends up concluding that it doesn't really matter who is speaking. But then Foucault's interests in the initiators of discursive practices must be abandoned too, for by his own definition when we think about such writers we are led among other places to the mysterious relationship between them and the texts they produced. We cannot escape the brute particularity of the author even in a world in which the author has died. Freud and Marx have to go too, then. They too must become nothing more than markers in the regulation of a discourse they themselves purported to understand. Either their own special functions within our discourse have to be disallowed as anything other than a manifestation of power relations, or we must concede that there is more to the subject than meets the eye, more to be discerned than the placement of it within the flows of discourse.

In this context we might recall Foucault's remarks about the earlier situation of the author: "In our culture—undoubtedly in others as well—discourse was not originally a thing, a product, or a possession, but an action situated in a bipolar field of sacred and profane, lawful and unlawful, religious and blasphemous. It was a gesture charged with risks long before it became a possession caught in a circuit of property values. But it was at the moment when a system of ownership and strict copyright rules were established (toward the end of the eighteenth and beginning of the nineteenth century) that the transgressive properties always intrinsic to the act of writing became the forceful imperative of literature" (p. 124, 25). We know today that for the most part discourse is now indeed a "possession caught in a circuit of property values," a function within an all-encompassing system of ownership that has reduced both author and self to precisely the two-dimensional status to which Foucault relegates them. And we understand the ways in which this alteration in the nature of discourse was directly related to the demise of the bipolar field of sacred and profane: once the sacred sphere collapsed under its own weight, once the profane sphere of economic activity overwhelmed the socius, it was inevitable that the author would become a marker of property rights. This also meant that the threat of the text disappeared, that its "transgressive properties" diminished steadily in intensity until today when it would seem that any text can be neutralized in the briefest of spans. In this sense, writing is no longer a gesture charged with risks, except when it comes to the risks inherent in violating others' property rights.

But if Foucault is capable of recognizing the changed status of writing here, surely he must also concede that there were some aspects of the bipolar field that could not be killed off by the economic flows. If the risks of writing have diminished, if the transgressive properties of it have likewise shrunk, and if the sacred sphere to which writing was at one time attached has almost totally dissolved, there is still the question of authority, the question of who is speaking, to be addressed. It is the remnant of the older flows that will not disappear, no matter how much cultural critics try to make it go away. It is the repository of the question of the author, of the question of the author's relationship to what used to be called the sacred, that made the writer not merely a marker of property rights but a bearer of certain responsibilities within the socius that were crucially dependent on the ways in which this awareness manifested itself in the flows of his own writing. It *does* matter that Foucault wrote "What Is an Author?" not specifically because it was Foucault, or because he possessed some secret knowledge that his genius allowed him to express in such a text. Not because his "product" is worth more with his name attached to it. And *not* because there was something about his creativity that should interest us in the least. These things truly do not matter.

"Foucault" *is*, however, a marker of certain forms of authority and responsibility, even as it is an indication of a specific kind of discourse within the flows of the socius. It allows us to discern particular values from an individual location within the discourse we ourselves participate in and prompts us to question our own relations to them. "Foucault" is nothing if not an assertion of a very specific set of attitudes toward the social systems of the West in the late twentieth century, and as a declaration of those values, it likewise establishes an authoritative viewpoint on those attitudes through the values that are located within the text. It is a reflection of the remnants of the sacred domain as well to the extent that the writing to be found in "Foucault's" work is both aesthetically and philosophically *compelling*. Its authority is finally to be located in the forcefulness of the prose, and its legitimacy stems from that alone. We might say in this context that the flows of discourse are measured out in such a way from "Foucault's" location within them that they present themselves to us in a particularly useful and meaningful way—they carry *authority*—and that therefore we have come tentatively to recognize "Foucault" as a mark of a system of values that expresses certain interests with which we need to be acquainted.

We can further surmise that the authority and value of "Foucault's" work has something to do with the actual person named Michel Foucault who once lived and put his name to those texts, though we need not be interested in the investments of the subject and the manifestations of creative genius. If there is an enigmatic relationship between the author Freud and his work, there is a similar relationship between Foucault and his work, even if he himself was not an initiator of a discursive practice (no doubt he *hoped* that he was). And whereas we can recognize that the work of "Foucault" has had considerable effects on the regulation of discourse beyond the mere disposition of property rights, we cannot through the work that is to be found in "Foucault" find a useful way of speaking about the authority that manifests itself in the texts simply because they themselves were articulated out of a conviction that it didn't matter who was speaking. (Though again, it is not altogether credible to assume that Foucault didn't have his own purely self-interested moments. It is hard to imagine a writer who invents a special category for "major" figures like Freud and Marx without imagining himself in the same category, without hoping that he too will achieve some special kind of status within the flows of discourse, even if his arguments are devoted to the death of the author and the unimportance of the subject.)

As is the case with all of the major work that can be loosely characterized as post-structuralism, Foucault's writing prompts us to reconceive the questions of cultural discourse given the death of the author and the self, but it fails to recognize that the collapse of the sacred domain upon which these deaths rest—and from which therefore our changed attitudes toward discourse derive—did leave something in its wake along with the political disposition of property rights within an endless flow of self-interest: it left the aesthetic out of which the sacred was originally constituted in the first place. As I have argued at length elsewhere,[2] the death of God and the dissolution of the self and the author had such monumental ramifications that we lost sight of the fact that the original site of the sacred was indeed the aesthetic.

Nietzsche, the writer who did most to establish the altered nature of our discourse and to delineate the effects of the changes, was also the last one seriously to recognize that the death of God did not mean the death of the aesthetic as well. Instead, it allowed us to see that the sacred derived from the aesthetic rather than the other way around, prompted us to recognize the ways in which the authority underlying our discourse was *always* aesthetic in nature rather than grounded in the sacred disposition of the subject or of God. After Nietzsche, we have been insistent on understanding the world purely in terms of the will to power and the ways that will disposes of itself in the regulation of our modes of discourse. But there is another project that works alongside of the critique of culture and that provides it with an orientation toward authority—its own and that of the political system it seeks to discredit—that no purely post-structuralist assay can contribute because the fundamentally aesthetic nature of discourse has been abandoned.

Foucault himself, in his disdainful attack on Derrida's work, is quick to dismiss the aesthetic foundation he perceives to be at the center of the play of signs, as we saw in his remarks about the problems inherent in granting a primordial status to language. From his perspective any such viewpoint "simply reinscribe[s] in transcendental terms the theological affirmation of its sacred origin or a critical belief in its creative nature" (p. 120). The very use of the word "primordial" in this context reinforces the notion that a writer like Derrida does indeed confer upon language such a status, though Derrida himself would hardly be inclined to characterize his attitude toward language in such a way. Foucault wants to discredit Derrida's viewpoint toward discourse because it smacks of the theological, because it seems to do little more than transfer the earlier transcendental affirmations onto yet another sacred location. That Derrida never says any such thing, and that he is hardly inclined to assert the "creative nature" of language, is beside the point at the moment. What is most revealing here is the way in which Foucault distorts Derrida's views in order to distance himself from what he perceives to be the sacred, when in fact what he is doing is simply denying the existence of the aesthetic, that "joyous affirmation of the freeplay of the world" to which so much of Derrida's work is devoted.

And one can well understand why Foucault would choose to distance himself from any view toward language that acknowledged its fundamentally aesthetic nature, for that would deflect attention from the larger enterprise of cultural critique. It is not an accident, after all, that until recently Derrida's work, which is so much more interested in the aesthetic nature of language than Foucault's ever was, had little to do with socioeconomic concerns. The joyous affirmation of the freeplay of the world focusses our attention on that aspect of language that creates and authorizes our world—that is what it has in common with Foucault's work—but it does so in such a way that it is possible to ignore altogether the particular investments in the regulation of discourse that exist at any given moment. One concerns oneself with the ways in which the aesthetic has been sacralized through the ruses of the book, and that is the extent of one's critique; it remains a general exposition of the flawed nature of the ontotheological system of values, but it doesn't concern itself with the ways in which those ontotheological values impede the flow of discourse right now.

Foucault wants to deal only with the politics of discourse, not with the aesthetics of it, and so it is inevitable that he will turn away from the aesthetic nature of language. Derrida—at least in his earlier manifestations—is so inclined to see the joyous affirmation of the freeplay of the world in the older aesthetic sense—that is, as an affirmation that exists more or less in a void, apart from any socius or experiential context that would allow that affirmation to establish a different set of values *in the world*—that he loses sight of the aesthetic connection of language to the pragmatic measuring out and regulation of the flows of discourse. And the more he concerns himself with Foucault's interests in the regulation of the flows, the less he remembers his more appropriate Nietzschean commitment to an aesthetic vision of the world that affirms life in the midst of all of its horrors. In this sense neither Foucault's nor Derrida's work takes the aesthetic nature of language seriously enough, and for that reason both of them miss the most fundamental feature of the world they concern themselves with: its modes of authorization are aesthetic in nature, and nothing they have written can either get away from this fact or properly address it. Given the original connection of the aesthetic to the sacred, Derrida and Foucault are simply too wary of it, too preoccupied with the concern that they too might be investing in yet another sacred system of creative genius and authorial autonomy, to notice that even their work—*especially* their work—needs to account for its own authority, that it is not enough to argue that all authority is a function of the will to power and the endless attempt to manipulate property rights for the benefit of the regulators of discourse.

Discourse is authorized by its aesthetic nature, yet such a statement leaves us with too little knowledge. What could it mean to assert that the aesthetic nature of a text is the repository of its authority, and how is that a different mode of authority than that to be found in the expressions of the will to power? The first thing to be noted is that whereas all aesthetic events have interests involved in them, they are not exclusively driven by self-interest, as is the case with the will to power. By definition an aesthetic situation is one in which the boundaries between "self" and "other," or "world," have loosened precisely because the demand to sustain the self and its fictions is not in question. It is worth remembering that writers like Derrida and Foucault can carry on at such length about the death of the author, the death of the self, and the death of the ontotheological system that engendered them because Nietzsche's essentially aesthetic perspective of the world has come to be the regulative form of at least some of the modes of discourse in the West. Nietzsche declared the world itself to be an aesthetic place, thereby overturning the more traditional Kantian offshoots that suggested the aesthetic was a place removed from the real. The self is recognized to be a fiction—just as the author is—precisely to the extent that one perceives it and its artificialized essences to be extruded offshoots of the play of forces within aesthetic fields rather than constitutors of those fields. That Foucault in particular ignores the aesthetic context that first dissolved the self and the author, displacing their authority to the aesthetic play of the world itself, is again a reflection of his own political ardor and social commitments.

Language has not become, as Foucault suggested, a primordial or transcendental supplement that extends the ongoing ontotheological chain, even if it appears that way at times in Derrida's work. Language itself is merely one field through which the aesthetic flows of the world play, and when they do so, they are distinguished in qualitative terms from those linguistic flows that are deliberately manipulative of others' discourse. I need to emphasize that this statement doesn't mean that all aesthetic discourse takes place in poems and plays, for if literature itself has not quite disappeared in the way the intertextualists might have hoped, the linguistic manifestations of the aesthetic can occur within any domain where the flows of language take place. Likewise, it is also true that the aesthetic manifestation of language is no guarantee of the absence of the will to power either, for all sorts of reasons. First of all, most vested interests do not recognize themselves as vested, most prejudgments remain beneath the screens of consciousness, and so inevitably any linguistic artifact manifests self-interest or the will to power to a certain degree. Further, in some cases the will to power plays more than a subsidiary role in linguistic events that also manifest aesthetic events. The hard truth in this context is the most obvious one: the presence of the aesthetic field of play within the flows of discourse or any other process is no assurance of purity because no aesthetic context is pure. We are capable of recognizing to a greater or lesser degree an aesthetic event, but having so recognized one, we can no more be sure that the presumed authority of such an event is legitimate than we could in any other non-absolutist, ungrounded context.

From an absolutist perspective, the fact that the presence of the aesthetic is no guarantee of a legitimate authority is the fatal flaw in the Nietzschean perspective. It is simply impossible *ever* to be sure that the aesthetic authority to be discerned in a particular situation is indeed legitimate, and this is a serious issue because an aesthetic event requires an aesthetic response from those who are involved in it, which also inevitably means that self-interest will at least temporarily recede as the central concern of one's vision. And if the will to power is not dominating one's viewpoint, one is more vulnerable in the face of other locations within the fields of discourse who might make use of aesthetic effects for their own interests. So if one asserts unequivocally, as I do, that the aesthetic manifests an irrefragable authority, one must also concede that that authority is *never* definitively legitimated. It must always be questioned further, must always be open for further inquiries into its legitimacy.

Nevertheless, as I hope to make clear in several ways in the remaining sections of this book, the aesthetic is the one regularly recurring way we have of locating an authority that is at least *potentially* beyond the self-interests of the will to power.[3] We all recognize that our viewpoint changes when we experience the world aesthetically, that we are no longer specifically concerned with how what is happening might play into our own interests but are generally willing simply to see what unfolds. We all acknowledge that a powerful aesthetic event carries with it the force of religious revelation, even if there is nothing religious to be revealed, even if any "truths" to be discerned within such an event will always remain in question. And we all also tend to note that even if we can never be quite sure what we are sure of when we are in the midst of an aesthetic event, we do know that we are never surer of what we are sure than when we are within the flows that are marked by beauty.

Of course it is precisely because we can never be sure of what we are sure of within the aesthetic that its authority is so problematic for us, and this is also why the aesthetic is always vulnerable to the endless manipulation by charlatans of various stripes that human communities have witnessed from their very beginnings. And given our inability ever definitively to validate the nature of this authority—its very groundlessness, after all, is the reason why we can never establish what we are sure of or determine conclusively its validity—we have tended to ignore its existence, retreating always either to the absolutist perspective that demands definitive responses from the world or to the nihilistic perspective that asserts that none of us has anything more definitive to go on than our own self-interest.

If the aesthetic is the marker of authority yet its presence is never a definitive mark of legitimacy, the world in a sense becomes a devilishly difficult place in which to pass judgment on the nature of things, and the uncertainty implicit in such an aesthetic view, as Nietzsche himself well knew, is perhaps the major obstacle to an appreciation of the value of the aesthetic both in our lives and in our relative understanding of the ways in which authority is measured out in the world. In another sense, though, once we learn to discern those circumstances under which an aesthetic perspective is useful and viable from those situations in which such a viewpoint would become a threat to our lives—it doesn't do, obviously, to consider an onrushing tiger from an aesthetic perspective if one has the least bit of interest in preserving one's life, any more than an aesthetic perspective on the land would make crops grow that could sustain one over the long term (though an aesthetic perspective on the land *could* contribute both to a more ecological orientation toward the land and consequently to a more useful implementation of farming techniques)—there are degrees of assurance that one develops over the course of a lifetime that, while not definitive, do have a sense of certitude to them. That is, there are some things over time about which one can be fairly convinced, others about which one has some degree of understanding, and still others whose certitude remains seriously in question. And if even those things about which one is fairly convinced can be easily enough overturned by an aesthetic event that reveals a former truth to be a self-interested convention, the habit of the aesthetic itself becomes an increasingly valuable and comfortable mode of being to adopt.

One could be still more precise in the formulation of this concern by saying that even if an aesthetic viewpoint fails to provide any definitive marks of authority in any of the contexts it manifests itself, this is hardly the great obstacle it appears to be. What this means in the practice of everyday life is that for the most part the world and the situations with which it presents us are understandable and clear enough for us to deal with in a fairly ready fashion. The only time the perpetually inevitable lack of final certitude within the aesthetic becomes problematic is when something crucial to one's sense of the world is at stake, and in such situations the lack of certainty is almost always present within those who maintain a belief in absolute standards too, or even in those whose will to power hasn't completely exhausted their vision of the world. Any situation that seriously calls into question how one makes one's way in the world will engender uncertainty in *anybody,* so the fact that the authority of the aesthetic does not definitively manifest itself is not really any more of a limitation to this viewpoint than the presumed certitudes of the absolutist are easy comfort for the conscientious individual who has had something seriously called into question.

The ready example to explain the lack of essential difference in certitude comes when one imagines a situation in which a serious debate about some fundamental principles is occurring between two individuals who have a great deal of respect for each other. Even if one is an absolutist and one perceives things aesthetically, a true dialogue in such a situation would inevitably prompt the aesthetically-inclined individual to wonder if maybe the absolutist isn't right, and the absolutist in turn would seriously question whether or not the aesthetically-inclined viewpoint was more accurate. Both individuals would experience the anxiety of uncertainty, as they well should, and in this situation—the only really relevant one when it comes to the question of authority in the end—neither individual has any more certitude than the other. In a more threatening situation when, say, both an absolutist and an aesthetically-inclined individual have to assess whether or not something within the flows they are experiencing is a manifestation of a self-interested effort to regulate the discourse or rather a genuine attempt to reach an agreement, the threat would again be the same for both the absolutist and the aesthetically-inclined individual.

The final fact of the matter is that in the end absolutism is no more a guarantee of the comforts of certitude than an aesthetic viewpoint is—the true virtue inheres not in absolute values *but in one's ability to interpret*. And given this fact, the aesthetically-inclined individual is better prepared to face the flows of the world because his viewpoint assumes from the outset that everything is interpretation, and that therefore everything finally depends upon one's ability to assess the flows of the fields of discourse in intelligent ways. Interpretation is in this sense always an aesthetic phenomenon, and it is always inevitably associated with the aesthetic. Those who have come to understand the world in aesthetic ways are invariably the ones who are the master interpreters of the fields of discourse, whether they be science, painting, theology or whatever.

Given the fact that an aesthetic viewpoint emphasizes the continuing inevitability (and, it should be said, the continuing *desirability*) of interpretation, one who construes the flows of the fields in aesthetic ways is also more likely to be adept at recognizing and interpreting those contexts in which the aesthetic orientation is neither relevant nor useful, and perhaps even harmful, as it would be in the context of a charlatan who would seek to convince one through the beauty of his words of the value of something that might well indeed be quite pernicious. The aesthetic perspective is no guarantee of anything then, but it is at the same time also at least arguably the best viewpoint to take up because of the potentially comprehensive nature of the vision that will derive from its measuring out of the flows of the fields, and because it is the one viewpoint that emphasizes the necessity of interpretation and therefore turns it into an activity of profound value.

Again, qualifications need to be made. I have been referring somewhat awkwardly to an "aesthetically-inclined individual" rather than an "aesthete" because the term that has been applied to one who perceives the world aesthetically has been corrupted by the decadent and escapist vision of the aesthetic that has dominated so much of the modern era. If an aesthete is one who assesses the world through an aesthetic that differentiates itself from the real and values itself precisely because it is an escape from the real, then one must when speaking of the Nietzschean form of the aesthetic refer to aesthetically-inclined individuals. And experience has taught me that it is almost inevitable that individuals will interpret "aesthetic" as "an artifact that is by definition pleasingly removed from reality in its confections, a human construct that is measured exclusively in the terms of taste and tone, feeling and delight."

As I am employing the term here, I am defining it in a way that opposes the more common definition: the aesthetic is *not* that into which one retreats in order to escape from the pressures, anxiety and/or tedium of everyday life; rather, it is the real in the midst of which we find ourselves everyday, though not necessarily the real that engenders the pressure, the anxiety, or the tedium. It is the real of the world in the midst of which we find ourselves when things are going well, which is most of the time most of the day. *That* reality seems nonexistent to most people because it doesn't call attention to itself. *That* reality is the undisclosed aesthetic in the midst of which we live the vast majority of our lives. The *other* reality, that portion of our lives through which we agonize over choices and worry about future and past events and face conflicts with humans and within ourselves, is the artificialized real that comes from centrifuging out of the processes around us a context that focusses upon the flows of the world in exclusively self-interested terms. We *need* to focus on the world in self-interested ways in order to survive, and self-awareness of this sort is both *useful* and *compelling* in its own right. But it is *not* the real; it is rather the artificialized vision of ourselves stripped of the contingent flows all around us, and the "real"—really the unreal—to which it points is in the end a relatively small, albeit most-often recognized, portion of everyday life.

The self-awareness to which one refers when one imagines oneself outside of the flows of the fields is one of the distinguishing features of human existence, and it is most to be prized, but I would argue that it is most to be prized when its mode of perception is attached to the more comprehensive vision of the aesthetic perspective, which embraces the large flows of existence in all their joy and horror. It is precisely that aesthetic vision of the joys and horrors of the world that allows us to frame in a meaningful way the values of the self that makes choices every day in the world; it is precisely that aesthetic vision that allows us to have the authority in our own lives and in the lives of others that we all so desire as members of the human community; and it is also that vision that asserts unequivocally that it does indeed always matter who is speaking, even if the reasons why this is so are radically different once we declare the author and the self to be dead.

Until we come to realize how fully our vision can be informed by the aesthetic flows around us and begin to discern the ways in which it establishes the contexts through which we gauge the world and assess the legitimacy of those features within it to which we grant credence, we shall never be able adequately to deal with the fallout from the cultural critiques inaugurated by Nietzsche's work and pursued with such vigor in the past century or so. And if it is in our interests to overcome the resistances within the flows of discourse that seek to perpetuate a mode of regulation that works to the benefit of those in power, it is also to our advantage to recognize that there are equally powerful interests that continue to resist the full implications of the aesthetic authority with which their critique of our culture began and to which their critique must always finally return.

# Chapter One

# Charismatic Authority

Given the radically opposed meanings that are attached to an aesthetic perspective, and given the controversial nature of the assertion that the aesthetic is the primary locus of authority in the human world, we need to explore several contexts where a similar notion is in play. In our own century, one of the potential analogues for the aesthetic viewpoint I am arguing for can be found in Max Weber's discussions of the three types of authority, where his definition of charismatic authority embodies some of the features of what I would characterize as an aesthetic viewpoint and which will therefore help us understand better some of the defining features of the aesthetic.

Weber, we know, delimited three basic forms of authority, legal, traditional, and charismatic, and whereas I shall be devoting most of my attention to his remarks on the charismatic form of authority, it is worth remembering what Weber had in mind in his remarks on legal and traditional authority as well. His most-quoted definition of the types of authority is as follows:

> There are three pure types of legitimate authority. The validity of their claims to legitimacy may be based on:
> 1. Rational grounds—resting on a belief in the "legality" of patterns of normative rules and the right of those elevated to authority under such rules to issue commands (legal authority).
> 2. Traditional grounds—resting on an established belief in the sanctity of immemorial traditions and the

legitimacy of the status of those exercising authority under them (traditional authority); or finally,

3. Charismatic grounds—resting on devotion to the specific and exceptional sanctity, heroism or exemplary character of an individual person, and of the normative patterns or order revealed or ordained by him (charismatic authority).[1]

In some respects it has grown increasingly difficult over the past century to distinguish between legal and traditional authority, particularly in our own era when more and more of the legal tradition is seen as another repository of traditional authority, and where traditional authority is increasingly construed in the manner of Foucault, as little more than an attempt to regulate the flows of discourse for the benefit of those who have power. The legal authority of our societies is in many respects derived from the traditional authority of the ontotheological system upon which most everything has been based, and even if the rules themselves differ both in the support they garner and in the relative respect in which they are held, still the border between the two forms of authority remains tenuous at best once one begins to consider the grounds of reason and rational patterns of normative rules.

One might also assert that the origin of most forms of authority is the charismatic variety which, as Weber demonstrates, comes to be bureaucratized through a gradual process of routinization and therefore loses its charismatic flavor and becomes traditional; over still more time it may in turn be seen as a legal form of authority. Just as many linguistic expressions begin their lives as fresh and vibrant articulations of the world and move gradually to a general way of speaking and finally turn into a cliché, so too authority can move in these directions; and given the role that language plays in all charismatic contexts, there is more than simple parallelism at work here. Just as, say, Jesus's words become profound utterances that change the fabric of the world for those who accede to their meaning, so too they become part of a general framework of life over time and even turn into clichéd versions of facility that are uttered like magic words to cover certain situations in the everyday world.

It is also worth remembering that even in our own highly contentious age, traditional and legal forms of authority remain paramount. The paternalistic structures of authority are still very much in evidence today, though they are also considerably discredited in the eyes of many, and most of the forms of everyday life are derived in some way from the patriarchal authorities that established the grounds of action and motive in our society. The legal authority we subscribe to has even more force today, particularly in an overly litigious society like the one to be found in the United States. Our system of rules and elections guarantees a fairly credible association with the legal codification of our structures, and most of the laws through which we construe our daily lives remain unquestioned.

There are always marginal areas within the legal form of authority in which its rules are contested in various ways, and there is more sustained activity on those fringes today than ever, particularly as they intersect those aspects of the ontotheological or patriarchal system that are found to be most objectionable by those who are most insistent on calling into question the rules of the discourse. It goes without saying that even among the most contentious of individuals, traditional and legal authority still play by far the greatest role in everyday life and form the base from which any other structure of authority is hypostatized and through which the same forms are undermined. Legal authority in particular can usually be altered in peaceful ways only by making use of the same legal authority to undermine it, and this is the operative procedure today, as it has been for some time.

If our lives are generally conducted under the aegis of traditional and legal authority, though, charismatic authority is usually the most appealing form of authority and the one to which we are most often attracted, as the writing on Weber over the years would suggest. His concept of charisma has been discussed more than any other feature of his work, except, perhaps, for his linkage of the Protestant ethic to the spirit of capitalism, and his assertions seem most compelling when he is dealing with the nature of charisma and the way such authority functions. As Weber himself acknowledges, "charisma" has the original sense of a gift or a manifestation of grace and is linked to the Greek *chairein,* to rejoice, so it combines both the power of authority and the exuberance of ecstasy. More specifically, Weber tells us that "The term 'charisma' will be applied to a certain quality of an individual personality by virtue of which he is set apart from ordinary men and treated as endowed with supernatural, superhuman, or at least specifically exceptional powers or qualities. These are such as are not accessible to the ordinary person, but are regarded as of divine origin or as exemplary, and on the basis of them the individual concerned is treated as a leader" (p. 358, 59). Charismatic individuals are generally clearly recognizable to others, even if not everyone sees their charisma as useful or beneficial, and most of us have little difficulty denoting such types.

The borderline of the charismatic is somewhat fuzzy, particularly inasmuch as the word has come to be overused and overgeneralized since Weber's formulation, and we might indeed find the most compelling cases of charismatic authority at the fringes of it today, in part because so many individuals in Western societies would be chary of the more powerful manifestations of charisma. There are certainly some indications of a reemergence of religious fundamentalism both in places like the United States and in Islamic countries, and these groups quite often depend on charismatic leaders of one type or another; but the subsidiary features of these truly charismatic figures keep many people from expressing an interest, even when attracted to the general presence of charisma itself. And inasmuch as charismatic figures like Hitler have given its presence within the political context a rather horrifying cast, most of us are reluctant to embrace such powers in the sociopolitical arena, though we do often expect our leaders to have a kind of charm that approaches charisma.

In some respects today, as was perhaps always the case, charisma is most attractive to the disgruntled, to those who find their lives to be less than satisfactory. Most of those who adhere to the traditional values of our society, the mythologized ones in particular that emphasize the independence of the autonomous subject and its unilateral freedom, are not inclined to embrace charismatic authority, for it compels obedience of one kind or another. The power of such an authority inevitably requires submission from the disciples, just as it compels a submission of sorts on the part of the charismatic individual himself. The tight series of rules through which charismatic authority originally manifests itself is articulated by Weber in the following manner:

> It is recognition on the part of those subject to authority which is decisive for the validity of charisma. This is freely given and guaranteed by what is held to be a "sign" or proof, originally always a miracle, and consists in devotion to the corresponding revelation, hero worship, or absolute trust in the leader. But where charisma is genuine, it is not this which is the basis of the claim to legitimacy. This basis lies rather in the conception that it is the *duty* of those who have been called to a charismatic mission to recognize its quality and to act accordingly. Psychologically this "recognition" is a matter of complete personal devotion to the possessor of the quality, arising out of enthusiasm, or of despair and hope.
>
> No prophet has ever regarded his quality as dependent on the attitudes of the masses toward him. No elective king or military leader has ever treated those who have resisted him or tried to ignore him otherwise than as delinquent in duty. Failure to take part in a military expedition under such leader, even though recruitment is formally voluntary, has universally been met with disdain. (p. 359, 60)

Although the recognition of charismatic authority is indeed "freely given" and would be a contradiction in terms if it were thought of as compelled by force, the demands, the *duty* to which such adherents are called, are demanding indeed. And the "recognition" upon which the duty to the charismatic individual rests is usually "a matter of complete personal devotion to the possessor of the quality, arising out of enthusiasm, or of despair and hope."

In a literal way one gives oneself up to the authority of the charismatic figure and ceases to be a free agent in the world. As one serves the authority out of a sense of duty, so too one is absolved of the need to engender authority through one's own acts. If freedom and autonomy are the compelling signs of one's existence, a charismatic figure is less likely to attract one in the first place because one will be reluctant to accede to the demands of the discipline authority requires. But if one sees the freedom and autonomy of the individual as burdens to bear, anxiety-provoking manifestations of the alienation of the self from others, then charismatic authority can be compelling indeed, precisely because it relieves one of the burden of choice and valuation, precisely because one no longer has to be responsible for one's own authorization.

There are always manifestations of this richest form of charisma in play in the world, most often within religious contexts where the figure believes and compels others to believe that he or she has some divine mission to fulfill. There are people like Jim Jones who can convince others to go to the jungle with them or to drink poisoned Kool-aid, and most of us are wary of this type of charisma even if we also recognize its attractions. And one by no means has to believe in the great myth of the free and autonomous individual in order to be wary, for even one who sees life in terms of all of its contingencies and complexities is generally unwilling to offer himself up to an authority who has all the easy answers. Charisma works through the benign solution, the simple plan that lays the fabric of the world bare, and only one who remains committed to such a vision of the good life is likely to value positively the most obvious forms of charismatic authority.

To the rest of us, these figures remain more of a threat to the larger socius than a benign influence, and again for obvious reasons: "Charismatic authority is . . . specifically outside the realm of everyday routine and the profane sphere" (p. 361). Inasmuch as such authority works outside of everyday routine and the profane world, it by definition inevitably calls into question the activities within the daily sphere of life, and most of us are usually satisfied to a greater or lesser degree with the profane world in which we live, even if we might also believe in the sacred as well. "In this respect," as Weber says, charismatic authority is "sharply opposed both to rational, and particularly bureaucratic, authority, and to traditional authority, whether in its patriarchal, patrimonial, or any other form" (p. 361). The charismatic figure always calls into question the other forms of authority that dispose of the business of our lives, and the conflict between forms here is most important:

> Both rational and traditional authority are specifically forms of everyday routine control of action; while the charismatic type is the direct antithesis of this. Bureaucratic authority is specifically rational in the sense of being bound to intellectually analysable rules; while charismatic authority is specifically irrational in the sense of being foreign to all rules. Traditional authority is bound to the precedents handed down from the past and to this extent is also oriented to rules. Within the sphere of its claims, charismatic authority repudiates the past, and is in this sense a specifically revolutionary force. It recognizes no appropriation of positions of power by virtue of the possession of property, either on the part of a chief or of socially privileged groups. The only basis of legitimacy for it is personal charisma, so long as it is proved; that is, as long as it receives recognition and is able to satisfy the followers or disciples. But this lasts only so long as the belief in its charismatic inspiration remains. (p. 361, 62)

The charismatic figure is inevitably a "revolutionary force" because he denies the past and repudiates the forms of authority that exist around him. Precisely because charismatic authority is based on irrational grounds, it cannot peacefully coexist with the relatively rational grounds of either rational or traditional authority. The precedents and rules of tradition are that which a charismatic person must call into question, and the "intellectually analysable rules" of rational authority are even more an obstacle to the revelations of the gifted one. This explains why it is generally those who are disgruntled either with themselves or with the socius as a whole who find the appeal of the charismatic figure to be most compelling, and usually those who are disgruntled with the socius are also disgruntled with themselves and therefore willing—rather *eager*—to have all the structures of their lives overturned through the grace of an otherworldly intrusion into the secular.

Weber is careful, though, to keep the definition of charismatic authority broad enough to include more than the extreme and most obvious forms of zeal, as when he tells us that a charismatic individual "is set apart from ordinary men and treated as endowed with supernatural, superhuman or at least specifically exceptional powers or qualities." If the extreme forms of charisma bear a metaphorical relationship to that aesthetic form called the sublime, the "lesser" forms bear a similar relationship to what we characterize as beauty. If those who seem to have supernatural or superhuman powers are recognizably revolutionary in their mode of being, those who manifest exceptional powers or qualities are also touched by the revolutionary force, though perhaps the nature of their revolution is less obviously compelling. And if we broaden our sense of charisma to include at least some of its sense today, we should have to assume that a charismatic figure is any individual who by means of the force of personality is capable of compelling change within the lives of others and in prompting those others to effect changes within their world. Charisma in this sense is by no means the same thing as being "telegenic," for that is at best a minor subset of the category: one can be charismatic without being telegenic, and one can be telegenic without being charismatic, though there is no doubt that television has been a medium that has been useful to a number of charismatic—chiefly religious—figures like Jimmy Swaggart and Jim Bakker. Given the ways in which television has changed our conceptions of things, we might indeed be increasingly likely to define the charismatic figure in terms of those individuals whose appeal comes across most compellingly on television, but for now at least one must assume that a powerful presence on television is not a sufficient characteristic of a charismatic figure.

The lesser types of charismatic figures are inevitably always more in evidence than the major types simply because the "qualifications" are lower. If there are few individuals at any given time who could compel people to leave their former existence behind and take up residence in a jungle or an isolated community in Oregon, there are considerably more whose force we notice on a regular basis, from the prominent figures in any way of life or discipline to the people who rise to the occasion when some form of grass-roots politics provides a need. These are people who, we might say, *have* charisma but who are not quite charismatic figures; their discourse is powerful or moving and prompts us to reconsider some of our ways of doing things, but their activities and dispositions are such that they don't demand fealty or radical changes in our way of life. They might prompt us to alter completely our ways of thinking about this or that thing, and they might likewise prompt us to change some aspect of our behavior, but they do not require a complete redefinition of who we are any more than they compel us to abandon the secular world. And if the more powerful manifestations of charisma are capable of a totalizing kind of authority, the lesser manifestations are equally capable of a localized form of authority.

The charming CEO of a company, for example, may well not demand a total change of life in his workers, but if he is sufficiently compelling he will convince many of them that their work is part of a larger "mission" and will thus go some way toward shaping their attitude toward their work—and thus toward themselves—and will in so doing change their sense of the shape of their daily lives, turning perhaps what might have been drudgery into something of great value because it contributes to the greater cause, profits, or whatever. The major figures in the academic world, be they individuals like Derrida or John Silber, do not as a rule demand a total change of life either, though it is possible, as it is with the CEO, that their words will have that effect. The intellectual figure obviously hopes through the force of his or her words to change the ways people look at things, and thereby also to change the way individuals live their lives, but most often the visions of these figures are not comprehensive enough to include regimes of discipline that give form to the entire life. Deconstruction may be a useful form through which to measure the effects of certain texts, and in mutated form it may be a useful analogue for interpretive activities in other modes of discourse, but it is not a means through which to construe one's life and does not provide a sufficient system of values to compel complete change, perhaps because it lacks almost totally any positive formulations. So deconstruction can change the interpretive means at one's disposal, it can alter the discipline into which it intrudes itself, and it can modify one's way of thinking about one's life, but it cannot provide the necessary components for an entirely revolutionary system of the type that would be proffered by the extreme form of charismatic figure.

Inasmuch as most of us are committed in some fundamental respects to the secular world—even if we also have a belief in the sacred—these lesser forms of charisma are more compelling for us than the major manifestations that change the lives of the disgruntled. In this respect it is almost always those who have charisma without necessarily being truly charismatic figures who effect the major changes in the world, for their charisma is such that it makes them recognizable authorities—though obviously also authorities that must always be seriously questioned—and yet doesn't compel a complete change of life. Indeed, we might say that their charisma is more effective precisely *because* it doesn't require a complete change of life, for many of us would tend in the end to choose the very lives we have even if we have complaints about the ways our lives are going, and therefore don't want the revolutionary effects of the charismatic leader and remain most wary of any individuals who might offer such a thing. The person with charisma, by definition because he *has* charisma, prompts us to attend to his authority, to recognize him as someone with whom we must deal, but he doesn't overwhelm us with his authority in the way the charismatic figure does. If such an individual is capable of effecting more changes in the world—and I am, of course, ignoring for the moment the fact that a charismatic figure like Jesus obviously effected more change in the world than any person with charisma ever will, because Jesus marks the rarest form of charisma precisely in the magnitude of change He engendered—that may well have everything to do with his "lesser" powers, which, because they are less intimidating and yet are still compelling, provide him with authority but don't engender the kinds of insecurity or anxiety the most powerful manifestations of charisma would.

We have yet, however, to define what "specifically exceptional powers or qualities" an individual with charisma might have that would give the person the authority we all tacitly recognize in such types, and Weber is curiously unhelpful in this respect, for he fails to tie the gift of charisma to any specific qualities at all, even if he does provide examples of charismatic individuals and thereby gives an idea of the kinds of qualities he has in mind. Aside from the examples, though, Weber only states in a general fashion what the charismatic person is like. In speaking of the exceptional power or qualities of the charismatic individual, Weber asserts that they are "not accessible to the ordinary person, but are regarded as of divine origin or as exemplary, and on the basis of them the individual concerned is treated as a leader," but he doesn't tell us *why* these qualities should have that effect, other than to point out that they are exceptional in nature and recognized as such.

Likewise, in his original definition of charismatic authority, Weber asserts that it rests "on devotion to the specific and exceptional sanctity, heroism or exemplary character of an individual person, and of the normative patterns of order revealed or ordained by him," and whereas he is a bit more precise here, still we are left wondering just what constitutes such authority. We may simply be forced to say that we all recognize this "exceptional sanctity" when we see it, that heroism is such that we can all easily identify it too, and that an exemplary character cannot fail to be noticed. For the charismatic character is by definition one that is easily recognizable; that in itself is one of its distinguishing features. If one had to submit to the lengthy questioning of a board of authority in order to determine how much charisma one had, one would clearly not have any, for it would have to be apparent to all for it to command authority in the first place.

"Exceptional sanctity," though, is an elusive phrase, even if we may in some senses know what it is; heroism is also difficult to note, particularly the variety that compels a sense of duty in others; exemplary characters are perhaps unavailable in this era because there would be so little agreement about what should be considered exemplary. In effect, these definitions do indeed say little more than that we all recognize a charismatic presence when we see one, for even the second half of the definition only establishes linkages that would be considered irrelevant in another context. The charismatic figure may indeed assert "normative patterns of order revealed or ordained by him," but so might many another individual, and the only way to sort out those revealed orders that have authority from those that don't would be according to whether or not one considered the person charismatic, simply mad, or an incarnation of pure evil. Weber is aware that to a certain extent charisma is in the eye of the beholder, that there must also be something in the followers of the leader that prompts them to be attracted to the special force of his charisma, but he doesn't explore at any length the ways in which the special manifestations of power in the charismatic person do indeed depend on the local context, on the values that leader and followers share *outside* of any particular attitude toward the charismatic individual himself. One person's charismatic authority is indeed another person's madman, and there are no definitive steps that allow us to establish independently which is which simply because charismatic authority is *always* completely contingent on the immediate circumstances of its manifestation.

That which sets the charismatic person apart, then, is recognizable by all, even if they don't always characterize it as charisma—they might think it madness instead. But the specific qualities of charisma are always context dependent and thus contingent on the values of the individuals who recognize the person as charismatic in the first place. Nevertheless, the power of the individual with charisma must surely have some features that are more specifically identifiable than this, and at the very least I think we can assume that a person with charisma has some kind of gift of language. Often charismatic types do not come from the most educated realms of a social system, so their gift of language clearly doesn't come from their vocabulary, something that might be very limited indeed. And their rhetorical powers are usually not something that they have had to learn, for the very nature of their charisma would suggest that what moves them so powerfully must come from some internal source. But if the charismatic individual is going to move people, he will almost always have to do it with words, which means that inevitably he will have to have some kind of eloquence.

Now, we no more know specifically what constitutes eloquence than we understand the source of charisma, in spite of all our great scientific machinery, but we do know that rhetorical prowess is characterized in terms of the choice of words and their placement. The rhythms of speech of a master of discourse partake of the aesthetic and induce attitudes within an audience through their repetitions and periodicity that alter the people's orientation toward the world. The power of the words comes from their ability to transform the audience's way of thinking about its mode of being, prompts those who are listening to reconsider their place within the scheme of things; and for such reconsiderations to have the power that they do, the eloquence of the speaker must be capable of making the auditors forget their usual ways of thinking and the ordinary language through which they constitute their everyday lives. We have known for millennia that a powerful speech and a great poem have many things in common, from rhythms that are capable of altering the flow of a person's thoughts to ideas that seem so striking as to jar one out of one's complacency. And any charismatic person by definition must have these aesthetic gifts, must be able through his linguistic elegance to charm the audience away from its normal patterns of thought. In this way charisma is always crucially linked to the aesthetic authority of language itself and cannot be separated from it. As before, eloquence is not a sufficient condition in itself to guarantee the value of any charismatic authority, but it is a necessary condition for any possible value nevertheless.

The language of those who have charisma is an essential feature of their gift, but that gift is in turn expressed in another way when we say that it is always also connected to a specific kind of recognizable order, an order that must be transparently simple in some respects for it to have the power it has over other individuals. Most of the truly charismatic types who have had some effect on the world, after all, have been able to have that effect precisely because of the simplicity of their utterances. It is not only that someone like Jesus had the gift of parables, the ability to master a narrative in order to reveal metaphorically some spiritual condition, though that is one way that both the linguistic and the orderly method of the charismatic manifest themselves; it is also that the conceptions underlying the order are simple and straightforward in nature. The order itself may demand devilishly difficult regimes on the part of the converted, but the ideas underlying the discipline need to be clear to all. And inasmuch as such figures invariably have considerable effects on less well-educated audiences, their simplicity of order is necessary for that reason as well.

At the same time, though, a transparent order is not contingent on the needs of an ignorant audience. Simplicity itself, after all, is one of the features scientists regularly list as an essential element of powerful scientific concepts, and any aesthetic condition to be found in painting or poetry is connected in some respects to what at least appears to be a transparent and straightforward order. And it is the *feeling* of its simplicity, the "Of course!" that it engenders in the audience, that is one mark of its power. It seems an inevitable offshoot of the ways things are, so inescapable that one might wonder why one hadn't thought of it oneself. It may be an order contingent on magic numbers or geographical locations or a definition of the group in terms of some obviously "hostile" force or whatever, but the features must be readily identifiable and clearly focussed. That is precisely what it means for a charismatic figure to have authority.

Given these requirements for the charismatic forces inherent in an individual, we might pause a moment and ask ourselves why some of the features of order and language tend to repeat themselves, particularly in those cases where a more rational person would wonder why they tend to appear as often as they do. Many charismatic orders, for example, do indeed depend on sacred numbers of one type or another, be they numbers like seven and nine, or prime numbers or numbers said to characterize certain powerful forces in the universe. Is this an arbitrary feature of charismatic authority, or is it intrinsically related somehow to the gifts such figures have? The easy response to this linkage would be to say that charismatic types tend to pick particular numbers precisely for their simplicity and therefore the numerology helps to clarify the goals of the order. But there may well be something akin to what is found in a disease like Tourette's Syndrome—whose victims are given to involuntary outbursts of curses and repetitions that seem to come from another part of the person altogether—that is the origin of the charismatic tendency to speak in terms of magic numbers and recurrent phrases of various sorts. This is not to say that charisma is a disease, though it could be argued that its most extreme manifestations do indeed have linkages to some forms of mental illness. Rather, it is to suggest that charismatic language and the powers it manifests are connected in some mysterious ways to special regions of human discourse that lie beyond the ken of both audience and speaker.

Most of us are not likely to be swayed by the magic in a number like nine, for example, yet I have known people who have built up entire political systems on the basis of the number nine. Every order was based on some factor of nine, every contingency that would threaten the system was somehow contained by the number nine, and the entire legitimacy of the system was dependent in the end on one's belief in the "rightness" of nine as a cornerstone for a political vision. The gift of magic numbers is connected in turn to the capacity for facile phraseology as well, for the lucid phrase or epigram that encapsulates in a memorable way an idea with charm and simplicity. Indeed, it is precisely the charm and simplicity of the phrases and magic numbers that make "outsiders" so skeptical of the authority of charismatic figures of this type, for the simplicity of numbers and phrases also suggests the incredible unreality of the entire apparatus.

In the case of the individual I knew who based his political system on the number nine, he was convinced that the number itself legitimized the system, and the euphonious phrases through which he articulated the basic political program of action reflected in their own way the same kinds of legitimacy: they simply *sounded* right to him, and even to a skeptical individual they had their own recognizable force. Yet the marvelous system in the end seemed totally absurd to a skeptic precisely because the numerology and facile encapsulations covered over an incredible naiveté about the nature of human systems. In the politics of nine, for example, the individual involved assumed that humans within a socius as large as ours could in effect come to some consensus every week on the nation's most compelling problem, and once that consensus was arrived at through a series of meetings that were based on nines and that all took place on Saturday, the leader could spend the next week dealing with the agreed-upon problem. It would then be eliminated, and the following week the groups of nine could arrive at a consensus about the next most-compelling problem, and so forth on into utopia. If the world were constituted in such a way that leaders could indeed focus on one problem a week and then forever eliminate it, or if it were constituted in such a way that citizens could so easily agree on that which most needed to be addressed at any given moment, the planet's problems would have been reduced greatly over the millennia. But the very implausibility of such a scheme was part of its attraction as well. To hear the inventor of this system talk about it, one would think that everything in the world would be fine within a year if only he were given a chance to let everyone know about his new political system. And it was, naturally enough, a given that when people listened to his description of this amazingly simple system, they would all immediately be convinced of its veracity (or so the inventor thought).

It is also not an accident that most such charismatic types have what we might characterize as a somewhat paranoid attitude toward the prevailing systems of authority. Inasmuch as their benignly simple orders compel total assent—there cannot be a partial implementation of the politics of nines, for the entire package must be in place for it to work—their structures must inevitably be at odds with the givens of the socius. This is why charismatic authority is "sharply opposed both to rational, and particularly bureaucratic, authority and to traditional authority" as well. The charismatic person's plan of action is inevitably revolutionary in that it unequivocally denies the authority of the prevailing systems and asserts a radically different version of order and authority. As Weber phrases it: "Within the sphere of its claims, charismatic authority repudiates the past, and is in this sense a specifically revolutionary force. It recognizes no appropriation of positions of power by virtue of the possession of property, either on the part of a chief or of socially privileged groups" (p. 362). The simplicity of the order, the perfection of its system, depends totally on a denial of the givens, so the charismatic individual will be inclined to promise great changes in the world and in the lives of those who follow him, but *only* if the vision and the order are universally applied, which means *only* if all the prevailing human orders are overturned.

Part of the authority of the charismatic person thus stems from the language he or she uses so eloquently, and part of it derives from the transparency of the order, but these in turn are related to the greater vision underlying both of these features: the order can institute *great* change, revolutionary change, and it can forever eliminate those features—or at least some of them—that we find most in conflict with our ideas of the good life. The promise of the charismatic figure must be of this magnitude because his demands are also great: as Jesus explained, one would be forced to put off the clothes of one's old life, leave behind the comfortable, if also anxiety-provoking, ways that one had employed for years, and become washed in the blood of the lamb, take on a new form that would repudiate not only the abstract past of the social and political systems of which one was a part but also the *personal* past. The virtue of the charismatic leader is that he promises a *totally new* order; the limitation is the same, and therefore the appeal of the leader is always contingent on those who most desire a totally other world in which to live. In that case, the magic numbers and mysterious phrases with their incantatory logic help to convince the individual that there is indeed a different order of things that one simply had not noticed sufficiently before, that one can truly live in a constant state of magic and bliss.

I have been discussing charismatic authority in extreme situations, not to discredit charismatic authority per se, for I have also asserted that authority is aesthetic in nature, and clearly Weber's charismatic type derives his or her power from an aesthetic conception of things and linguistic eloquence. Rather, by discussing certain aspects of extreme forms of charisma, those kinds we might call paranoid, for example, I hope to locate some of the features that are to be found within all charismatic individuals, even those who are only individuals with charisma rather than the charismatic types to which Weber devotes his remarks. A more ordinarily charismatic individual would also have the gift of language, for example, and the phrases through which the vision of the person was articulated would doubtless be couched in memorable rhythms and images, but they wouldn't necessarily be of the variety of totally implausible visions of the kind of which I have made use. It is true that

Jesus's message was contingent on memorable images, compelling anecdotes, and magic numbers, but to say so is not necessarily to discredit the entire vision, and there are obviously many forms of charisma that aren't dependent on magic numbers and simplistic visions. Jesus's vision, after all, might have been simple, but it was not simplistic. And it might have appealed exclusively to the disgruntled or the politically astute, but that is not to say that it didn't have its own great value.

At the same time, it is not enough to establish that the distinguishing feature of a charismatic authority like Jesus, that which would separate him from a cracked and paranoid figure who would have us all drink poison to get to heaven more quickly, is his sincerity any more than it would be his ethical commitment. There are, to be sure, charismatic types who are charlatans from the beginning, whose self-interest is so evident in their appeal that we cannot mistake it even from a distance. Whatever self-interest a figure like Jesus must have had, though, it was clearly not the main reason for the program of action; rather, Jesus was sincere, truly wished to help others, and had an ethical plan of action that would transform the lives of those who were willing to listen to Him. Still, the authority of a figure like Jesus cannot be based on this sincerity, for we know that that is not a sufficient criterion for authority—many people are sincere in what they believe and in what they promulgate, but many of these are also indeed truly mad, and many are simply misled by the magic of their own words.

Sincerity is a condition of charisma, but not a sufficient one. It is necessary—at least the appearance of it is necessary—because the charismatic individual's *complete* conviction in the rightness of what he is doing would not be possible without it. One must at least appear to be willing to lay down one's life for one's ideas if one is going to have any hope of compelling others to do equivalent things, and that cannot occur without sincerity. Likewise, at least in most cases, the sincerity must be connected not just to a plan of action but to a *virtuous* plan of action. The system has to be an *ethical* order because only a structure based upon the *right* could compel unequivocal assent, only a system that made one feel that one would truly be completely virtuous in taking up the values of it could create the necessary fervor to gain zealous adherents.

A charismatic figure, then, must not only be eloquent, and must not only have a transparent order of great simplicity to offer, but he must also provide a sincere and clear vision of the good and convince others that they too will be good and virtuous if only they adhere to the proffered order. And this, I would argue, is true of the entire range of charismatic possibilities, whether in the extreme form of a madman, or in the guise of a leader who changes the world, or in the pattern of a writer whose work compels assent, or in the context of any other aesthetic manifestation in the world. Given that, and given the fact that sincerity can always be faked and isn't always necessarily good in and of itself, the virtue itself, like the authority inherent in any context, is not to be taken as a given. The difficult assessments only *begin* once such an authority has been located. They don't end there, and if they have too often stopped there, this is because the seemingly magical powers of charismatic types induce individuals to assume that the greater powers are a reflection of greater probity and higher truth. For too many, the manifestation of charisma is in itself a demonstration of virtue and authority when in fact it should rather be the point at which one seriously begins to question whether or not virtue and authority are truly associated with the individual and the plan of action that comes with the charismatic person. The mere *difference,* the mere presence of a seemingly exemplary life, should no more compel our assent than an individual's seeming ability to bend spoons should convince us of his godhead. "Charisma" in this sense, in whatever form, is the beginning point of our individual and cultural investigations into authority, not the end point, as we have thought; it is that which we all recognize as a *possible* location for assertions of authority, but always only a possible location.

Given the ways in which past eras have construed both charisma and authority, it is important to point out that whatever powers inhere in the charismatic individual, they are not a function of an essential self. God is dead, the self is dead, and the author is dead, and so we should not think that the individual with the powers of authority is gifted *in himself* because of who he is in his selfhood. This is an illusion of longstanding that can be easily demonstrated because of the similarities in charismatic types. If one were to do an analysis of the patterns of language, the kinds of order articulated and the emotional fervor with which the order is asserted, we would find that there is an amazing consistency to them. After all, this is only another way of explaining why we can recognize charismatic types in the first place. But this also suggests that even if the characteristics of the charismatic individual always inhere in particular individuals—where else would they be located?—yet they are hardly something for which the individual himself can take credit. And given the end of the self in the conventional sense, we can begin to understand the relationship between the charismatic individual and his gifts in a new light.

One of the characteristic features of charismatic types is humility, feigned or real, and this is a crucial marker of the relation of self to the gifts of authority. For if the individual is humble in the face of that which sets him apart, he is so for a reason: he legitimately doesn't feel that he can take credit for those features which distinguish him in the eyes of others. Often the circumstances of charismatic individuals are quite modest, and there is no ready way to account for the virtues the person has. If Jesus was a carpenter's son, that too is exemplary in many respects and reflects the fact that the powers of the charismatic cannot be readily attributed to anything the individual himself has done. The gifts are indeed *gifts* and do not arise from anything for which the person could really take credit. And if one who has charisma can also learn over time how to exaggerate the value of the self as a result of the power of authority, those who remain steadfast in their relation to their charisma never lose their humility in the face of their ability to move others.

Although it is no doubt true that the good fortune or special gifts of most humans cannot be directly attributed to the individuals who possess them—outside of the willingness to work hard to develop them or the self-discipline that is needed to harness them—the case is somewhat different for the charismatic person for two reasons: first, the gift is such an obvious marker of difference from normal people that the idea of achievement or "credit" seems altogether alien to it; second, the gifts themselves are essentially *aesthetic* in nature, hence *selfless,* and thus the very feelings that accompany the abilities are demonstrably non-egocentric. The skills and virtues of others are often deliberately manipulative in nature and frequently explored precisely because of a concern for the fetishization of the self. Such skills are also doubtless attached to the aesthetic in some ways, but the primary orientation is first and foremost one of self-interest.

For the charismatic type, the self-interest almost always follows from an initially non-egocentric perspective: the gift of inspiration, or of poetic utterance, or of political persuasion, is something that seems to come from outside of the self, not within; and if one does learn how to take credit for it, quite often that is because those who most admire the possessor continually seek to give him credit for that which at some level he knows he has no responsibility for. As is always the case, aesthetic effects can be bound to self-interested contexts but are not initially so, and whereas we may have become adept at binding them in this way, and whereas the individual with charisma may find it hard to resist such binding over time—accounting for, in part at least, the many "falls" from grace to be found within those religious individuals who have charisma—it never begins that way.

Certainly the original conception of inspiration relied upon this notion of humility, for it was based on the idea that the poet or the sage had the breath of a god breathed into him. Not only did this account for the powerful feelings the charismatic one felt and inspired, but it also characterized quite well the sense that the gift was not something that "belonged" to one at all; one was only a "vessel" for the message of a higher calling. And the subsidiary characteristics of such extreme forms of charisma as are to be found in legends of old and in poets on and off throughout the millennia add to the mysterious feeling that the power passing through one indeed comes from somewhere else. Although religions traditionally developed ritual contexts through which the breath of the lord might be more likely to come, and although any charismatic type develops routines through which to attempt to guarantee the appearance of the eloquence or force that comes and goes, the fact remains that it is still generally the case that it continues to come and go of its own seeming bidding. No human can contain or guarantee a moment of charismatic power, even if over time one becomes more adept at harnessing it and thus is more likely to help engender it. If the powers of the charismatic have a mind of their own, so to speak, then the temporary possessor of them hardly feels as though he or she is the origin of them.

To put the same matter in a slightly different way, we could say that most all charismatic states are inherently ecstatic in nature, leaving the individual feel as though he is outside of himself, as he is in terms of his normal sensibility. He truly is in some sense taken over by a force that is not part of his ordinary disposition, a force that displaces his self-interested perspective, makes him feel more powerful than normal, and perhaps also makes him feel as though he is the vessel of a god. However these states are used by the charismatic individual, a circumspect person would inevitably be somewhat careful and humble in the face of such forces because they do have the power to displace the ordinary self—where does it go when it goes?—and thus have seemingly magical properties to turn one into something that one is not. Such powers are not to be trifled with, and only one who has lost sight of the uncanny nature of them as a result of a subsequent egomania is likely to ignore the potential perils also to be found in such ecstatic states. The individual can *learn* how to take credit for the powers of the divine, but at least initially does not see them in that context at all. Likewise, if the one with charisma becomes a repository for authority of one sort or another, he is also usually very circumspect at first about the nature of his authority, carefully declining to take full responsibility for it precisely because he no more knows the origin of it than do those who follow him. Even without a sense of the fragility of these powers in the face of the much larger traditional and rational structures that will inevitably oppose the charismatic authority, the person would instinctively be likely to recognize that in a real way the authority stems from his *lack* of authority—he speaks for *another*, not for himself. He achieves authority only by becoming the vessel of authority for someone or something else.

If Weber is insistent about the non-secular nature of charismatic authority, surely the reason for its difference from the ordinary world is to be found here in the paradoxical context of a self gaining authority through the abandonment of self to another authority, losing the self and yet gaining authority in the process. The humble person with great persuasive powers capable of garnering great numbers of adherents in a real way has no idea whatsoever where his or her utterances come from or how they are given shape. In this the person is no different from the poet or any other figure who participates in the aesthetic, for in all these contexts the degree of manipulation on the part of the "artist" is less than often seems the case. This isn't to say that much, if not most, art is not composed according to very careful formal experiments on the part of the artist, for it may well be. But the artist himself may well have absolutely no idea of the basis for his own gifts. What makes this dab of paint "right" in this context rather than that dab is something the artist "knows," and no doubt that knowledge is dependent on experience and practice, but it is also a knowledge that comes with gifts that remain forever beyond that person's knowledge.

Martin Heidegger was fond of saying that "Language speaks man," and this statement is related to the phenomenon that is in play within the context of the charismatic individual. In part Heidegger was referring to the fact that the traditions and history built into the language we use always antedate our usage of language—it always comes before any particular individual who uses it and thus shapes the way the individual speaks (and thinks) rather than the other way around. Far from being the speaker, we are the spoken, and the shape we give to things is dependent on the way we are assumed into the language of our culture. But language also speaks us to the extent that we are taken up by it, particularly in those moments of eloquence that drive a poem or a passionate speech, and we are even less the possessors of language at these times than we are normally when we seem to be in control of the flow of our discourse. One of the limitations, finally, of Foucault's perspective in "What Is an Author?" is that he failed to acknowledge the degree to which language speaks us rather than the other way around. The frequent references to the regulators of the flows of discourse prompt one to think that there are specific agents in the world who, like the French academy, deliberately mark out what can and cannot be uttered, what will and will not be sayable. It is most certainly true that discourse is regulated, and that it is regulated to a significant degree by those within any system of discourse who have power, but what Foucault misses is how much even those with special interests in the flow of discourse are incapable of manipulating it for their own purposes. They can, and they do, and their manipulations need to be resisted and redirected to the extent that this is possible. But language speaks them as much as it speaks us, and as with the charismatic types, they can ignore this only at their own peril. To the extent that they do ignore it, the flow of discourse will eventually manipulate them rather than the other way around, and perhaps it will in any case.

If we are much more assumable into the vast flow of signs of which our cultures are a part than the other way around, we must inevitably come to recognize that our position is not as we thought, yet at the same time such an awareness is antithetical to the practices of everyday life, where the ability to know who and where one is and how to manipulate this or that event according to one's needs are paramount considerations. If language speaks us, we have reversed our ways of conceiving the world, turned in opposition to the language of the master that we are brought up to think is that which we should possess, or at least desire. The gift of speech may make one rich, but that is a paradoxical effect rather than an inevitable factor in its appearance. The redirection of the flows of language *away* from any particular self-interested location to some larger context that always somehow manages to remain unnameable is that which keeps charismatic authority a deliberately revolutionary medium.

❦

To put the final link in the chain, we need to remember Weber's remarks that "Pure charisma is specifically foreign to economic considerations. Whenever it appears, it constitutes a 'call' in the most emphatic sense of the word, a 'mission' or a 'spiritual duty.' In the pure type, it disdains and repudiates economic exploitation of the gifts of grace as a source of income, though, to be sure, this often remains more an ideal than a fact" (p. 262). Particularly in our money-obsessed age it might strike one as peculiar that charisma and economic considerations don't go hand in hand, even more so given the fact that many of those who once would have assumed at least relative vows of poverty in order to remain pure now feel not the least bit uneasy about living as royally as any king or queen. If even modest ministers in small congregations no longer want to avoid the middle-class dream and even less want to be perceived as people set off from the ordinary run, we might think that there is nothing intrinsically antithetical between charisma and economic considerations.

Weber is careful to emphasize the word "pure" in his assertion and to state unequivocally that this might well be a rule obeyed more in the breach than otherwise, for after all even charismatic people have to eat and need shelter, and the alternatives in our economies are not what they were in Jesus's day. Weber is also insistent that the reason why pure charisma is foreign to economic considerations has to do with the special "calling" that the individual with charisma perceives himself to have, the "mission" or spiritual duty that is so all-consuming as to eliminate from the mind any serious consideration of economic well-being. The pure type takes no thought for the morrow, we might say, because his mission and powers are such that he is sure that the one whose mission he is undertaking will surely provide for him. One might also add, though it is clearly a subsidiary element in the context, that any individual who perceives himself as having a mission, and who wishes to gain adherents to that mission, must inevitably be able to convince those who will listen to him that the mission is *not* one of self-interest, and the most obvious way to do that is to repudiate any interest in the material and economic worlds, to deny any relation to them whatsoever. Inasmuch as many people remain convinced that money rules the world, and that the cynical manipulation of discourse on the part of those whose money runs the world is the norm rather than the exception, the best way to convince others of the purity of one's intentions is to abjure an interest in the prevailing values of the day and refuse to participate in them. Only in doing so can one convince the skeptics that one's authority is not a lure designed to entrap the weak and steal from them their own place within the economic system.

I would emphasize, however, that the so-called pure type of charisma is not in the least dependent on this more manipulative form of repudiation; there is something in the nature of charisma itself which prompts it to deny the force and value of the economic, and not merely because one believes that one has a special mission in life. The feelings of well-being and power that charisma denotes are sufficient in themselves as food for life, or so it would seem; if one is possessed of such strong and beautiful feelings, what need would one have for great fortune? What could it buy one that one didn't already have? If great well-being is that after which all humans seek, and if no greater well-being is felt than in the presence of the charismatic forces that flow through one, then mere pelf seems the most repugnant of lures known to humans, a pale substitute and dirty ruse designed to take one away from the much more pleasing values one already possesses.

It is true, then, that the mission of the charismatic and economic considerations are antithetical, but to say no more is to miss the very real chasm that inevitably appears between the two because they compete for the same human energies. The pure charismatic cannot but be repulsed by the idea of self-interested drives, even if he too is driven by them to a degree—perhaps unacknowledged—and no one can fail to note the self-interested motive inherent in the economic sphere. Even more, the psychological states engendered by self-interested manipulation as opposed to aesthetic utterance are such that the aesthetic would inevitably feel contaminated by the self-interested, again, even when it is present. It is the one thing that cannot be acknowledged without a serious reappraisal of the relationship of one's gift to the authority it provides one with to the self-interests that authority inevitably serves.

Another way of expressing the same inevitable opposition is to suggest that the pure type of charisma engenders feelings that lead to a devaluation of self-interest at the same time that the attention they call to the individual prompts others to focus upon him or her in such a way as to create the same effects that would ordinarily be achieved through self-interest. The charismatic type may well not be after success by any traditional standard, not seeking wealth or great social status or even the role of iconoclastic force of opposition, yet the greater the degree of success the individual has, the more he or she is going to have at least some of those aspects of success. At the very least the person will achieve a social status of some magnitude, if not throughout the socius then at least within the circle of his devotees. The role of iconoclast, of breaker of the profane images, is a necessary component of the charismatic authority, as Jesus came to discover, regardless of whether or not one chooses to take it up. And wealth is almost always readily available for one who is truly charismatic because those who are devotees are willing to give the person everything they have out of gratitude for the ways their lives have been changed into rich and meaningful constructs with goals and genuine passion. Indeed, as we know from far too many examples of writers and movie stars gone "bad," one of the most serious problems a charismatic individual ever faces is how to deal with all of the self-interested things that come one's way in spite of one's initially non-self-interested perspective. And precisely because in many cases the traditional routes to social status and wealth were never pursued, those who suddenly find themselves with them as a result of their gifts are the least likely to be able to know how to deal with them.

The final paradox of the charismatic authority is the one for which Weber is best known, the problems inherent in the "routinization of charisma." It may be that the charismatic individual has no interest in secular power, status or wealth, and it may be that the order articulated by the individual is in opposition to precisely those things. Nevertheless, the more successful the individual is at gaining adherents, the more people there are who are dependent on him and his values for their way of life. The structures of dependency grow into a fairly complex network even as the inherently unstable force of the charismatic leader is incapable of addressing the problem. As Weber has noted, the *only* basis of legitimacy for charismatic authority is the personal charisma of the individual, and yet that authority must be continually proved in ever-new contexts. Just as yesterday's prognostications are no longer of value, so too yesterday's miracles are never sufficient for long to keep the disciples in line. New wonders must be conjured up, new heights of mastery must be demonstrated, new attempts to overturn the old order and impose the new. And yet there are mouths to feed, and shelter must be found and maintained, and so the non-secular disposition of charismatic authority always runs up against the limitations of the everyday.

Weber establishes the rationale underlying the inevitable attempts to routinize charismatic authority in the following way:

> In its pure form charismatic authority has a character specifically foreign to everyday routine structures. The social relationships directly involved are strictly personal, based on the validity and practice of

> charismatic personal qualities. If this is not to remain a purely transitory phenomenon, but to take on the character of a permanent relationship forming a stable community of disciples or a band of followers or a party organization or any sort of political or hierocratic organization, it is necessary for the character of charismatic authority to become radically changed. Indeed, in its pure form charismatic authority may be said to exist only in the process of originating. It cannot remain stable, but becomes either traditionalized or rationalized, or a combination of both.
>
> The following are the principal motives underlying this transformation: (a) The ideal and also the material interests of the followers in the continuation and the continual reactivation of the community, (b) the still stronger ideal and also stronger material interests of the members of the administrative staff, the disciples or other followers of the charismatic leader in continuing their relationship. Not only this, but they have an interest in continuing it in such a way that both from an ideal and a material point of view, their own status is put on a stable every-day basis. This means, above all, making it possible to participate in normal family relationships or at least to enjoy a secure social position in place of the kind of discipleship which is cut off from ordinary worldly connexions, notably in the family and in economic relationships. (p. 363, 64)

If the group that is attached to the charismatic individual is to manage to have any significant effect on the socius it is determined to change, it realizes fairly early on that there is a need to organize its forces in more systematic ways. If in some senses it is true that the pure form of charismatic authority can "exist only in the process of originating," if it is incapable of stability, then it has no choice but to seek to become either traditional or rational, losing at least some of its fervor in return for a structure that will be capable of greater effects.

The difficulty, of course, is that whereas charismatic authority is reflected in the fervor and instability of the leader, that is precisely what undermines the leader's effectiveness once a group has been established. In order seriously to maintain the goals with which the group began, it has no choice but to find some way of normalizing things in order to engender some kind of ordinary life to go along with the larger plans of the group. Just as the fury and enthusiasm of a crowd cannot continue for long but must burn itself out in one way or another, so too the group must organize to avoid the inevitable dissolution that will come once the energies are no longer as intense as they once were. If there are no compensatory gestures put in place, the authority of the charismatic figure declines, and the group is bound to lose its effectiveness and solidarity. Born of a context that spurns both economic realities and everyday concerns, charismatic authority must finally bend to these forces as much as any other kind of order does.

The other aspect of this routinization of charisma that so affects its future disposition concerns the ways in which the authority begins to be delegated to bureaucratic units within the group, yet again something that would have been inconceivable in the beginning. As Weber puts it:

> Concomitant with the routinization of charisma with a view to insuring adequate succession, go the interests in its routinization on the part of the administrative staff. It is only in the initial stages and so long as the charismatic leader acts in a way which is completely outside everyday social organization, that it is possible for his followers to live communistically in a community of faith and enthusiasm, on gifts, "booty," or sporadic acquisition. Only the members of the small group of enthusiastic disciples and followers are prepared to devote their lives purely idealistically to their call. The great majority of disciples and followers will in the long run "make their living" out of their "calling" in a material sense as well. Indeed, this must be the case if the movement is not to disintegrate.

Hence, the routinization of charisma also takes

> the form of the appropriation of powers of control and of economic advantages by the followers or disciples, and of regulation of the recruitment of these groups. (p. 367)

Inasmuch as the group feels the need to consolidate, it first establishes means of succession and also determines the ways in which various members of the group can continue to administer the authority that originally resided exclusively in the leader himself. Weber's assumption here, doubtless a correct one, is that there are always only a limited number of individuals who are willing to give their lives exclusively to the cause of another, regardless of how important it is perceived to be; once the group expands past that limited number, it has to find ways of appealing to those who might be interested but who are also sufficiently committed to the values of their current lives that they would be unwilling simply to lay them down and totally transform their lives, as, say, Jesus's disciples did.

To provide for the needs of this larger group, and to guarantee that their bonding to the group will remains strong, the leader and the "staff" that emerges to help in the structuration of the group must find ways of providing a sustaining way of life for the larger number of people and of using that way of life to reinforce the value of the group. The need for routinization in this sense is inevitably connected to size, to the number of people involved, and again in both metaphorical and literal ways the necessary changes are a result of the effects of numbers. A small group's enthusiasm is much more self-contained and focussed than a larger group's is, whether it be at a rock concert or a religious revival. The larger the group grows, the more the energies will be dispersed. It will still be capable of large effects, and its enthusiasm will not necessarily disperse altogether—though that is certainly possible—but it will not be as organized and disciplined as it would be with a smaller number. Once, for example, the opportunity for genuine eye contact with the leader declines, the ability to hold the audience's attention on a single object or intention also declines, and pockets of "anarchy" or "entropy" appear within the crowd: most people may hold the leader in rapt attention, but some people's minds will wander because they lack the holding force of eye contact or even the close meshing of a small number of bodies.

The group cannot afford too much in the way of pockets of entropy, either in the context of a singular event or in the overall disposition of the career of the cause, for the more of them there are, the more the enthusiasm of the leader is wasted, and the more it is dispersed, the less effective it finally is. As Weber concludes, routinization of charisma is a necessary and inevitable event, one that may be resisted, and one that surely means the end of the original group's full enthusiasm and complete attention, but one that also gives the group a chance to survive and allows its effectiveness as a political mechanism to grow and move in new directions. Given these forces, that which was anti-economic must become economic in nature, must accommodate itself to the needs of everyday existence within a social system; once that principle is accepted, the charismatic authority in a real way begins its journey toward a different kind of authority.

After charismatic authority is routinized and turned into a permanent structure, in a real way it ceases to exist. Once it adapts itself to the larger needs of pragmatic and economic reality, it does indeed become more and more either rational or traditional in its form of authority, and the more it does so, the less the charismatic authority itself continues to exist as the *raison d'etre* of the organization. The tight solidarity of a local political group metaphorically moves from regular sessions of enthusiasm with the leader to occasional meetings with him to perhaps a television transmission of his image and voice from another location. The first-name basis of the group disappears, the structure of authority covers up the gaps in the previous arrangements of solidarity and replaces the emotional fervor that compensated for the inevitable differences among individuals.

And this is the *best* that can happen to such a group. The worst, as is again most often on display in the context of certain religious charismatics, is that in some unknowing way both the group and the leader succumb totally to that which was previously antithetical to their goals. If they have spurned economic necessities, they might well end up unintentionally devoting themselves to them once they are forced to accommodate them. The group subsists more on its own in the beginning, but if it grows beyond a relatively small size, the need for fund raising arises, and once it becomes a necessity to raise money in order to help the group to get its message to a larger audience, it is all too easy for the need to raise money to overtake the other goals: what began as charisma ends as a boiler-room operation devoted to the need to beg for money from potential adherents, hoping that their dollars will fund the existing structures of fund-raising and allow them to expand in order to reach still more people. Precisely because the charisma that originally drew the people to the organization keeps them in ignorance of the powerful forces of the economic flows, they fail to note in time the ways in which those flows can thoroughly come to dominate the activity of the group, placing the original mission into economic submission and clear subordination: it becomes the "message" in an "advertisement" that is designed to raise money more than raise spirits or change lives. And that marks the eventual end of the authority of the charismatic leader, even if it quite often takes a while for the group to lose its effectiveness.

Weber is no doubt right, then, both that charismatic authority must eventually become routinized if it is to continue to exist and that in a real way it ceases to exist even if it becomes routinized. Though Weber himself does not draw this conclusion as specifically as those who build upon his work, it does seem inevitable in the very way he describes it. He accounts, for example, for the need to establish a line of succession from the original leader, and by definition any successor is going to have a different form of authority, even if he too possesses charisma. There will inevitably be a displacement of the importance of charisma in general and an increasing focus on a bureaucracy to manage the day-to-day events of the group as a whole. Once that happens, the effectiveness of the charismatic authority has disappeared, as has its reason for existing. It has capitulated to precisely those forces it originally resisted. It began as an authority that was radically opposed to the status quo and completely determined to alter the way lives are lived, and it ends as yet another structure devoted to the perpetuation of a seemingly rational form of authority or a comfortably traditional authority. The nods to the leader, alive or dead, become ritual gestures of an emerging past, one that will eventually be part of that which is repudiated by yet another charismatic figure somewhere down the line. If charismatic authority is in some respects the most genuine form of authority known in human communities—if also the most unruly and potentially destructive as well—it is at the same time the one kind of authority whose very success is guaranteed to destroy its genuine powers and to transfer them to some lesser guarantor of rights and privileges.

If we, like Weber, can imagine such authority in a pure form, we can assert that charismatic authority is the one authority that at least potentially can be in some fundamental respects disinterested in the older sense of that word. Certainly the charismatic authority has an interest at heart in his assertions, but it is not predominantly his *self-interest* that is at stake. The authority he achieves comes from his ability to manifest a message and a plan that are clearly untinged by special pleading for himself and by self-aggrandizement; these are the marks of his personal charisma even as they manifest themselves in the larger domains by his repudiation of the past and the economic forces that consume other people's lives. That charismatic authority is not driven by self-interest in its original manifestations is no guarantee of its value, we know, for it could still be a misguided form of enthusiasm that proffered a seriously demented version of reality or that unintentionally managed to undermine the fabric of life for those people it sought to "save."

But if there is no guarantee that such an authority will indeed be worthy of legitimacy, it has more of a likelihood of avoiding the main reason other forms of authority are never as legitimate as they purport to be: self-interest is not the goal of the system. Both rational and traditional authority are finally based on self-interest, even if we think of them in their pure form too. Rational authority is in many respects little more than traditional authority that has been around so long it now appears to be based on reason rather than tradition, and hence its forms of self-interest are less available to scrutiny than they were as traditional forms, where the self-interested groups' interests are clearly on display. It is possible to develop structures of authority that purport to be purely rational, but again, for the most part this only means that they are developed out of an ignorance of their original presuppositions. Still, one of the necessary goals of human communities should surely be the task of implementing a truly rational form of authority in a disinterested way. Even then, once authority begins to disperse itself, it becomes a relative marker of power, and, as with the transformation of a non-economic charismatic form of authority into an economic machine of considerable force, once the relative measures of power are put into play by the bureaucratic structures that are developed, the fight for a self-interested assertion of that power begins to develop and will eventually threaten thoroughly to undermine the original intentions of the group.

This account of the forms of authority, however, has all too much of the cast of the four ages about it. It is as though all authority begins in the golden charismatic age, and as it is routinized it gradually comes to the silver age where the original mission is still intact and even some of the old fervor is still present but the goals have somehow been modulated through structures that diminish their importance. From there it is a small step to the bronze age in which the routinized structures have become so wedded to the economic and pragmatic needs of the group, and the group itself has grown so large and heterogeneous as to become less a group and more an agglomeration of individuals, that the original forces are all but spent. And finally in the iron age there is no longer even any pretense of upholding the original mission. Self-interest once again becomes all, enthusiasm is devoted to purely secular forms of expression, and decadence is the inevitable rule, only to be overturned yet again by another form of charismatic authority that will rise up to rouse people from their dogmatic slumbers.

One might even go so far as to posit a law on the basis of an equivalent physiological phenomenon called the habituation response. Just as that which is new becomes that which is given, so too it becomes part of that to which attention is no longer paid. Once we become habituated to the pleasures of this or that phenomenon, they cease to be as pleasurable as they once were; they become "routinized" and are not capable of providing us with the charge of pleasure they once had. In such a situation one can adjust to the habituation of one's pleasures and accommodate oneself to lesser forms of intensity, or one can seek out other non-habituated pleasures to obtain the enthusiasm for life that one originally desired. All enthusiasms suffer under their inevitable habituation, and their "bureaucratized" form is thus going to be something of a different manifestation of them than they were. So too charismatic authority is eventually in each of its particular manifestations something to which we become habituated, and once we do its form inevitably changes to something else, either a traditional or rational form of authority whose chief values reside precisely in its habitual continuities rather than in its great enthusiastic forms of explosive energy. And if it is in some respects both inevitable and preferable for this unstable form of authority finally to give way to the traditional or the rational, the crucial question in the end is whether or not those other forms of authority are at least potentially capable of maintaining the same relatively disinterested perspective that was to be found in their charismatic origins. This fundamental problem of authority is the one to which we shall return again and again, for it remains the final litmus test of the values of any form of authority.

❦

Up to this point I have confined my discussion chiefly to the parameters that Weber himself establishes with only an occasional reference to the linkages between the charismatic form of authority and the aesthetic, and I have thus also concentrated far more on charismatic individuals than I have on individuals who have charisma. Inasmuch as the major forms of authority as they manifest themselves in our daily lives come from these "lesser" forms of charisma, from individuals or contexts whose authority is declared by their charisma but who at the same time are part of rather than radically distinguished from the socius as a whole, our main interest in this form of authority ought to reside in a consideration of these more localized versions of charisma. In referring to these lesser forms of charisma, I intend only to suggest that their manifestations are such as to keep them within the bounds of the everyday world to a greater or lesser extent, either because of their lesser intensity or because of their regionalization in a specific location that doesn't repudiate the entire structure of life as it is lived within the given culture. If the distinction is metaphorically the one between the sublime and the beautiful, I am more interested in the manifestations of beautiful authority than I am in sublime forms, and thus I should like to explore how individuals (and other forms of cultural life capable of engendering aesthetic events) create a kind of authority that is to be distinguished from the radically repudiative versions of the "sublime" charisma and the rational and traditional forms that we all recognize around us every day.

It is also worth noting that our culture, like many of those before it perhaps, has more often than not been preoccupied with the sublime forms of charisma rather than the beautiful ones. Its apocalyptic tendencies, its deep-seated needs for constant and radical change, its tendencies toward gullibility, are in a real way all somehow dependent on the cultural features that reflect our considerable dissatisfaction with the inevitabilities of our lives. Given the myths through which we have constituted ourselves, and particularly the American myths that emphasize the autonomy of the individual and the ability of that individual to live a largely free life capable of great transformations and a total denial of the past structures that made it what it is, it is no accident that we should prefer the sublime to the beautiful any more than it is a coincidence that such a culture should be responsible for the development of nuclear weapons.

One might go back to Nietzsche and argue that the West is based upon an essentially nihilistic, life-denying apparatus, whether filtered through the Platonic world-view or the ascetic perspective of Christianity which places a greater emphasis on a better world to come. Given our dissatisfaction with life as we know it, and given our need to will regardless of our dissatisfactions, we would, as Nietzsche liked to put it, rather will nothing than not will at all. As a result, we are easily subject to the lure of the sublime, the apocalyptic, the intense adrenal flow that overrides everything in its wake, and we have tended to develop our cultures in terms of such grand gestures of enthusiasm. If a country like the United States is both reviled and admired for the way it has institutionalized late adolescence as the quintessential form of human existence, and if it has done more than any other society to extend this state into the later years of the human span, that is surely because the West in general has come to define itself more and more in terms of intensities, *great* intensities, and we don't need Wordsworth to tell us that those intensities are most in evidence in late youth when the hormonal surges and chemical imbalances set in play by the onset of maturation have yet to modulate themselves into the flows of adulthood, have yet to become "routinized" by the succession of years that gradually habituates one in both a bodily and a psychic way to the strange wonders of the world.

Accustomed as we are to the need for great intensity, condemned as we presently are to a generally life-denying, nihilistic attitude toward the commonplaces of the routine world, we have defined ourselves in terms of the extreme forms of charisma and the aesthetic, the revolutionary leader and the sublime experience. Indeed, one might suggest that we have pushed this mode of human being to its limit, even as we have explored to the maximum the consequent forms of charismatic authority and sublime intensity. Nietzsche himself in this respect would be a call to another vision of things, a revolutionary figure devoted to the extraordinary idea that life itself is worth affirming in all of its joys and terrors and doesn't necessarily need the constant stimulus of the apocalyptic and the decadent. Perhaps we ought to turn away from our metaphorical preoccupation with Wagner, just as Nietzsche finally did, and recognize the far greater virtues of the beautiful in the midst of which we are always capable of finding ourselves.

The region of the beautiful, the lesser forms of intensity to be found in those locations that have charisma yet are not exclusively defined by its presence within them, is the most compelling feature of our world, yet it has been far less explored than the extreme forms, as perhaps, is only to be expected inasmuch as it is always easier to articulate the nature of extreme forms than "mixed" ones. But again, the reason these forms of beauty remain less explored in the culture at large is also because they truly are mixed, and our culture, like most others, has been committed to *pure* forms. If Nietzsche wanted to embrace the world in all of its joy and terror, the only reason this is such a striking notion to us is that we should prefer to embrace the world only in its joy and forego our connection to the terror. In the mixed world, the impure world, in the spot where we inevitably live out our lives, there has been too much with which we have fundamentally disagreed, far too much with which we have taken issue. We, like the highly charismatic figure, have preferred to repudiate the world as we know it in the hope that something better will be forthcoming, either in an existence after death or in a community that will come about as a result of some charismatic figure who will show us the way to a purer world of great intensities.

The impure world of beauty is also more difficult to locate because of its inevitably mixed hues. If we have found that the problem with all forms of authority is that there is no guarantee of their veracity or their virtue, so too the problem with beauty is that we cannot easily separate its constituent elements from other aspects of our world that are decidedly *not* beautiful. And inasmuch as its pleasures are also of a lesser intensity than those of the sublime, it remains unquestionably a less glamorous region of the social world. But it is also the location through which the richness and the fundamental authority of our world plays itself out, so we need to investigate it more carefully than we have been inclined to do, and we should determine how its forms of authority measure up to those of the sublime on the one hand and the traditional and rational on the other. Without such an inquiry, we shall not be able to assess the possibilities for authority in a world in which there are no longer grounds for *any* form of it, regardless of its charismatic, traditional or rational orientation.

When we think of how the intensities and authority of beauty might differ from those of the sublime, we must first ask whether we are only speaking of differences of degree in these two manifestations of charisma, or whether the differences of degree are also a reflection of a clear difference of value as well. The primary difference of value would seem to be that the qualitative value of the beautiful tends to focus the mind on the everyday world whereas the power of the sublime inclines one toward a state that is more likely to renounce this world in favor of another, more powerfully manifested one. But the beautiful is like the sublime in its tendency to be disinterested and unattached to the economic system, though it too is certainly capable of merging its interests with the economic, as we see in those artists who prostitute their gift for money or fame. If it can be attached to these forms of social discourse, though, its tendency is to repudiate them too because its perspective is largely nonegocentric. The distinguishing feature of the beautiful is that its authority comes from its ability to place us within the attractions of this world and to demonstrate to us the ways in which we are always a part of the various flows around us rather than purely self-interested, alienated spectators in a show that goes on regardless of us.

Having established the major difference between the sublime form of authority and the beautiful one, I should also add that to a great extent even this difference is culture-dependent rather than purely intrinsic. If the sublime forms tend so radically to repudiate this world and conjure up another, if they tend too often to be tied to essentially nihilistic forms in the modern West, that is because we have devised theological systems that are oriented toward that other world. In a culture that finds the presence of God everywhere, the sublime would not direct our attention away from the presences in this world but would rather serve to reinforce the locations where that presence manifested itself. So it is rather the strict delineation of a sacred space that is unconnected to the profane space of everyday life that tends to link the sublime authority to a mode of assertion that denies the value of the world through which one lives one's life and makes a living.

Inasmuch as both the aesthetic and the various forms of authority have been attacked and presumably discredited in the past century, though, we need to consider the relationship of beauty to a disinterested state, particularly since the disinterested perspective of the realm of judgment is a Kantian principle that has long been called into question by the followers of Nietzsche. As I am using the term, however, there is no purely disinterested perspective: again, inevitably and as a matter of course, he who finds himself obtaining authority through the flows of the aesthetic will clearly "profit" from them to the extent that people listen to him and look upon him as an authority. In this sense self-interest is an inherent part of *any* kind of authoritative discourse, even those forms in which the speaker seeks to repudiate and deny his or her authority, for there the authority itself is increased through the humble act of repudiation. Even if the individual thinks his discourse is pure, then, it simply cannot be so, and more than likely any individual who has placed himself in the midst of the flows of the beautiful or the sublime has a good idea that at the very least people will think more highly of him as a result of his utterances. Still, even here it could be argued that there is a temporal problem, for *in the midst of* his utterance, he will likely *not* be thinking of self-interest at all; that is something that is part of the overall circuitry of the process but not essentially related to the moment of utterance itself. Rather, *after* one has felt the force of one's own utterance or seen its effects on others, one begins to recognize the ways in which even those who attempt to speak from a purely disinterested perspective inevitably forward their own interests in the process.

All aesthetic discourse is also self-interested to the extent that it expresses the values of its location, its placement within a particular space and time, culture and body, domestic and social heritage. The charismatic figure may well repudiate the status quo and the base world of economics and self-interest, but his form of repudiation is still based on precisely that world, and his formulation of an alternative world is likewise based on the way that the profane world is conceived. In the interstices of such a repudiation there is a different kind of self-interest, an utterance that is based upon the tacit presuppositions about the nature of what is that are easily enough caught in the web of class interests and other limiting elements without the knowledge of the speaker himself. These kinds of "self-interest" are inevitable in any discourse, and the greater and lesser forms of charisma no more escape them than any form of aesthetic discourse does.

Still, it is crucially important to the sense of values any culture possesses to distinguish between this form of self-interest and the more obvious kind that dominates the everyday world of economic and class interests, first because they are products of two different psychological states, so even in "scientific" terms we should have an interest in preserving distinctions between states that are readily recognizable; and second because even if every human event has a degree of self-interest attached to it, we still must act on the basis of certain kinds of authority, and one of the ways we do so is through an assessment of the individual's own self-interest in the nature of his aesthetic propositions. As I have suggested before, at the very least we need to recognize the effects that come from the different *placement* of self-interest within the nature of the discourse, for self-interest in aesthetic discourse is clearly subordinate to the utterance or event itself rather than the dominator of it. Whereas charlatans manipulate their words for the purposes of self-aggrandizement and general self-interest, truly charismatic figures of both the lesser and greater varieties are more manipulated by the flows of their discourse than they are the manipulators of it, and not only does this mean a change of state, but it also reflects a change of orientation that affects the way we see the situation of the speaker, the self, and finally the location of authority in general.

If the flow of discourse takes precedence over the location through which it flows, as is the case in a charismatic or aesthetic context, the discourse itself provides us with a pattern of authority that is dispersed rather than centralized, that emanates not from the individual himself but rather from the manner in which the flows flow through him. This orientation toward discourse and its flows inevitably engenders a different way of looking at the world, one that emphasizes our own nugatory status within it, one that prompts us to recognize the degree to which our lives are shaped by the flows that we usually think we are in control of, and one that suggests to us a different placement for our needs and interests within the overall flow of the world beyond the one of pure human interests. If charismatic figures are capable of gathering to them many disciples who are zealously committed to a radically different world than the one they are accustomed to, that is because the aesthetic nature of charisma places leader and disciples into a framework that subordinates self-interest to the flows of the field as they are conceived on the basis of the charismatic utterance. Such a discourse could construe that framework in purely religious or purely secular terms; it could be a vision of heaven or a description of the ideal human community. But whatever it is, it is as comprehensive as it is precisely because the aesthetic perspective of existence is antithetical to the self-interested egocentricity that governs much of our daily lives. And this is not merely the *appearance* of a lack of self-interest any more than the force of the charismatic figure depends solely on the emotional power of his words. Rather, the revolutionary nature of the discourse, its emotional fervor, and its disinterested perspective are all reflections of the same fact: that the aesthetic utterance is one in which the self is subordinate to the flows of utterance itself. If the self has died and the author has gone elsewhere, and if God Himself was the original casualty from which the others derived, that is because we came to understand the essentially aesthetic nature of human discourse. We realized that our placement within its flows was precisely our placement within the fields of the world in general: we may have interests, and we may even see ourselves as essential selves in opposition to the natural world or the social world or some other greater structure, but we are really part of flows that are far greater than any ability we might possess to control them. The grief and the wonder and the joy and the terror in life emanate from precisely that fact: the flows flow through us rather than being controlled by us.

The aesthetics of the beautiful reveals the flows through which our lives constitute the "selves" we have and demonstrates that those selves are simply the codified history of a location within the flow of a field, a manifestation of energy within fields of force that are constituted out of the collations of energy as they manifest themselves in the natural and the human worlds. The aesthetics of the beautiful convinces us through its power that it is indeed a disinterested location, one through which different kinds of flows are occurring, one in which we can find an authority that has something to it that traditional and rational forms do not. We are convinced of this authority *not* for hierarchical reasons—*father* says so, or the Queen says so—*nor* for rational reasons—we know through reflection that this or that is not the thing to do in this particular context—but rather because the *orientation itself* is authoritative—not the individual manifestation of it in the charismatic figure or the particular words themselves but rather the ways in which the individual and the words come together into an utterance that both charms us and has conviction.

The problem with charismatic utterances, though, like all aesthetic authority, is that it is difficult to sort out the nature of the conviction and the charm: does the charm engender the conviction, or the conviction the charm? Do we recognize the aesthetic truth of a moment because of the powerful feelings of pleasure or joy that course through us, or do we experience joy because we are in the presence of truth. Is "truth" the (empty) illusion at the center of any aesthetic moment, the lure that draws us onward like the charismatic figure who has seen a better world, or is it the mark of our certitude about our place within a series of flows from which we all too often feel cut off and differentiated? Given the nature of the experience, it would seem that there is no way to determine such things, and there is no reason why we should need to do so.

What is important is not whether the pleasures of beauty are the mark of truth or truth the engenderer of the pleasures of beauty—such questions of origin have been legitimately undermined by Derrida and others—but rather that both pleasure and truth do indeed exist in the same moment. It was the illusion of the moderns that "poetry" or the aesthetic was unrelated to any kind of truth, and that illusion prompted them to separate the pleasures of the aesthetic from the very real truths that are at the center of them. That illusion also prompted them to ridicule such statements as those by Keats—"'Beauty is truth, truth beauty,'—that is all / Ye know on earth, and all ye need to know"—because they felt that the very abstraction of the utterance demonstrated the total vacuity of the notion of truth that was essential to it. But of course Keats was right: beauty *is* truth, the mark of the most profound truths about the world we have, and truth *is* beauty precisely to the extent that in the end the two are indistinguishable. We shouldn't need a Grecian urn to tell us about this any more than we should need Keats to, but we do because whatever truth the aesthetic moment has, it does not correspond to the kinds of truth we have developed out of our rational and traditional discourses, and so it seems nonexistent within the beautiful. That this should be more of a problem in a rational and scientific age goes without saying; that it should also be a problem in a nihilistic age in which everything is a question of the will to power also goes without saying, so there is every reason why we should need to be reminded again and again that truth is indeed beauty and beauty truth.

❦

Still, such gnomic utterances return us to the heart of the problem, which is that whatever truth there is in the aesthetic or the charismatic, it remains elusive. And whatever authority emanates from the aesthetic or the charismatic, it cannot be definitively established or repudiated in a single moment or even over a short period of time. The truths of such contexts require the continual testing of a great many people over a considerable expanse of time, moving through the alterations of demotic discourse of several generations at least, if not several epochs. But we can at least begin to get a grip on the nature of that elusive authority if we start with the relationship between the aesthetic and the charismatic and if we question what the relationship is. After all, if I have been using "aesthetic" and "charismatic" almost interchangeably, Weber himself did not, and one might wonder what the relationship between the two is. If the charismatic always partakes of the aesthetic, still the charismatic is not all there is of the aesthetic. The charismatic is that aesthetic context in which a human location plays an important, if not necessarily central, role. We obviously experience aesthetic events in a great many contexts, some of them in purely natural locations, others in larger social situations with no central figure to be found, and in these situations the word "charisma" does not apply. There is no readily identifiable *agent* for the wonder of the aesthetic experience, and even more importantly, there is no *desire to find an agent*. The experience stands by itself because we feel no need to locate the origin of it. If we spend half an hour appreciating the beauty of a sunset, we are not likely to wonder *where* it came from but rather are willing to let the experience stand on its own terms.

Of course, there are those who will relate the beauty of the sunset to God's wonders, just as there were those who originally thought of God in the midst of such wonders: the great power of the beauty of the natural world is surely one of the origins of the gods, and thus at least some of those who sat and watched a sunset were given to looking for an agent of its beauty. If we today are less inclined to seek an agent in this context, that is because our understanding of the flows of discourse has prompted us to see the beauty as agentless, as something that occurs which may well manifest certain truths about the world and our placement within it, but not an event that points to an agent of the beauty of the world or to an individual or god who would be capable of explaining to us the point of our placement on the planet.

Likewise, in some social situations we are not finally interested in the agency through which the moment of wonder has occurred, though within the flows of social discourse we are clearly more likely to look for agents. If one appreciates the beauty of a work of art, for example, one can choose to focus on *who* did it and question the nature of the agent and become exclusively preoccupied by that; indeed, we know that our own era has particular proclivities in that direction in spite or because of the very real death of the author or the self as an agent of any particular value. But one can just as easily participate in the aesthetic event of the painting without even thinking about the agent involved. To be sure, reflection on the event will usefully prompt one for knowledge about the context out of which the painting was generated, and this will lead one to historical, cultural, and personal information that will be most useful in further appreciation of the painting. Still, one can experience the beauty of a painting without wondering in the least about the origin of its special value. One can simply recognize it as valuable and note its usefulness in one's own life and leave it at that. Or one can be part of a spontaneously formed crowd that comes together into an aesthetic event and not be concerned about any particular agent of the event. One *might* be interested in how such an event came about; indeed, one is almost invariably interested in the how of an event because one should like to have such events occur again in the future. But one need not think of that how in terms of a who at all. The death of the author and the death of the self would instruct us precisely *not* to think of a who but rather to think of a how.

In a charismatic context, though, it is difficult to separate the question of aesthetic agency from the question of aesthetic authority, and this is one of the reasons why the charismatic location within the aesthetic flows of the world is both the most dangerous and potentially the most promising of moments. Within the charismatic context we tend always to attribute the authority of the utterance to the seeming agent, the charismatic figure, even when the individual himself insists that he is only a vessel for someone or something else, be it the voice of God or the aesthetic flows of the universe. We want to insist in turn that he is indeed the agent because we have become habituated to the need for origins, and the most compelling origin would be the agent right in front of our eyes. And as charismatic figures well know, one of the immediate offshoots of the tendency to focus on the agent rather than the event is that the agent himself becomes fetishized and the event recedes into the background, even though the distinguishing feature of an aesthetic event is that the event itself takes precedence over the agents who are present within it. The agent is also foregrounded instead of the event because our ordinary ways of conceiving of things center on agents and power, and so it would be natural for us to think of even extraordinary events in such a way. Nevertheless, the moment the event is displaced in favor of the agent, its effectiveness begins to disappear and the authority to be found in the context also dissipates, usually without either agent or audience being aware of that fact.

If there are dangers in those contexts where there is a readily identifiable agent for the aesthetic event, and if both agent and audience can lose themselves in an aggrandizement of the agent, it is also possible for the charismatic figure to turn the attention of the audience to the event itself as a marker of authority that doesn't reside in the individual himself or even in the audience but is rather to be found in the unfolding of the event and its discourse. To the extent that attention can be focused on the real locus of authority in the event, one can begin to pursue the question of authority within its proper domain with the right perspective on it. And if the orientation toward authority can be directed in this fashion, one can begin to get a better sense of how authority is established in the world, what its crucial links to contingency are, and how far the authority of any one event, utterance, or discourse can and should extend. These are always questions that need to be answered on the basis of a particular set of circumstances, and so there is no way to establish any set of rules to cover the terrain or to convey the sense that something has been definitively nailed down that will never need to be addressed again. For better or worse the question of authority will need to be reconsidered on every occasion in the future when authority is at stake, and the only thing that has changed is that one will be better able to assess the value of the authority that announces itself. Even then, though, the focus must always be kept on the authority of the event rather than the agent, lest the fetishization of self begins to corrupt the authority and undermine its value.

Even if the linkages to the authority of the aesthetic are exclusively to be located within the event rather than within particular agents, though, we need to recognize that there are locations within events that are capable of having a greater awareness of the nature of the authority that the flows have, and such a location used to be called the "agent" or the charismatic figure. To focus on the authority of the event is not to deny that the event itself is at times best assessed through the most obvious manifestations of its aesthetic force, and that would be the figure through whom the utterance is given expression. The agent has been displaced from the central role within the aesthetic context because we came to recognize that the authority we had attributed to him was in fact a function of his location within the flow of discourse and not an essential feature of the individual himself. In some cases this means that the charismatic figure himself is not a reliable guide to the nature of authority that manifests itself in the aesthetic event—in traditional literary criticism this is called the intentional fallacy, assuming that the author's intentions are a reflection of what indeed occurs in the poem or novel, something that is not necessarily true.

But if the agent isn't the primary locus for the authority of an aesthetic event, and if the agent isn't even always the one to turn to for an interpretation of the event's significance, it is still true that the agent *can be* an authority as a result of the aesthetic events in which he participates, and he *can be* the one whose interpretative mastery of the event is the one upon which we rely. As always, these are factors that can only be determined in local situations and cannot be established in any unilateral fashion. If I emphasize the point here, it is only because the tendency is always to move from one excess to another: having displaced the agent from the locus of authority and dispersed the authority into the event itself, our inclination is to deny the agent any authority at all and to assume his understanding of the event is no better than ours, and perhaps worse as a result of the self-interest that might well take over once the event has passed. The author may be dead, but only in a metaphorical context, and we need to recognize specifically what that means.

If one speaks of aesthetic authority in less abstract contexts, referring to, say, the creation of a poem or a painting, we can see the obvious value of the agent even in a world where his authority has been displaced. The productions of a writer or painter are clearly dependent on him or her in any number of ways, though we would not be inclined at this point in our development to attribute that dependency to any particular form of genius. Any poem or painting is the result of a complex event whose direction is not exclusively the function of the "creator," even if he or she is usually in a better position to know how the event took place. The production of a poem is dependent on the location within the culture through which its form and manner passes, and that location always has what we would think of as certain "gifts." Any agent of production has worked to cultivate those gifts in order to learn how to employ them more fully to create better poems or paintings: art is not simply a matter of waiting for the call, even if it isn't a matter of total self-control either. The artist employs a discipline that allows his or her gifts to frame themselves in compelling ways within the painting, and the artist's discipline and gifts—whatever they may be, from an extraordinarily well developed sense of light and color to an acute notion of pattern and repetition to a mastery of the history of painting within the culture—are obviously the most important features of any aesthetic event.

The death of the author does not signify that magic visits itself upon individuals from the outside as they paint or write poems any more than it should mean that such figures are seized by the local fervor of their class or culture-bound interests and display them without thinking. The productions of any aesthetic agent are dependent on these interests, as the nature of the event is also dependent on the particular circumstances of the agent, but if there is an authority present within the event who is most capable of expressing the nature of it and most likely the repository of any residual authority it manifests, it is inevitably the author or the painter, as it should be. Such creative agents have been displaced from the central locus of authority, but they still almost always derive an authority from the events in which they participate, as they well should, having demonstrated their acuity through them.

Most specifically, we could say that there is no guarantee that any agent within an aesthetic event—be it artistic, religious or political—is the locus of a kind of discipline or wisdom that would grant him or her the authority that derives from the event itself, but there is a likelihood that the agent will possess a larger degree of these factors than the other participants in the event will, and thus both authority and responsibility should at least tacitly accrue to such a person. We need to remember too, that if we content ourselves with a description of the world in which the author and the self are truly dead, as some post-structuralists want to do, we shall be left with a society in which no humans have responsibility for their actions, for responsibility is connected to authority, and if we are content to attribute authority exclusively to events rather than to the agents within them, we will have stripped the world of any locations of responsibility. An event cannot be responsible for anything, can take neither credit nor blame, cannot be redone or refined in order to address whatever consequences came from it. Once it is over, it is gone. Only the agents within events remain behind, both to assess and to take credit or responsibility for their part within the event—after all, we do always inevitably live within a social world of weights and measures that is not to be avoided regardless of one's charismatic enthusiasm, and it is fitting within such a world for the effects of events to be measured and valued. This is what social systems do, and for them to do so, there must be locations of authority that are willing to assume responsibility for the consequences of the events in which they have played a part. The one with charisma is the likely source for that form of authority and responsibility, regardless of the decentralized role he or she occupies within the aesthetic event.

In this respect it is also worth stressing that aesthetic events have other agents as well, and these too share to a certain extent in the authority and responsibility for the event. The degree to which the other agents play a part in the event is dependent on the context—a reader of a poem clearly participates in the event of the poem in a way, as the reader-response theorists would remind us, but such an individual plays less of a role in the production of that event—the production of the poem itself, that is—than the audience of a charismatic speaker participates in the production of that kind of event. Clearly a speaker's charisma is dependent on the ways in which the audience responds to his words. If they show no interest or shuffle randomly about and talk to their neighbors, the speaker's words will have less effect than they will if the audience becomes wrapped up in the enthusiasm he expresses. And any charismatic figure knows full well that charisma itself is not enough, for the sweet eloquence of words is not always sufficient to move people, just as the words are not always forthcoming in the ways one would like them to be. Their greater or lesser pleasure is dependent upon the circumstances of production, which includes especially the auditors of the speech.

In addition, one would have to say that the word "agent" within aesthetic events exceeds the bounds of merely human presences, for there can be agents that have little or nothing to do with the human community per se and that at the very least don't inhere in a specific body. A poet's productions, for example, can be dependent on the local circumstances at any given moment. If it is an extremely hot day with high humidity, the kind of day that might make the poet uncomfortable in his body, the weather itself could become an agent in the production of the poem, just as a totally striking day with astonishing clarity and brilliant features could be the central agent in the production of a poem. More obviously, the language itself becomes an agent for the poet, just as the medium of paint or words in other contexts becomes an agent for a painter or another type of charismatic figure.

Nevertheless, it is fitting that we attribute authority more to one agent within a context than to others, and it is appropriate that we find that agent to be the poet or the painter or the charismatic speaker. It does indeed matter who is speaking precisely because within any flow of discourse there are locations of greater and lesser importance, and the location of greatest importance—beyond the flow of language itself, which is the most significant factor inasmuch as it is that which is produced through the event—is almost always the poet or the painter or the charismatic speaker. If the authority of the aesthetic context is distributed over the event as a whole, and if it is measured out in terms of the various agents within the context, still the greatest share of authority—and thus both credit and responsibility—for the event goes to the one upon whom the event itself was most obviously dependent. Without this looser sense of the authority of agents, the possibility for understanding the complexity of aesthetic events dissolves into the endless play of signs and the total meaninglessness of such a play outside of locations of authority, credit, and responsibility.

❦

The problem all human communities face as a result of this clear yet dispersed form of authority within aesthetic events is a result of the routinization of charisma, for if Weber intended that phrase to apply only to those contexts in which a revolutionary figure sought through his or her eloquence to overturn the authority of the secular world in one way or another, it also applies to other aesthetic contexts and displays the same problems. If the quandary for a religious leader with charisma is how to maintain the authority that has developed out of his charisma without sacrificing the number of adherents to his viewpoint, how to maintain that authority over time, the problem for an artist or for any other individual whose authority depends on charisma rather than on tradition or reason is the same: how to maintain the authority he or she established over time without dulling its force and effectiveness.

One of the main difficulties in this context is one that Weber himself didn't seem interested in, for his focus was more on the ways in which the authority calculated the need to perpetuate itself over time. If another feature of the inevitable routinization of charisma comes from the changes in relations between the charismatic figure and his audience and from the charismatic figure's relation to himself, we can see that the problem has to do with more than the simple questions of economics and perpetuation with which Weber concerns himself. These difficulties are more obvious in our day because there are so many more people competing for charismatic authority, particularly in the "entertainment industry," and we have learned a great deal about the ways in which the contexts that engender authority are inevitably stripped from those who eventually acquire authority from them.

The politician whose skills depend on his own acute assessment of what is going on in Peoria can no longer check out the way things are in Peoria because he now travels with a retinue of bodyguards and gaffers who attend to his every need, thus removing him from the situations in the everyday world on which politicians must inevitably depend. The author whose work derives from an acute awareness of the play of discourse between individuals becomes celebrated and hence fetishized, and so the nature of discourse that takes place in his midst changes and becomes something other than the dialogic exploration it once was. It turns into a series of one-way communications with no real purpose beyond the vatic praise of the master, cutting the writer off from the nuances of everyday speech upon which his authority depends. The charismatic religious leader whose powers emanate from an understanding of the suffering of the average individual, like the politician, becomes too important a figure to be exposed to this suffering anymore—the larger the audience, the more the need to dispose carefully of the figure's time, to make sure that he attends only to the events that are most important to his overall ministry. Events that have to do with real suffering quickly become symbolic rather than real.

Again, cut off from the source within the everyday world that engendered the productions of authority to begin with, the chief agent loses that upon which his authority depends. People may continue to attend to the figure with the same reverence and depend upon him for utterances of authority, but his very authority may have disappeared in the needs of other agents within the event whose very estimation of the value of the charismatic figure have so routinized him and his life that he no longer can provide that which they depend on him for. These problems of routinization are at least as relevant when it comes to discussing the very real limitations of charismatic authority as are those that concern the general economic establishment of stability to which Weber attends.

The problem of the routinization of charisma and the consequent routinization of authority has another angle to it as well, and that comes from the mere repetition of aesthetic events and the difficulty any agent within them has in keeping them from being habitual and hence non-authoritative. Given the exceptional nature of a charismatic situation or an aesthetic event, both agents and auditors have an interest in the repetition of them, for they are among the most highly valued of human contexts both as a result of the pleasurable feelings that are generated within them and because they manifest a truth and authority that humans have always depended on. If the auditors are agents themselves in some respects, still they are generally dependent on the chief agent, the charismatic figure, for the manifestations of charisma to occur. Their disadvantage is that they tend not to be able to produce such events themselves, but their advantage is that therefore they do not have to provide the discipline and the wisdom of whatever variety is necessary to produce the event itself. The level of participation in the event requires only a readiness to respond to the forces around them and be taken up by them.

The chief agent too is responding to forces around him in the production of the event, but he is the main location through which these forces are given shape, and thus the event is more dependent on his capabilities than on the other agents. He also values the event for its authority, truth, and pleasure, and he too therefore wants such events to occur again in the future. Even more, he comes to gain social advantages as a result of his primary participation in such events—he is looked up to and acquires a general prestige that has great value in the social world—so he has both a further inducement to produce future events and a growing obstacle to their production, the added burdens of being a figure of prestige whose authority is now not dependent on the moment of charisma alone but also on the way the rest of his everyday life is disposed of within the social world. All these factors contribute to make the agent more and more a differentiated and self-conscious individual when his very agency depends on an undifferentiated and non-self-conscious event. He therefore may well find it more and more difficult to participate in and help produce those events upon which his authority depends.

Inasmuch as some routinization of charisma seems to be an inevitable factor within any series of aesthetic contexts that perpetuates itself over a considerable period of time, there is another criterion in play to determine the continuing value of the authority that manifests itself in these situations. Whereas it is relatively easy for us to assess the value of the authority that displays itself in any single aesthetic event, it becomes more difficult for us to discern the value of authority within a series of events that persists over great time. Part of the problem has already been discussed, and that has to do with the fact that the authority that manifests itself over a series of events requires a different—or at least an *additional*—set of skills. This is most apparent when it comes to the agents themselves, whether the context is literary, political, or religious. Some novelists are capable of writing one or two truly distinguished books yet can find no way to develop and perpetuate their skills over time. Indeed, some would argue that this is a particular problem when it comes to American writers. If today a good part of that problem comes from the fetishization of the author about which we know so much, that is not a sufficient explanation of the phenomenon.

Likewise, there are religious authorities who achieve great status within the religious community and acquire huge audiences, and these figures are usually of the highly charismatic sort. Yet some manage to develop and extend both their authority and their charisma, whereas others somehow burn themselves up through the intense energies of their charisma. We might say that there are three general possibilities for the agents of aesthetic events:

1. Their authority might inhere in a very few localized moments or productions and yet fail to manifest itself over any significant range of time—their authority thus is dependent on those very few events, remains localized within them, and quickly dissolves.
2. Their authority might initially depend on a series of aesthetic events, but they manage over time to parlay the authority that accrues to them as a result of these events into some more routinized form of authority, one that becomes either traditional or rational—the zeal and fire of the original charisma declines, but the effectiveness is not lost because bureaucratic structures have been put into place to continue the authority in a lesser form.
3. Their authority might begin as it does with any charismatic figure, but they manage to perpetuate it through an ever-new and ever-expanding series of contexts through which their charisma and authority can manifest itself and thus grow and change—this situation is not quite the same as the more routinized version of the second possibility because the agent has managed to overcome the severe pressures involved in routinization and has refused to subordinate his gifts to the need for permanent structures.

Admittedly, the third possibility sounds something like Mao's permanent revolution, certainly something that cannot exist in the larger social world, where all revolutions inevitably decay into routinization of one sort or another.

And authority of whatever stripe eventually modulates itself into some kind of traditional or rational form. Nevertheless, there are agents and authorities that manage to avoid becoming routinized over time, even if this is the rarest form of charisma and authority, even if such events and figures occur only as a limit to human possibilities rather than as the general condition. There are writers who have kept their gifts from turning into routinized tools for the production of self-interested value and authority, writers who have managed to create new and important aesthetic events over the greater course of a lifetime. There are painters of this type as well, and perhaps political and religious figures too, though these arenas and their more complex forces are generally the ones most susceptible to the inevitable routinization Weber finds inherent in all charismatic structures.

The chief problem in this respect is that we have no real way of accounting for the presence of the third possibility for charismatic authority. The first we understand as a function of a discipline and a discourse and a context through which these can play themselves out; the second we recognize in the function of habituation that is written into our nervous systems and every other element of our perceptual and social world; but the third seems to depend on skills whose nature we truly don't understand. We can resort to clichés and talk about the need to make it new or to *keep* making it new; we can assert that the good life is one that finds ever new things to be interested in and recognizes the degree to which even the slightest changes make everything new; we can suggest that humans need to work at keeping their original curiosity alive throughout life; or we can assert that true genius is capable of discovering ever-new possibilities throughout a lifetime; but none of these formulations accounts for that special blend of charisma and continuity upon which the ability to engender meaningful aesthetic events throughout a lifetime would be based. Perhaps the least reductive formulation of such a combination of gifts would be that the agent of such an aesthetic would have on the one hand a continuing awareness of and appreciation for the history of past aesthetic events and their authority, and on the other would maintain an essential rootedness in the everyday out of which comes the wonder and curiosity that prompts the production of aesthetic events in the first place. This would allow him to preserve a balance between the ever-enlarging sense of the *history* of aesthetic events and the knowledge that every moment presents new possibilities for further aesthetic events. This too is an evasion of sorts, for it doesn't properly encapsulate either the difficulties of such a discipline or account for the rarity of those who are capable of such a way of life. But it at least suggests that such a possibility for aesthetic agents would offer the fullest expression of what humans are capable of and thus provides us with a measure of our own attainments as well as a guide to the authority of those whose agency we recognize in our own lives.

There is one final element to this problem of routinization that needs to be established, and it concerns yet again the relative shift in the location of the agent within aesthetic events. If Weber was convinced that all charismatic authority must inevitably be routinized into traditional or rational authority, he also based his conclusions on a view of the world in which the agents themselves were the central figures. He demonstrated how the charismatic figure's authority was modulated over time into a routinized form of authority that might well bear little resemblance in the end to the original revolutionary fervor with which he began. In assuming that the locus for such authority is always inevitably dependent on the agent himself, Weber was conceding what appeared to be the case: authority is contingent upon those charismatic individuals who first formulate values in such as way as to inspire followers to subscribe to them, and even as it transforms itself into bureaucratic structures for the maintenance of those values in the everyday world, it remains contingent on the agent of their formulation. This fetishization of the figure of authority is indeed a general feature of human culture. The only question is whether or not it is a *necessary and inevitable one*. If we live at a time when the author has been declared dead, and if we now recognize the degree to which the author's authority inheres in a context of which he is always only a part, can we produce out of this decentralized vision of the authority of the agent a system of values through which authority can manifest itself over time within an aesthetic context without modulating into traditions whose authority has lost its original aesthetic impetus? The possibility for this comes about precisely because the author is dead, because we can at least imagine a world in which figures of authority are not fetishized because we recognize their crucial yet limited role within the production of authority. If we begin to focus on the overall context of authority rather than isolating the most obvious agent of it, perhaps we can alter the flow of forces within the aesthetic context in order to guarantee its perpetuation over time with an ever-unfolding sense of charismatic value. This is not exactly the dream of perpetual revolution and is in some senses antithetical to it, for any perpetuation of authority in this way would manage both to be aware of the values and limitations of the aesthetic (historical) context out of which it grew and at the same time to recognize precisely those situations within that aesthetic history that had yet to be addressed and were thus best capable of moving the aesthetic events—and the human community that develops out of such events—into ever-new directions.

It may be that humans are incapable of such a decentralized vision of things. It may be that it is inevitable that they will fetishize particular agents of authority for their own psychological and biological reasons. And it may be that human communities can thus constitute themselves in no other way than through an endless play of charismatic eruptions that transform themselves over time into the traditional and rational structures with which we are always more familiar in our everyday lives. But it is also possible that the altered status of the agents within aesthetic events—and the important yet displaced authority that is to be found within the chief agent of production in particular—will allow us to develop our communities in different ways and will provide us both with a greater understanding of the nature of the authority on the basis of which we establish our individual and collective lives and with a better set of means through which to allow such authority to express itself over time without succumbing to the numbness of routinization.

Inasmuch as I have assumed throughout my discussion that the central locus for value and authority inheres in the charismatic or aesthetic variety of it rather than in its traditional and rational forms, I should explain briefly what the limitations and virtues of the traditional and rational forms of authority are in order to establish further the degree to which all authority depends on the aesthetic context out of which it originally grew. It is true that much of what passes for rational authority is genuine and essential, particularly the structures that reflect the ideals of a given society's people. If legal authority is based upon a rational assessment of the prevailing aspirations of a people, it is reasonable to assume that such an authority will indeed reflect the will of the majority of the people. In this sense it is not necessarily "rational," for its legitimacy could very well reflect totally irrational and mutually exclusive concepts.

But according to Weber's criteria, we must assume that those forms of authority that persist over time as embodiments of human aspirations and attempt to effect them within the social world are indeed rational, when in fact they seem more traditional than rational. The problem is that the traditional forms of authority as defined by Weber tend to be based "on an established belief in the sanctity of immemorial traditions and the legitimacy of the status of those exercising authority under them" (p. 328), and this is an insufficient description of the most valuable kinds of non-charismatic authority. In part the problem with traditional and rational forms of authority, then, lies in their very definition, at least in an age like ours that would be unwilling to accept the assumption that any form of authority is truly rational.

Nevertheless, there would seem to be a category of authority somewhere between rational and traditional authority that can over time establish a legitimacy that embodies the aspirations of the socius, and it would be traditional in the sense that there would be no rational grounds for such an authority, yet it would not necessarily be caught up in the inevitable self-interest of traditional systems either. Its legitimacy would not be contingent on the particular authorities who were said to uphold its authority but rather on the *way* they upheld it; the legitimacy would inhere only in the general structure of values that allowed certain agents the privilege of upholding the rights inherent in them. This kind of authority, potentially self-interested but never necessarily so, is of the sort to which any long-term charismatic authority must attach itself in some ways, for not all aspects of charismatic authority necessarily depend on the continuing aesthetic events through which its legitimacy perpetuates itself, and the continuities that are necessary to any system that persists over time require the establishment of at least some general parameters that can regularly be relied upon. In a very basic way, we might think of traffic signs as a manifestation of this kind of authority, something that is essential to the disposition of the members of society who need to have their various interests mediated on the road in a disinterested fashion. And far richer concepts like equal rights for all would also occupy this category of authority, for they embody the kind of aspirations all humans share at a basic level, at least as long as they consider their own rights in the context of others.

These contextual rights are determined through the collective will of the society as it plays itself out through the flows of discourse within it, and they are always somewhat imperfect, just as they are therefore always subject to refinement, improvement, and occasional abandonment. It could not be said, though, that such authority has been routinized from the more charismatic version, for even if many of the structures of this contextual authority might have originated in an aesthetic context, still they are not dependent in the end on the kinds of aesthetic deployment that charismatic authority must employ in order to continue to be viable. To the extent that the contextual authority does not effect the structures that would let traffic flow or that would permit people to live together more or less as equals, charismatic authority will eventually work to force changes in the structures that militate against such forms of legitimizing, but beyond that the forms themselves remain independent of aesthetic contexts.

One more serious problem with the traditional and rational forms of authority as Weber establishes them is that they are dependent on the same kind of authorial self that has been dispersed in the past several generations. Traditional authority clearly does depend on particular figures who can embody its forms, most obviously within paternalistic or patriarchal contexts where there are always special authorities whose legitimacy derives from their perpetuation of the legacy of paternalism. The system is nothing if not an essentialized version of the author who dispenses authority on the basis of who he is rather than on where he finds himself. And rational authority is dependent on a conception of objectivity that is distinguishable only as long as one assumes that charismatic authority is somehow subjective or affective. Once the so-called subject/object split is seen for the ruse that it is, any conceivable objectivizing authority loses its legitimacy. If the subjective, essentialized self dies, so too does the objectivizing, rational authority that depends on rules that transcend the group. There are still "normalizing" authorities who operate through "normative rules," but the origin of those normative rules is no longer to be found in reason but rather in the needs of the culture as a whole. This may seem a minor difference, yet unless it is taken into account, the entire schema of authority falls apart.

It should also be said that Weber's emphasis on the affective, religious, or rational context for disinterested authority also misses the mark. It is true that charismatic authority has a strong affective component to it; nevertheless, this is not its essential feature but rather a *mark* of its essential feature, which is an aesthetic event in which the self and the other are not construed as opposed but rather are seen as part of the same flow of discourse. And in this sense it cannot be rational either, for no rational authority could have a connection to an aesthetic event. If the religious forms of disinterested discourse are indeed legitimate in some senses within their own field of play, they derive their authority once again from the aesthetic context that is a complex event of many contextualized layers. If both the religious and the other forms of charismatic authority depend on affective states, that is still not the distinguishing feature of their discourse.

Weber's remarks, however, suggest otherwise:

> The legitimacy of an order may be guaranteed or upheld in two principal ways: (1) from purely disinterested motives, which may in turn be (a) purely affectual, consisting in an emotionally determined loyalty; or (b) may derive from a rational belief in the absolute validity of the order as an expression of ultimate values, whether they be moral, esthetic, or of any other type; or (c) may originate in religious attitudes, through the belief in the dependence of some condition of religious salvation on conformity with the order; (2) also or entirely by self-interest, that is, through expectations of specific ulterior consequences, but consequences which are, to be sure, of a particular kind. (p. 126, 27)

Here the notion persists that outside of purely self-interested motives, the only forms of legitimacy finally rest in emotionally-determined loyalty, rationally conceived notions of ultimate values, or religious expressions of some form of salvation. The charismatic form of authority we have been discussing throughout is not intrinsically dependent on any of these forms of authority, for it is not specifically self-interested; it is clearly not rational in nature or contingent on beliefs in rational authority; its linkages to the religious are more historical than anything else, and the most profound linkage is to the aesthetic context from which the religious authority itself derived; and its connections to emotional states do not necessarily depend upon a particular individual in whom those affective states are thought to exist or upon whom they rely any more than its exclusive feature is its affective functions. These ways of speaking of charismatic authority are finally too yoked to the authority of a rational system that has been discredited along with the author and the self, and if they give us pointers toward the very real legitimacy of the charismatic or aesthetic context, they also are capable of pointing back toward directions we have moved away from.

In the end, the problem of authority is clarified by Weber's insightful discussion of charismatic authority to the extent that we connect his remarks to the changes in our own forms of authority as they have developed out of the existentialist and post-structuralist modes of discourse that have gone so far to define our present context. Indeed, even if Weber's analysis is connected to an older system of rational authority that has since been discredited, it has the additional advantage of reminding us of the limit point to the seemingly endless discussions about the death of the author and the dissolution of the self. Weber demonstrates that all authority depends finally on an agent or self, even if that authority inevitably inheres in a context and not in the self per se. He forces us to recognize once again that it *does* matter who's speaking and shows us how the speaker and his or her authority emerge from a charismatic context that is capable of extending itself over a small or a large range, depending on the nature of the utterance and the flows of discourse into which it inserts itself. And Weber's own professional and emotional investment in the category of charismatic authority—particularly given his rational commitments—suggests as well the compelling nature of this form of authority in the face of all of its legitimacy *and* its potential instability. We have yet fully to confront either that legitimacy or the instability that is to be found within it, but Weber has given us the orientation through which we can begin such an inquiry.

# Chapter Two

# Behold the Man!

If we are to pursue the nature of the authority inherent in aesthetic events, we can best go about doing so at this point through an analysis of a particular text, one that will allow us to test its claims and measure its legitimacy. For practical purposes it is best to look at a work that is several generations old simply because we shall have a better grip on those utterances within the text that were supposed to be supported by charismatic authority but clearly don't measure up under any context of authority in our own time. For symbolic reasons, it is worthwhile to pick a text of Nietzsche's inasmuch as the very nature of our return to charismatic authority and the dissolution of the older forms of authority are inevitably linked to his name within our tradition. And for a work that will certainly test the ways in which aesthetic events engender the forms of authority and legitimacy upon which we depend in ways large and small every day, we could do no better than to look at *Ecce Homo,* a text that hovers on the threshold of Nietzsche's madness, and yet a document that carries its own great authority, in part as a result of its location at the edge of the abyss, in part because it also reflects the very sure authority that Nietzsche possessed more than any other individual of his era, and perhaps our own. It also demonstrates that the very basis of Nietzsche's authority is to be found in assertions that are grounded on nothing more than his own contextual understanding of the aesthetic nature of the world.

There are no rational claims to authority made in *Ecce Homo,* and there are certainly no traditional claims that are asserted; the authority is established throughout exclusively on the basis of Nietzsche's assessment of his place within a series of flows of discourse. One might think that this would inevitably be the case given the autobiographical nature of the book, but in fact most autobiographical works seek to ground themselves in some larger form of authority than the individual self they are meant to reflect well on. Nietzsche seeks no ground for his assertions about his life or his work; he assumes that they can be sufficiently measured on the basis of the context they establish and that nothing more is necessary for their evaluation. This is the aesthetic context par excellence, so it provides a fitting point of entry into the problems posed by aesthetic authority. And inasmuch as aesthetic authority can always only be measured by local contexts, whether those contexts are books and their localized reflection of larger flows or the everyday situations we employ aesthetic authority in as a matter of course, any series of assertions about the nature of such authority must weigh itself against a sufficient number of particular situations in order to determine its adequacy.

A good point of origin for an assessment of *Ecce Homo* would be a few of Walter Kaufmann's remarks about the text as he released his English translation of it in 1969. He first tells us that "*Ecce Homo* is one of the treasures of world literature. Written in 1888 and first published in 1908, it has been largely ignored or misunderstood. Yet it is Nietzsche's own interpretation of his development, his works, and his significance; and we should gladly trade the whole vast literature on Nietzsche for this one small book."[1]

This statement frames the context as Kaufmann construes it through which the work has come to be seen, yet it quite clearly is also his bold assertion of a contrary series of hypotheses about the work. First, he calls it "one of the treasures of world literature," hardly minor praise for any work of any era; second, he declares that the work "has been largely ignored or misunderstood"; then he informs us that "we"—that is, Kaufmann—"should gladly trade the whole vast literature on Nietzsche for this one small book," not only because it is Nietzsche's own interpretation of his career but also because of the great power of Nietzsche's authority here and in other contexts. These points suggest a revaluation of the text to which we should attend and remind us of some of the central features of most of Nietzsche's later work.

If Kaufmann emphasizes the literary value of *Ecce Homo*, he does so both because he sees the book as a literary masterpiece of sorts and because Nietzsche saw his work at least partially in aesthetic terms. Indeed, the true distinction of Nietzsche's work in the end is that it broke down the barrier between philosophy and literature and questioned endlessly their relationship. To assert that authority is charismatic in nature is in its own way to state the same fact, that the validity of an utterance comes not from some traditional or rational source but rather from the context out of which it emerges. So Kaufmann is right to suggest that the first measure of *Ecce Homo* is an aesthetic one, just as he is justified in saying that the last five books Nietzsche wrote "are such brilliant works of art" (p. 201). He lets these statements stand on their own and doesn't provide specific evidence for the quality of the prose style, but this too would follow from the assumption that it is immediately apparent that the works are brilliant pieces of prose whose aesthetic qualities are readily recognizable.

Kaufmann also insists that *Ecce Homo* has been "largely ignored or misunderstood," and this too fits in with the nature of the text, part philosophy, part literary criticism, and part autocritique, hardly the kind of work that would be expected either of a philosopher or of a literary writer. Instead of being pure philosophy, it is a mixed breed. Instead of providing a standard autobiography, it offers us what Kaufmann would probably characterize as an impressionistic piece. And instead of providing us with a comprehensive assessment of each of his works, Nietzsche fills in the context of their composition and goes straight to the heart of the argument within an individual text that he wishes to link to his own life's path and to the other works he created. These are definitely unusual traits for a text to have, particularly when they are all mixed together into one piece, but they are at the same time for that very reason a reflection of Nietzsche's own authority.

Kaufmann approaches the qualitative nature of the work best through his discussion of its "self-portrait": "The self-portrait is not naturalistic; hence, it was widely felt, it is clearly insane and to be disregarded. This prevalent view is doubly false. The lack of naturalism is not proof of insanity but a triumph of style—of a piece with the best paintings of that time. And even if what might be interpreted as signs of madness do occasionally flicker in a passage, that does not mean that the portrait can therefore be ignored. In both respects Nietzsche should be compared with Van Gogh" (p. 202). It is certainly true that Nietzsche's depiction of himself and his work and the place of the two in the larger scheme of things is hardly "naturalistic," if by that we mean a description that adheres to the traditional strategies of recounting a life and its work, but this is indeed "a triumph of style" all its own, a reflection of a different kind of reality that Nietzsche sought to articulate throughout the course of his life. If the assessment of the text seems unreal, even mad, that is because it has that so-called "affective component" of the charismatic event as an essential element of the depiction, as a mark of the reality of the statements.

Given Kaufmann's general approach to Nietzsche, one that emphasizes the self and the existential writers that will follow from Nietzsche, it is perhaps natural that he would use such phrases as "triumph of style" and would compare the "artist" to someone like Van Gogh. Both reflect a tendency to take seriously the subjectivizing tendencies that are in part called into question by Nietzsche's work and thoroughly undermined by the writers who followed in his wake. It seems less appropriate today to talk about triumphs of style and to refer to literary geniuses in the age of the end of the author, and Van Gogh is not the painter one would like to have associated with one's life, particularly given the fact that the painter's madness seemed much more clearly connected to and present in the work itself. If *Ecce Homo* does indeed have "signs of madness" that "occasionally flicker in a passage," one would not like to connect the value of the work as a whole to the pressures of insanity that we know were just on the horizon for Nietzsche. Again, the portrait is too much the one of an existential hero, one who holds off the chaos through his brilliant constructions and staves off the madness that comes upon him as a result of the torturous world of which he is a part just long enough to produce some truly great work. This way of speaking of the text is surely in line with the egomania to be found in *Ecce Homo,* but we might also think of such egomania as a reflection of Nietzsche's *worst* traits rather than his best, might assume that it is that which comes between him and his authority on too many occasions.

If the work has proved hard to understand, though, and it has, that is because the realities to which it refers are indeed unnaturalistic; they are aesthetic realities, and Nietzsche expects both his life and his work to be assessed in terms of the charismatic authority they carry with them as a matter of their aesthetic power. Once one recognizes that Kaufmann is right to argue that the value of the portrait is to be found within this aesthetic construction and is to be judged by its ability to reflect the aesthetic through which Nietzsche's work as a whole is to be assessed, then one can properly place the context for the work. And if we are grateful to Kaufmann for providing the means through which this context is established, we should also recognize that he was able to do so because he was both a careful reader of Nietzsche and one who understood the history and culture from which Nietzsche came. That is, the interpretive skills of Kaufmann here come from a region that is open to us all; it is best reflected in Kaufmann's expertise, but Nietzsche's work should theoretically be able to speak for itself. It is only its revolutionary nature that engenders the misinterpretations and the deliberate refusals to confront it seriously.

As for Nietzsche's interpretations of his own work, Kaufmann argues that we should surely prefer to have the master's own assessments in place of the vast heap of critical garbage that has been assembled at his feet, and certainly in Nietzsche's case this is the truth. Kaufmann's statement need not depend on the intentional fallacy that authors understand their intentions better than others do, for this is certainly not always true. Rather, the assertion relies on a careful reading of the text and the conclusion that Nietzsche does indeed understand his work, understands it far better than his critics, even if, as here, his assessments are occasionally tinged with the flavor of madness. Again, this is an assertion of Nietzsche's authority that Kaufmann makes on the basis of his own extensive reading of the work, and it seems to me to be an assessment that holds up quite well. Nietzsche *does* understand his work better than most of his critics, even if there are aspects to it that remain hidden from his view—in the case of *Ecce Homo,* the odd flickers of madness among other things. In part this better understanding comes from the terrible misunderstandings that have surrounded his work from the very beginning, but in part it also comes from the fact that the master writer is so because he is first and foremost a master interpreter of experience and language, and he can apply these skills to his own work as much as he can to Wagner's or anyone else's.

To delve further into the authority of the book, we need to look at the curious blending of autobiography, literary criticism, and philosophy the text is and ask why the author would create the work in this way. Perhaps the most ironic feature of these linkages is that Nietzsche reestablishes the notion that the work and the life cannot be separated, a strategy that contrasts greatly with those philosophers who preceded him who sought to keep their writing on a different plane, who through rational means and logical arguments would construct philosophical confections that had no connection to their own lives or to human existence in general. Their very unreality is their distinguishing feature in Nietzsche's view, and the unreality itself comes from the notion that one can separate one's discourse from one's contextual situation in the world. To transform philosophy once again into an aesthetic enterprise, which is precisely what Nietzsche did, is to assert unequivocally that the life and the work are in some crucial respects inseparable. "Nietzsche the man" *should* be in his texts, for they do, after all, depend on what he lived and what he suffered. *Ecce Homo* provides an excellent example of this blending of the life and the work, as we shall see.

The irony inherent in this shift in the nature of our discourse is that Nietzsche's consequent madness, also quite clearly a part of his life, came for a long time to define his work more than any element of the life he lived while he was writing. Those who would strenuously argue against the linkage between the life and the work would at the same time denounce Nietzsche's writings as the products of a madman, thereby using the life to attempt to discredit the work. Nietzsche clearly understood the inevitable relation between the work and the life, and he would not be opposed to measuring the work by the life. But he would surely object, as we should, to the notion that any writer's rich corpus should be assessed chiefly in terms of a madness that is demonstrably not present while most of the works were being composed.

The very issue of the relationship between the life and the work and the endlessly troublesome problems that it raises were behind the original attempts to separate the two, and both Nietzsche and *Ecce Homo* demonstrate fully why there was such an attempt to remove the consideration of the work from the life itself. And they demonstrate why we have tried hard not to see the aesthetic nature of authority, for to do so is to recognize that Nietzsche was right, that the work and the life are interdependent and need to be considered together. But to think of them together, and to link them in turn to the sociohistorical context in which both are to be found, is to make the task of assessment far more difficult than it would be if we merely interpreted the words on the page. From one angle, after all, it makes perfect sense for us to investigate Nietzsche's work in terms of his ultimate madness. Regardless of whether the insanity came from some physical debility or not, it inevitably follows from his life that we need to determine the degree to which his work itself could be said to be madness-inducing. This is an important question not only because we should prefer to keep madness-inducing work from those who might lose their sanity as a result, but also because it would provide us with an essential perspective both on the work and on the nature of ideas in general. It would establish not only that Nietzsche's ideas were truly "toxic" in some ways but also that ideas themselves *could* be toxic, a notion that has never been sufficiently investigated because the possibilities are more threatening than we should like to admit.

And if we think of *Ecce Homo* in this context along with the rest of Nietzsche's work, it should be said that we cannot finally determine whether or not it is madness-inducing. Kaufmann himself obviously wants to put this question out of play, seeks to defend the text from the easy denunciations that would come its way as a result of Nietzsche's madness, so he defends the text against those accusations while admitting that there are indeed "flickers" of what might be considered madness. In his own way, Kaufmann unintentionally blunts the force of the work by seeking so assiduously to put out of play a very real and serious question that *Ecce Homo* in particular *demands* that we ask. Its final authority depends on our assessment of this question perhaps more than any other query we might put to it, even if it can't ever be definitively answered. And its power and legitimacy depend on our awareness that its revolutionary perspective could indeed be one of which humans are finally incapable. How can we therefore *not* think of *Ecce Homo* and at the same time ask if it and the other works were either products of a madman or else aesthetic events that helped push a wise but fragile intelligence over the edge into insanity? If we are to take Nietzsche's arguments seriously, these questions need to be asked.

❦

If we ask the question about Nietzsche's madness, a good bit of it can be put out of play in the way Kaufmann does. The two features that most obviously suggest the work of a madman are the egomania and the tendency to dwell on features of the landscape that would seem to be totally irrelevant to the texts and to the production of texts. If a writer asserts that "I am much more interested in a question on which the 'salvation of humanity' depends far more than on any theologians' curio: the question of *nutrition*" (p. 237), we might think that at the very least we are in the midst of a misguided utterance, at most in the presence of one who is deranged. Surely questions of nutrition are less important in the overall scheme of things than the much more important issue of our final salvation. From the traditional perspective, Nietzsche could indeed be conceived of as being mad for making such a statement, for its seeming misconstrual of the relationship between the profound and the trivial is obvious to all. The only question is whether he is *right* to suggest nutrition is more important than salvation or whether he is *mad* to say so. In our own day, we have definitely come to appreciate the great value of nutrition, and we recognize its force in our lives more every year, so that would suggest that in strictly physiological terms Nietzsche was perhaps more correct than he could have surmised.

As for the idea that nutrition is far more important than any question of salvation, we can recognize at this late date that Nietzsche is establishing two different qualitative ways of measuring the value of human existence, the one characterized by him as essentially nihilistic and life-denying—that mode which thinks most on human salvation and thereby denies the value of the life we have in this world—and the aesthetic viewpoint—that mode whereby the concrete circumstances of life (including such seemingly banal things as nutrition) would clearly be more qualitatively important because they would prompt us to recognize the value of our everyday existence and sway us away from our tendencies toward nihilism. In this context the statement itself is hardly a reflection of insanity. It *does* suggest Nietzsche's revaluation of all values, and our own assessment of its worth depends on whether we side with Nietzsche or prefer the road to salvation, but the utterance itself is a mark of a profound assessment of the realities we confront every day and is hardly the statement of a madman.

Still, when we think of the consequences of the revaluation of values that is to be found in Nietzsche's declaration of the importance of nutrition, we cannot so easily escape the threat that madness brings to the text, for even if the statement itself is sane, even brilliant in its effectiveness, it remains to be seen whether the consequences of this way of thinking would prompt the madness. Thus, we might argue, there is great honesty in the assertion about nutrition, and perhaps even great courage involved in confronting the issues that are framed by the relative measuring of the question of salvation vs. the question of nutrition, but the fact is that the very way the question is framed demonstrates the final madness into which Nietzsche would lapse, for if we have for millennia been far more interested in questions of salvation than those of nutrition, that is because we cannot *bear* to face the realities that Nietzsche uncovered once again. The Greek and Judeo-Christian veneers we have laminated onto the top of our civilization exist precisely to keep us from confronting those most horrifying truths about human existence, and they do so because humans are fundamentally incapable finally of confronting them. So, the argument would run, Nietzsche may be profoundly right in his revaluation of values here, but he is also profoundly *wrong,* because he refuses to see that humans cannot face the world squarely without being driven to madness. And we would then link Nietzsche's own insanity to precisely this point. No one, we might say, stared more pitilessly into the abyss than Nietzsche, and no writer in our era has had more courage in the face of that abyss, yet even he could not bear to confront the full terrors of the abyss over the course of a lifetime. Indeed, he didn't make it too much past the halfway span of an average life, suggesting that only destruction can follow upon the revaluation of values that Nietzsche wanted to set in play.

*Ecce Homo's* values, then, truly could be said to be predicated on a dual madness, both the incipient insanity we can see in Nietzsche in some of the statements, and the madness that comes from thinking for long the very ideas to which Nietzsche and his texts are devoted. No one was more aware than Nietzsche of the difficulty of his thought, no one was more conscious of the perhaps inconceivable possibility of imagining a human who could actually accept the terms of existence as we have come to understand them. He knew full well that his thought might be literally impossible in this sense, even if he didn't construe that impossibility in terms of potential madness. He recognized the *danger* of his ideas, and we must perforce do the same thing, even if we don't want to argue that the text itself was the product of a madman who went insane precisely because he thought too long at the edge of the abyss. The quality of the work, its authority and aesthetic legitimacy, demands of us that we never move too far away from this concern. The moment we decide definitively that it is a mere canard to suggest that Nietzsche's work is the product of and is capable of producing madness, we have stripped some of the authority from the text.

The danger and the authority of *Ecce Homo* are inseparable, but then that is true of all profound work, and it is true of all charismatic events, regardless of whether they are religious in nature or against religion, as Nietzsche's work was. After all, if we take Nietzsche's arguments about the fundamentally nihilistic nature of Christianity seriously, we can see that the danger of a Christian viewpoint is that one could entirely waste the only life one has on perpetual attempts to deny the value of that life. One could die without ever having lived simply so that one might have the prospect of another life somewhere else. This is a dangerous idea to the extent that it costs one one's entire life, and it would not have had the profound effect that it did if it didn't come with that danger. There is a choice to be made there that costs one one's life, and the result could be that one wastes the only source of life one has, or that one "invests" that life wisely in the denunciation of a secular life for an eternal life to follow. Likewise with Nietzsche's work, there is the danger that one's attempt to face the world as it is will be too much for one, that it might indeed be too much for *any* human. Again, the choice of value might truly cost one one's life, or it might focus one's attention so clearly on the nature of what is that one comes fully to affirm it in the way Nietzsche argued we must. So of course Nietzsche's ideas come to us in a threatening form, and of course they involve potential danger.

That is a mark of their great value to us and a reflection of their authority.

Nevertheless, as soon as one begins to phrase the dangers of a text in such a way, one encounters two problems. First, one distances oneself from the dangers themselves—to put them forth as a mark of authority is in some respects to take them seriously only in an intellectual way, when obviously the dangers of Nietzsche's texts are inherent in the very assessments of life that they reach. We need to remember that it is indeed truly possible that Nietzsche's thought leads to madness, but if we grant his work the authority it deserves, we also have to conclude that we have no choice but to run that risk. To turn away from the dangers the texts present us with is to retreat into precisely those nihilistic structures that Nietzsche did so much to unveil for us, and to do that is to conclude that we have chosen instead the dangers of the traditional nihilistic way of life.

The second problem with the question of danger is that it is possible once one begins to formulate things in such a way for one to end up in a different kind of madness, the one Nietzsche himself was obviously on the edge of in *Ecce Homo:* the madness of divine egomania, the belief that one has become God, is also an inevitable danger when thinking through Nietzsche's work. It is this danger that attaches itself to Kaufmann's attempts to aggrandize Nietzsche himself and to turn him into an existential hero who faced the terrible abyss and brought his reports back for us to see. The problem is that Nietzsche was right in some respects to assert that his ideas were dangerous, that it took great courage to face what his work had led him to. This in turn, however, prompted him to assume that he must be truly great if he himself had done such a good job of confronting the terrors of life in the face of evidence that suggested 2,000 years of individuals who turned away from its terrors. One begins by uncovering certain contexts through which a different perspective of reality emerges; one learns over time that these contexts have been deliberately hidden because it takes courage to face them; one concludes that one is the first individual in two millennia to be able to look the world squarely in the eye; and egomania bursts forth into full flower.

Thus Nietzsche will every now and then make statements like this:

> My concept of the "Dionysian" here [in *Zarathustra*] became a *supreme deed;* measured against that, all the rest of human activity seems poor and relative. That a Goethe, a Shakespeare, would be unable to breathe even for a moment in this tremendous passion and height, that Dante is, compared with Zarathustra, merely a believer and not one who first *creates* truth, a *world-governing* spirit, a destiny—that the poets of the Veda are priests and not even worthy of tying the shoelaces of a Zarathustra—that is the least thing and gives no idea of the distance, of the *azure* solitude in which this work lives. (p. 304)

If Nietzsche was correct in his assessment that he had reached some profound conclusions about the nature of human existence—as I personally think he was—and if it is true that in some respects those truths are embodied in his creation Zarathustra—though I myself am not terribly enthusiastic about this bombastic and overly-wrought figure—it by no means follows that he has been the only individual ever to achieve such a supreme deed. To place those whom Nietzsche obviously valued very highly—Goethe, Shakespeare, Dante and the like—far below him in the second rank is unquestionably to mistake greatly the nature of his own achievement, for it finds its precedents precisely in those figures he cites. At the very least there are those who preceded him to the heights of his supreme deed; at best a good number of us travel there at least occasionally, and only a self that has lost control of its ability to appraise its value in the larger cultural context would be inclined to make such an absurd statement. Indeed, we might even go so far as to say that Nietzsche's madness is not reflected in the fact that he *thought* such a thing, for we might imagine any number of other "great" figures measuring themselves *to themselves* in terms of the other "great" figures and concluding that no one has ever come close to what they have done; the madness comes in the fact that Nietzsche was willing to display his innermost wishes and fantasies *in public.* The barrier that separates public and private space has broken down, the resistance to the imposition of fantasy onto the public domain is no longer there, and madness flickers like a harsh light over the visage of one who thought to demonstrate the obvious.

Just as important in the larger context, though, is the fact that Nietzsche's own words here finally belie his very profundity. In saying that "all the rest of human activity seems poor and relative" next to his concept of the Dionysian, he is denying the value of the minutiae of everyday life as much as any nihilist would, asserting that *only* the sublime heights of such a conception, and such an ecstatic *moment* of conception, have any real value. The rest is poor indeed, and hardly worth noting. Nietzsche doesn't recognize that he has denied his own work through the process of aggrandizing himself, doesn't see that his preoccupations with climate and walking and nutrition should not lead simply to the grand moment of conception but should enrich the life that is lived in the midst of the joys and terrors that also come one's way. Indeed, the very fact that Nietzsche has come to need such illusions about his "self" is a further reflection of how far away in some respects he has moved from his own thought, though again this too might provide the cautionary note of potential danger in the work as well.

One could argue that the self-aggrandizing tendencies are an inherent part of Nietzsche's work, but it seems more plausible to see them as a reflection of Nietzsche's own incomplete understanding of his writing. He who has recognized the fictitious nature of the self nevertheless comes to believe all too much in a fictitious construct that he himself has made. He who realizes that the self must die along with God grasps onto his own self more and more furiously as he faces his neglect in the real world and perhaps in the context of the onset of madness as well. Human, all too human. Nietzsche plumbs the depths of the human psyche with great courage and creates a number of authoritative texts as a result, but another consequence of those texts is the growing conviction that he alone understands and can face the world. Put in the context of his isolation, measured against the almost complete neglect his writings suffered, it is more than understandable that a kind of defensive construction could begin to emerge in the face of the human problems Nietzsche confronted. If people ignore his work and thereby implicitly condemn it as useless, he can gradually come to agree with them, or he can defend all the more fiercely the value of his work (to himself at least); if his work isolates him more and more from others rather than bringing him into more contact with them, he can convince himself that he is so far superior to the others that his only fitting interlocutor is himself.

And if it is perhaps true that the courage necessary to face the world as Nietzsche saw it becomes harder and harder to muster over time—perhaps as a result of aging, perhaps because the full consequences of that vision only manifest themselves over time—it is quite plausible that the formations of the self begin to cover over the abyss and yet make it yawn all the wider at the same time. After all, Nietzsche is no mere lion tamer; he is the one who has confronted the great terrors of the world and lived to tell about them; that no one wants to hear about those terrors is thus only a further reflection of his own greatness. One way or the other, all these possibilities are indeed possibilities, and at the very least they reflect the dangers that come from the reaction formations of self-aggrandizement.

❦

Nietzsche reconnected the life to the work, and he did so nowhere more strikingly than in *Ecce Homo*. Given this, and given the complexity of the text, we can translate the life into what it would become in the following decades—the tale of the first existential hero—or we can see how that tendency in the text—for there can be no doubt that Nietzsche's self-estimation was both accurate and wildly out of control at the same time—is opposed to another one, a tendency toward the awareness of how *little* aesthetic authority has to do with anything that could be self-aggrandizing. If the subtext of the entire book is in some respects "How One Becomes What One Is" (p. 215), surely that statement suggests that the powers of the text do not come from any Nietzsche who could take credit for them in the way he seeks to on and off throughout the text (and his life).

The most straightforward way Nietzsche puts this problem is in terms of his own lineage:

> The good fortune of my existence, its uniqueness perhaps, lies in its fatality: I am, to express it in the form of a riddle, already dead as my father, while as my mother I am still living and becoming old. This dual descent, as it were, both from the highest and the lowest rung on the ladder of life, at the same time a *decadent* and a *beginning*—this, if anything, explains that neutrality, that freedom from all partiality in relation to the total problem of life, that perhaps distinguishes me. I have a subtler sense of smell for the signs of ascent and decline than any other human being before me; I am the teacher *par excellence* for this—I know both, I am both. (p. 222)

The "fatality" of Nietzsche's life, the fact that he was born twice, as he says here, once as his father and once as his mother, once as a decadent and once as a beginning, is something for which he can obviously not take credit. It was simply part of the circumstances that generated him and his particular set of characteristics. It is clear throughout *Ecce Homo* that for the most part one becomes what one is as a result of circumstances one had no hand in choosing, which in turn diminishes the degree to which one can take credit for the accomplishments that come one's way. Just as we saw that the charismatic figure most often feels humility in the face of his gifts, so too should Nietzsche recognize that his own "greatness" is a result of great fortuity.

Nietzsche knows the many fortuities of his life, as we see in his description of how he came to be the teacher *par excellence* of both decadence and self-overcoming. He tells us, for example, that "To become what one is, one must not have the faintest notion *what* one is" (p. 254), suggesting among other things that only the fortuitous unself-conscious unfolding of the self through the contexts it finds itself in allows one fully to become what one is. Again, this can only mean that the self is no more exclusively responsible for such an unfolding than it can take credit for what becomes of it. In a more extravagant expression of the same situation, Nietzsche provides us with a viewpoint that goes against his own expanding egomania:

> This ultimate, most joyous, most wantonly extravagant Yes to life represents not only the highest insight but also the *deepest,* that which is most strictly confirmed and born out by truth and science. Nothing in existence may be subtracted, nothing is dispensable—those aspects of existence which Christians and other nihilists repudiate are actually on an infinitely higher level in the order of rank among values than that which the instinct of decadence could approve and call good. To comprehend this requires courage and, as a condition of that, an excess of strength: for precisely as far as courage may venture forward, precisely according to that measure of strength one approaches the truth. Knowledge, saying Yes to reality, is just as necessary for the strong as cowardice and the flight from reality—as the "ideal" is for the weak, who are inspired by weakness. (p. 272)

The extravagant "Yes to life" that Nietzsche's work insists upon as the central value may well be both the highest and the deepest insight, just as it may well be that to which all our truths and our science point, but even so, it hardly matters that Nietzsche had a hand in this precise formulation.

Indeed, if Foucault needs to acknowledge the ways in which it will always matter who's speaking, Nietzsche by this point in his life should recognize Foucault's truth: that in many respects it doesn't really matter who's speaking, that the agent is always subordinate to the authority that emerges from the aesthetic context and not the other way around. If anyone should know this, it is Nietzsche with his extravagant Yes, for he must utter that affirmation in the face of his own awareness of the fictitiousness of the self. If he is to oppose his rich affirmation of life to the nihilism he finds in the Judeo-Christian vision, he must also recognize that the fundamentally tragic affirmation he has in mind is thoroughly indifferent to who is speaking, just as it should be. Even more, he should realize that he is polluting his affirmation through his self-interested expression of it. Instead of focusing on the value of the Yes to reality, he concentrates on the fact that *he* discovered this vision and that so far *he alone* has had the courage to face everything that is required of that Yes to life.

Nietzsche's words indirectly reflect the same point at a different level because he concedes that "saying Yes to reality, is just as necessary for the strong as cowardice and the flight from reality—as the 'ideal' is for the weak, who are inspired by weakness." If we are to take him at his word, this means among other things that *he can take no credit* for the courage he musters in facing the fearful truths of reality because *he has no choice:* it is a *necessity* for him to do so, he is *compelled* by the circumstances that make him what he is to face these awful, yet affirmative facts of life. But anything done by compulsion is surely not something for which one should take credit; anything one had no choice but to do in the first place is something that one might or might not be grateful for, but it is not that which should contribute to the satisfaction of one's ego. Again, humility ought to be the response to the courage that was thrust upon Nietzsche for whatever reason, humility and *gratefulness* for the fact that he was fortunate enough to be in the position to articulate so eloquently the great Yes to life and to provide a full account of what is at stake in that Yes.

Instead, Nietzsche wants to hoard the glory that comes from such a courageous enterprise—a courage too, by the way, that *may* be exaggerated, though one can never be sure. He thinks he is entitled to the equivalent of royalties on his greatness and thus is prone to make grandiose claims for his self instead of for the work that came from him. In arguing that one cannot distinguish the life from the work in the manner of traditional philosophers and "objective" commentators of whatever sort, Nietzsche fails to recognize that even if they cannot be separated, they are still not the same. The work that came from Nietzsche was unquestionably as epochal in nature as he himself argues ad nauseam in *Ecce Homo,* and that work obviously connects to the life that was lived by the man who wrote those texts. But the texts themselves—as the mark of a *full* aesthetic event in which even the agent Nietzsche was subordinate to the larger flows—are the full manifestation of the truths that context offered both to Nietzsche and to us. For the most part, that which "Nietzsche" added—if by "Nietzsche" we mean that self-interested construct whose egomania is clearly at the edge of the abyss in *Ecce Homo*—is that which argues an opposing case, one that returns us to the tortures of selves in opposition to the world, of a world in which the aesthetic is that which keeps us from dying of the truth rather than that which allows us to perceive the truths of our world in the first place. *It is Nietzsche himself* in these later works who keeps getting in the way of his own insights and undermines the very power of his great affirmation.

Perhaps the clearest exposition of the absurdity of the self-aggrandizing tendencies we find in the later Nietzsche occurs in Nietzsche's description of inspiration, the flow of life out which everything of value comes:

> Has anyone at the end of the nineteenth century a clear idea of what poets of strong ages have called *inspiration?* If not, I will describe it.—If one had the slightest residue of superstition left in one's system, one could hardly reject altogether the idea that one is merely incarnation, merely mouthpiece, merely a medium of overpowering forces. The concept of revelation—in the sense that suddenly, with indescribable certainty and subtlety, something becomes *visible,* audible, something that shakes one to the last depths and throws one down—that merely describes the facts. One hears, one does not seek; one accepts, one does not ask who gives; like lightning, a thought

> flashes up, with necessity, without hesitation regarding its form—I never had any choice. (p. 300)

Anyone who is (quite accurately) willing to stress that "One hears, one does not seek; one accepts, one does not ask who gives" recognizes that no credit is to be attributed to the one who hears the voice—wherever it comes from, it clearly comes from somewhere other than the individual self, the Nietzsche who suffered and enjoyed life.

The charismatic associations of what Nietzsche is speaking about here are obvious even to him, most anti-religious of men, for he all but admits that he has experienced "revelation" and states that any description of revelation—that "suddenly, with indescribable certainty and subtlety, something becomes *visible,* audible, something that shakes one to the last depths and throws one down"—simply "describes the fact" of his own experience. He has acknowledged the mystery of the gifts that allow him to articulate with such authority his vision of things, recognizes that even for him it would be accurate to say that he is little more than a "mouthpiece, merely a medium of overpowering forces." If this is true, then his revaluation of values and its overpowering force cannot be attributed to Nietzsche but rather, say, to the flows of life within Nietzsche that overpower him through the joyous affirmation they allow him to express again and again in his work.

Though Nietzsche does not quite attribute these powerful aesthetic states to life itself, he clearly doesn't take credit for them either, and he isn't likely to link them to religious fervor or divine revelation, so their only possible location would have to be either life itself or the flows of language, which in themselves are but another manifestation of the flows of life. "I never had any choice" in the unfolding of my work, Nietzsche suggests; "like lightning, thought flashes up, with necessity, without hesitation regarding its form," and as a result the texts that Nietzsche produced come to be. This way of speaking about the nature of his own inspiration ought to suggest to Nietzsche that his authority does not come from his self any more than Jesus's authority did. He wouldn't even need to declare the death of God and the death of the self to recognize that he himself is only an agent and not a divine force in any essential way. Yet that perspective is almost entirely lacking here.

We need to remember that Nietzsche was indeed on the edge of madness when he wrote *Ecce Homo,* and we should consider the human situation as well. If any of us were faced with the rejection that he endured, and if we as a result were also forced into the chilly solitude he lived in, we might also develop precisely those structures that Nietzsche manifests through his egomaniacal declarations here. One thinks of such utterances as this one: "Then there is the gruesome silence one hears all around one. Solitude has seven skins; nothing penetrates them any more. One comes to men, one greets friends—more desolation, no eye offers a greeting" (p. 303). These wintry breezes are such that one wonders if any human could withstand them, and if pity is the last thing Nietzsche would want us to feel for him, yet these graphic depictions of his incredible isolation must be juxtaposed against the bravado of his equally genuine *need* for solitude: "The energy to choose absolute solitude and leave the life to which I had become accustomed; the insistence on not allowing myself any longer to be cared for, waited on, and *doctored*—that betrayed an absolute instinctive certainty about *what* was needed above all at that time" (p. 224). Even if Nietzsche is talking about an earlier period of his life here, he is also quite clearly trying to account for the great solitude that has taken over his life, and he does so by saying that he chose this regime because he had "an absolute instinctive certainty about *what* was needed above all at that time."

The instinctive certainty may well have been just that, but it was in that case a double necessity, first because it came from an intuitive level within Nietzsche and thus was not something over which he asserted any control, and second because in a very real way the instinctive certainty obviously derived from the desolate circumstances of his life that were already in place. As Nietzsche himself might phrase it, he chose what he had no real choice in choosing: he decided *after the fact* that he chose an absolute solitude that clearly developed out of something much larger than individual choice. And Nietzsche, to his credit, tries to the end of his sane life to keep the belief in his choice in the matter in play, for he must do so to continue to affirm his fated life.

At the very limit of his own sanity, Nietzsche reveals to us here precisely why the defensive strategy of egomania is never sufficient, why its protective projections can always only make matters worse in the end. From one angle, he acknowledges the "gruesome silence" that must have been the most painful thing he had to bear in life; from another angle he declares that he instinctively and rightly *chose* this gruesome silence and thereby became the great person that he was; and from still another angle we find outright delusions coming into play as well, as when he tells us that "wherever I go, here in Turin . . . everybody's face lights up and looks pleased at my sight. What has flattered me most so far is that old costermonger women won't relax until they have found their sweetest grapes for me. That is the extent to which one should be a philosopher" (p. 262). For all we know he may be right about the costermonger women, but surely it is a serious delusion to assume that everybody's face lights up when Nietzsche passes by. The great tragedy of Nietzsche's life in this respect is that he established the aesthetic perspective through which we have come to construe our lives—and on the basis of which we have recognized both the death of the author and the death of the self—yet in the end Nietzsche himself was too dedicated to the fabrications of the self and lost himself in the sea of delusion that such constructs present.

The uselessness of self-aggrandizement is something that is also recognized throughout *Ecce Homo,* just as we see that Nietzsche perceives the problems that derive from the fictions of the self. He boldly declares—in obvious opposition to some of his own work, notably on Zarathustra, and even in *Ecce Homo,* where the line between the construct and the human self is often hard to draw—that "The pathos of poses does *not* belong to greatness; whoever needs poses at all is *false.*—Beware of all picturesque men!" (p. 257). Outside of *Thus Spoke Zarathustra,* Nietzsche's greatest poses are to be found in *Ecce Homo;* the masks here are just as grand as those we find in the figure of Zarathustra, but now they are done up more clearly under the name of "Nietzsche" than they were before. Nietzsche, of course, waffled throughout his life between declarations of the usefulness of these constructions of the self and condemnations of the poseur who is at the center of every such construction. Poses here are antithetical to greatness, and picturesque men are the most dangerous because they are clearly hiding something through their artificial display.

The more general aesthetic formulation of this opposition was also present throughout Nietzsche's work, for he did indeed state unequivocally that we have art so that we don't perish of the truth just as he also firmly declared that true art is finally a laying bare of reality in all its joy and terror. Which one is the real Nietzsche? The creator of the poseur Zarathustra and the egomaniacal "Nietzsche" of *Ecce Homo?* Or the crafter of the *Genealogy of Morals* who recognizes the degree to which fate drives the truths that come from people rather than the essential genius within them? The man who gave to Apollo the divine right of illusions? The one who celebrated the Dionysian tearing asunder of the veil of maya? Or the composite Dionysus who possessed traits of both the early Apollo and the early Dionysus? In some respects, it would have to be said that there is finally no definitive way of choosing which "Nietzsche" was the "real" one because in some senses they were obviously *all* Nietzsche. And in another sense there would be no definitive way of choosing between these versions of Nietzsche because each one provides a different view of the aesthetic perspective to which Nietzsche's name is attached. But in still another respect we must finally decide which "Nietzsche" we are going to attach to those developments that come from the alterations in our ways of thinking he provided, and this too is finally a question of authority, both the authority of Nietzsche the man and writer *and* the authority of the texts themselves.

One of the main reasons for looking at *Ecce Homo* as an evaluative model for questions of aesthetic authority resides in the fact that there are mutually exclusive models of reality, and hence authority, in the text. How are we to establish this, and how can we determine to which one we should attach the name "Nietzsche"? First, we can say that the egomaniacal viewpoint that is to be found in the text and its complementary poses and the delusory structures that are needed to uphold them—reminiscent of the Apollonian in the early Nietzsche—do not belong in the same philosophical perspective as the so-called tragic vision of life for which Nietzsche himself claimed credit. There can be no denying that both the egomaniacal and defensive structures and the tragic celebrator of life beyond the facile distinctions of the fictive self lived within the same person, Nietzsche, but that is a different question. We need to recognize the points where the person and the philosophy merge into a coherent portrait and where they diverge as well. Regardless of how one phrases the matter, there are throughout two mutually exclusive perspectives, the one based on illusion and the false courage of artificial constructs—the one, that is, that asserts our need for the beauties of art to keep us from dying of the truth and that celebrates a nihilistic expression of the will to power that is dominated exclusively by self-interest; and the perspective that celebrates the truths that the human species has uncovered regardless of the terrors that are connected to them, that sees art as the chief means through which such truths are uncovered, that construes all truth, reality and value in aesthetic terms that deny the value of isolated selves and others from the outset, and that declares the will to power to be an expression of the overabundance of joyful life flowing through one and manifesting itself in the world through a wantonly extravagant Yes to life. There is no way these *perspectives* can be mixed, even if they always manifest themselves incongruously in some mixture within individual human beings as a result of their heritage and their limitations. One cannot deliberately *choose* both of these, for that is to lead to a hopeless muddle.

If there are these two mutually exclusive perspectives to be found in Nietzsche's work, we should state quite clearly that they are indeed both present, but then we need to look for that perspective which most accurately reflects what

Nietzsche *at his best* thought he was doing and that he indeed managed largely to effect. In terms of the traditions that have developed out of him, we can see that the tangled offshoot of the nihilistic vision of will to power died a fairly hasty death in the existential extension of it, which quickly led to the expositions of the death of the self and the author and to Foucault's fundamental indifference to who is speaking. The offshoot that continues to flourish has to do with the aesthetic perspective that celebrates *life* joyously, not the construct of the self or self-interest, not the will to power as nihilism, not the decadence to which Nietzsche himself succumbed even as he reviled it. Or if one should choose to look at the question of which perspective is most to be attributed to Nietzsche and which is most derivative of certain earlier modes of thought, there is again no denying that "Nietzsche" goes with the extravagant Yes to life in the face of all of its terror. Any way one chooses to look at the question of the "Nietzschean" perspective, it comes down to the exuberant celebration of life in the midst of its tragedy.

If we can agree on this definition of Nietzsche's perspective in the face of the obstacles presented to that definition as a result of his highly contradictory texts, then we can begin to assess the coherence and value of that perspective both through Nietzsche's egomaniacal expression of it in *Ecce Homo* and through the filter that would eliminate the contradictory self-interest that the egomania reveals. A fitting place to begin such an investigation would be Nietzsche's personal expression of the future of his name: "I know my fate. One day my name will be associated with the memory of something tremendous—a crisis without equal on earth, the most profound collision of conscience, a decision that was conjured up *against* everything that had been believed, demanded, hallowed so far. I am no man, I am dynamite.—Yet for all that, there is nothing in me of a founder of a religion. . . . I *want* no 'believers'; I think I am too malicious to believe in myself; I never speak to masses" (p. 326).

This is the utterance of a charismatic individual who understands well the force of his work and its consequences. It was indeed Nietzsche's "fate"—a word, again, that suggests how little in some respects he consciously had to do with it—to have his name associated with the memory of a tremendous crisis, a crisis that continues to this day and whose outcome remains as yet undetermined. To be sure, as the sentence suggests, Nietzsche doesn't say here that he is solely responsible for the crisis, for he knows full well that he is associated with it only to the extent that he declared it and established why it had happened. He did so by telling us what we always already knew, that God was dead and that we had killed Him. And in the West this knowledge has created "the most profound collision of conscience, a decision that was conjured up *against* everything that had been believed, demanded, hallowed so far." That as a society we still have not determined after more than a century how we are going to deal with the collision of conscience to which Nietzsche calls our attention demonstrates the profundity of the event; that even today Nietzsche's name is venerated and reviled suggests the powerful intensities that still swirl around the problems with which his name has become associated.

Nietzsche is right, then, to state that he is dynamite, right to recognize that if he himself is not a charismatic figure, his writings embody the charismatic authority of the greatest cultural forces that have been known. As always, it is important to recognize that here too Nietzsche misconstrues the nature of those charismatic forces and attributes them to himself rather than more properly attaching them to his *fate,* a considerably different way of accounting for them and one that would not link them to the self-aggrandizing tendencies of the statement. And even there Nietzsche is unintentionally right, for it is truly more his name than his work that has counted in the figuration of the crisis he mentions anyway. Although the effects of his work, for him and for us, ought to be such that we discontinue the practice of attributing such charismatic forces and their effects to individuals themselves and should prompt us instead to see the way they are always part of a fate that is embodied in a context that allows them to emerge without being exclusively the effects of an agent, we continue to fetishize the names that are attached to events rather than seek seriously to understand the events themselves. So it is indeed Nietzsche's name that has become associated with the event, and to a much lesser extent his work.

Even if Nietzsche's work bears the mark of charismatic utterance, he recognizes that "there is nothing in [him] of the founder of a religion." When he says he wants no "believers," we must surely take him at his word, for that which he has to espouse is neither a creed nor a statement of conscience per se. It is a perspective on the world and a critique of the history that has brought us to where we are, but it does not share the traits of a religious orthodoxy in any traditional sense. This is yet again why the self-aggrandizing tendencies so in evidence in *Ecce Homo* are decidedly out of place, for they belong more to the context in which a perfect master is venerated for his wisdom and for his ability to lead others to the truth. Nietzsche is neither Christ nor Buddha, even if in some respects his ultimate effects on the socius could be as profound, and he realizes that he has no doctrine to propound, no wish to acquire disciples, no desire to provide the discipline and ritual that adherents would require. The very distinction of his charismatic utterance is that it refuses to authorize such behavior, even as Nietzsche himself seeks an egomaniacal kind of authority. The consequences of the work itself destroy the very grounds of authority any religious figure would depend upon, force the need to deal with the aesthetic events and their interpretation onto the individual who must work through the problems of value and authority on his or her own.

Nietzsche also recognizes his elitism here, for if he never speaks to the masses, that is because he cannot bear to do so, fearing the proximity of the rabble to a greater and greater degree as he moves to the edge of the abyss. At the same time, it is disingenuous of Nietzsche to suggest that he doesn't want profound changes to come from his work, for otherwise he wouldn't be so sure of the great effects that will someday be associated with his name. If it will be attached to a great crisis, it also offers one path to the resolution of that crisis, and whereas Nietzsche regularly declares that he has no mission in the world—and is quite right about that from the traditional religious and moral perspective—still the full consequences of his work would be a revolution of the magnitude of the one associated with Jesus's or Buddha's name, as he knows full well. He doesn't keep pitting himself against Jesus by accident, nor does he name his autobiography after that famous moment when Pilate announces "the man" Jesus to the Romans without associating himself both with the sacrificial elements of Jesus's fate and with the religious fervor and ultimately profound changes that He introduced. That he doesn't have the gift for mingling with the masses hides his very real hopes for revolutionary changes that will be associated with the work he has done.

The revolutionary nature of Nietzsche's assertions, then, can never constitute a doctrine in and of themselves, though they do form a coherent perspective that is comprehensively established throughout his work, and it was his fate to have his name associated with the changes that have come about as a result of the crisis he declared and framed through his writing. But Nietzsche is also properly appalled by the thought of being turned into something he isn't as a result of the association of his name with this event. We must assume that the very writing of *Ecce Homo* comes about when it does because the growing egomania that heralds the onset of his mental illness suggests to him his true greatness even as he recognizes that he will—like all other revolutionary and charismatic figures—come to be misunderstood by the rabble. Anyone who begins his text with the following statement is obsessed with his place in the future: ". . . I have a duty against which my habits, even more the pride of my instincts, revolt at bottom—namely, to say: *Hear me! For I am such and such a person. Above all, do not mistake me for someone else*" (p. 217). Nietzsche seems presciently to know that his name will be mistaken even as he realizes that it will be associated with the profound crisis to come. He knows it will be misconstrued precisely because it will be associated with the crisis, perhaps because of the danger that attaches to being the messenger when the message is so revolutionary, perhaps because of the near-religious promise that a revaluation of all values suggests. One way or the other, Nietzsche is fully aware that he will be misunderstood, and it is worth noting that he is talking about *himself* here and not his work. He doesn't say that he is worried about his work being misinterpreted, though he has had more than enough examples of that in his forty-four years, and indeed these gross and regular misinterpretations of his work doubtless had something to do with his awareness that he himself will be misunderstood.

But why is he focussing on the self rather than on the more important work? And what has happened to make him willing to go against the pride of his instincts and revoltingly present his own personal case before the world? He has been misinterpreted and misunderstood for years, so that in itself is not sufficient cause. And whereas Nietzsche might have had moments of bombast in previous works as well, still he did his best to keep any personal special pleading out of his texts. After all, Nietzsche hated above all self-pity and its effects in the world, so the last thing he would want to do would be to create a situation in which he provided a portrait of himself that was laced with self-pity or that engendered pity regardless. He doesn't want the world's pity, even less, perhaps, its understanding. Still, instead of focussing our attention on the need to understand what his *work* means, and instead of seeking one more time to turn us away from our traditional preoccupations with selves, here he chooses to focus on his own self out of a desperate hope finally to keep from being mistaken for someone else.

We might think that the concern with being mistaken for someone else is a reflection yet again of Nietzsche's incipient madness. The borders of the self are beginning to waver. Just who he is and what his name is associated with are beginning to grow fuzzy for him as he becomes Dionysus or Zarathustra or Christ by turns. And there is equally no doubt that however much Nietzsche hates self-pity or pity that would be directed toward him, there is more than enough displaced self-pity in *Ecce Homo*. It comes in the guise of bravado, as always, under the rubric of "things I have suffered and lived through that have made me stronger." But the assessment of Nietzsche's life that we find in these pages is never far away from the fact that he has suffered mightily. All this may well have come together to give him a glimmer of an idea that a profound crisis is about to overwhelm him and threaten the very constitution of his self, and that he had better therefore establish clearly who that self is before it is too late. Regardless of the particular reasons, though, the awareness that he would be mistaken for someone else, devil or saint, was accurate enough and continues to be to this day.

Nietzsche's worries about the future of his name and being are, we know, proper enough given what happens to them, so the prescience of the charismatic figure was far from wrong even at the edge of madness. Likewise, there is good reason for his attempts to deflect the interests in him that he anticipates, for the attention he is likely to get will inevitably move away from the direction of his work:

> I do not want to be a holy man; sooner even a buffoon.—Perhaps I am a buffoon.—Yet in spite of that—or rather *not* in spite of it, because so far nobody has been more mendacious than holy men—the truth speaks out of me.—But my truth is *terrible;* for so far one has called *lies* truth.
>
> *Revaluation of all values:* that is my formula for an act of supreme self-examination on the part of humanity, become flesh and genius in me. It is my fate that I have to be the first *decent* human being; that I know myself to stand in opposition to the mendaciousness of millennia.—I was the first to *discover* the truth by being the first to experience lies as lies—smelling them out.—My genius is in my nostrils. (p. 326)

If Nietzsche does not want to be a holy man, he recognizes that the names of those who are associated with crises and the resolution of crises often become holy men, revered as fetishized figures rather than as authorities of a different nature. If Nietzsche became such, his work would have failed, would have been assimilated into the older forms of religious veneration.

That Nietzsche would rather be a buffoon than a holy man is doubtless no exaggeration on his part, for at least he would not have to deal with the artificializing structures of reverence and would theoretically be able to maintain some semblance of his original self (again, an utterance whose force is most ironic in this text, for *Ecce Homo*'s self-aggrandizing tendencies suggest a preference for veneration over buffoonery and imply that Nietzsche is more concerned with being ignored altogether or with being seen as a buffoon than as a holy man—even if he still has the presence of mind to recognize that his work depends on him *not* being seen as one). Given the gravity that is traditionally associated with holy men, Nietzsche thinks it would be better to be seen as being light and frivolous "because so far nobody has been more mendacious than holy men." If they have spoken nothing but lies, and if their mien has always been a grave one that would induce others to reverence, then Nietzsche would prefer to be associated with the opposite values. The problem with this way of looking at things is that it too self-consciously construes itself in opposition to the traditional ways of doing things, a course of action that is antithetical to what Nietzsche elsewhere suggests is necessary. Although it is a debatable point whether or not Nietzsche's work developed out of a simple opposition to and hatred of Christianity, I would argue that this is not the case. His critique of Western values came out of a genuine attempt to understand the implications of those values, and his revaluation of those values in turn did not simply mean overturning every "Christian" value and replacing it with its opposite. To do that would be to do little more than provide a mirror image of those values he opposed. Even so, that is precisely what Nietzsche is doing here, defining himself as the opposite of that which he loathes rather than assessing himself in terms of the positive values he espouses.

If the truth speaks out of Nietzsche—a fairly accurate way of saying that it is not precisely Nietzsche himself who speaks the truth—he recognizes that his truth is "*terrible;* for so far one has called *lies* truth." And given the terrible nature of "his" truth—again this false personalizing of a truth that may be associated with his name without being *his* any more than it could or should be anybody else's—it is perhaps better to be the buffoon, to buffer the message with the play of buffoonery so as to mitigate its harsh effects. The very terror hidden in the truth is more inclined to make him into a holy man, though, for the great and terrible truths of the world are associated with this type rather than the fool. Nietzsche wants a contradictory fate, then: he would like his name to be associated with a terrible truth, yet he chooses to be seen as a buffoon, or at least prefers that role to that of a holy man. The two states do not go together, even if one can imagine a figure who is associated with terrible truths and does not become a holy man.

The real crisis for Nietzsche here has to do with the problem he skirted throughout his later work: he seeks a revaluation of all values, yet he doesn't want this revaluation to be religious. He attempts to discredit thoroughly the holy and mendacious lies of his tradition and to replace them with the terrible truths he himself recognized, but he doesn't want his name to be associated in turn with the word "holy" or the word "morality" (or sometimes with the word "truth"). He would like to be a holy man of sorts, or would like his works to have equivalent effects, and yet he doesn't want the mantle that comes with such effects and prefers to stay away from the words that are always inevitably associated with such effects. Nietzsche seeks to provide a complete revaluation of values, and here declares himself to be the first *decent* human being—that, he tells us once again, is his *fate*—and yet he doesn't want the word "decency" to be linked in any way to morality and doesn't want his revalued values to have anything to do with morality. How can this be?

The contradiction at the center of Nietzsche's desires in *Ecce Homo* can be seen in other ways as well. Early on, for example, he insists that "The last thing *I* should promise would be to 'improve' mankind" (p. 217), and yet that is precisely what his work would do if it were to have the effects he would hope for it. True, as Nietzsche says, "No new idols are erected by me; let the old ones learn what feet of clay mean" (p. 217). His improvements would not depend on the fabrication of future objects of veneration, and he is right to work against that possibility as strenuously as he can. Still, the effect of his work would inevitably have to be a great improvement in mankind. The same situation is to be found at the beginning of the paragraph in which he pleads with us not to misunderstand him: "Seeing that before long I must confront humanity with the most difficult demand ever made of it, it seems indispensable to me to say *who I am*. Really, one should know it, for I have not left myself 'without testimony.' But this disproportion between the greatness of my task and the *smallness* of my contemporaries has found expression in the fact that one has neither heard nor even seen me" (p. 217). Not only do we see the flickering of Nietzsche's impending madness in this statement, for he clearly can no longer discern what he can and cannot do, even as he has lost sight of the fact that through his work he has *already* confronted humans with the most difficult demands ever made of them, but we also note that in part that madness is defined by his belief in his own agency and by the necessity for us to know who he is. These utterances come from the void Nietzsche felt himself to be in. His contemporaries were so small that they missed his great task altogether, didn't even recognize the threat of it; they simply denied him and his work's existence altogether. So *Nietzsche* needs to know who he is, and it is indeed tragic that he has been brought to this pass.

But it is not *Nietzsche* who is confronting humanity with the most difficult demand ever made of it—only a *god* could do that, and only a prophet or holy man could even hope to prefigure such an event. Rather, his work has unfolded the most difficult demand confronting humanity: a revaluation of all values that would create in us the will joyously to affirm life in the midst of all its terror. This is indeed exactly what Nietzsche thinks it is, the most difficult demand that has ever been made of the species; and it is true that the demand itself is to be found in Nietzsche's work. But we don't need to know who *he* is in order to recognize the value of this demand. It carries its own authority and doesn't depend on him in the least, even if he was the primary agent of its articulation. Again, Nietzsche wants to be a holy man and doesn't want to be a holy man, and only his work itself can set things straight, can establish the absurdity of holy men in general and demonstrate that authority within an aesthetic context is not determined by the agents within that context but rather by the context itself.

If Nietzsche's texts properly unfold the revaluation of values he has in mind, we will not really need to know precisely who he is, any more than what can be found of "him" in his works anyway, though naturally biographical and other kinds of information about Nietzsche might help flesh out the context more fully. The perspective that Nietzsche articulates provides its own authority in the end on the basis of its coherent expression of values and its clear and truthful depiction of the way human existence is to be perceived once we assume that the world is fundamentally aesthetic in nature (rather than "objective" or "subjective" or "religious" or "secular" or something else). The revaluation of values has Nietzsche written into it, for he was the agent of its articulation, but the Nietzsche written into the revaluation is not the Nietzsche who lived and suffered, even if his life and suffering were essential to the revaluation he achieved. So *we* do not need to know who he is, and his holy mission does not depend on him once his texts are written. Above all Nietzsche's work does not require him once it is written because it has dissolved the essential and sacred self to which the older authority attached itself. Nietzsche is the inventor of the charismatic *context;* it is that which he puts in place of the charismatic figure even as he displaces authority to the context itself as well. Yet that is precisely what he himself has forgotten by this point in his life.

Nevertheless, Nietzsche's fears about being mistaken for a holy man—and his desires for being so mistaken as well—reveal the dangers that are to be found in his work, only this time the dangers are different, are more akin to the problems inherent in Weber's routinization of charisma than in the possibility that humans will not be able to bear his terrible truths. The danger that is reflected in Nietzsche's own mistakenly egomaniacal attitude in *Ecce Homo* is not that we will confuse one person for another or misconstrue who someone is, not even that we will mistake who Nietzsche himself is; the danger is that we will misunderstand the importance of the individual, Nietzsche in this case, and lose sight of the truly significant event, which is not Nietzsche but the revaluation of values he helped bring about. We will in turn "routinize" his dangerous truths by reducing them to the utterances of a holy master who embodies these truths in a way we ourselves cannot. And in so fetishizing the master Nietzsche, we will reduce his truths and strip the revaluation of the effects it should have. The danger to which Nietzsche succumbs, then, is the very reduction of himself into a fetishized object that he presumably is seeking to avoid in *Ecce Homo*. His "testimony" should stand by itself within the flows of discourse into which it has been placed, but Nietzsche is unwilling to let it stand in that way, for then it no longer attaches to him in a way that would allow him to get credit for it. Such, at least, seems to be the state of things toward the end of his working life.

❦

The dangers of Nietzsche's work must be revisited from another context if we are to assess more fully the authority of it, and this can be accomplished by the statement in which Nietzsche cites the moment of truth for his revaluation:

> How I had thus found the concept of the "tragic" and at long last knowledge of the psychology of tragedy, I have explained most recently in *Twilight of the Idols*, p. 139:
>
> "Saying Yes to life even in its strangest and hardest problems; the will to life rejoicing over its own inexhaustibility even in the very sacrifice of its highest types—that is what I called Dionysian, that is what I understood as the bridge to the psychology of the tragic poet. Not in order to get rid of terror and pity, not in order to purge oneself of a dangerous affect by its vehement discharge—Aristotle misunderstood it that way—but in order to be oneself the

> eternal joy of becoming, beyond all terror and pity—that joy which includes even joy in destroying."
>
> In this sense I have the right to understand myself as the first *tragic philosopher*—that is, the most extreme opposite and antipode of a pessimistic philosopher. (p. 273)

Nietzsche's tragic philosophy is based on the need to say Yes to life even in the midst of "its strangest and hardest problems," the chief of which concern our temporal and mortal natures. It consists of the "will to life" itself as it is found within us, "rejoicing over its own inexhaustibility" in spite of the destructiveness and violence that is also attached to this will to live, and in spite of the fact that this affirmation can take place always only in the tragic circumstance of a life that is affirmed "beyond all terror and pity" in the midst of the eternal joy of becoming.

The revaluation of values, the attempt to weigh the things of the world anew, is based precisely upon this tragic vision of existence, this tragic celebration of the joys and terrors of life in the midst of all the woes they bring in their wake as well, without explanation, without justification, without another world to which we can turn at the end of this one. The tragic nature of this existence is framed by the fact that it ends *here* and doesn't point somewhere else, and is articulated through the awareness both that we have a fate and that we are fated, that much, if not most, of what happens to us occurs without particular reason or meaning and must simply be lived with and affirmed in spite of the fact that our will had no hand in its existence: "My formula for greatness in a human being is *amor fati:* that one wants nothing to be different, not forward, not backward, not in all eternity. Not merely bear what is necessary, still less conceal it—all idealism is mendaciousness in the face of what is necessary—but *love* it" (p. 258). Such is Nietzsche's tragic vision, and it does indeed prefigure a crisis even as it provides a resolution of the crisis through the tragic affirmation of existence of which we are all theoretically capable.

Nietzsche's *amor fati* can be measured in any number of ways, most obviously by the degree to which an individual or an utterance manages to affirm the value of the world in which we live in spite of whatever obstacles it might pose for us, but another way of phrasing this is to say that self-pity is the antithesis of *amor fati,* is that which is the mark of its absence. He who pities himself because the life to which he was fated did not treat him fairly or deal with him as he thought it should is he who would revise the past and who therefore refuses to accept it. If one truly wants *nothing* to be different, if one is willing to affirm *everything* that has ever happened in the world, then one truly is imbued with *amor fati.* Of course, no such human has ever existed, and perhaps none will ever be forthcoming. Nietzsche himself knew this very well, and if he sought as a goal for his own life to embody this *amor fati*—a goal, obviously, that he only partially succeeded in attaining, as the desperate clutchings after self in *Ecce Homo* suggest—he also considered this "formula for greatness in a human being" as a fitting measure for the unfolding of our everyday lives, even if in the end we could no more completely fulfill such a vision than Nietzsche did.

*Amor fati* is the positive individual limit and measure of that which is established through the revaluation of values, the limit we all can achieve at the very best of human moments, but one that is harder to attain in the ordinary circumstances of everyday life and harder still to arrive at in those worst of moments when our entire lives seem to be dissolving. This is a tragic vision not only because of its temporal and mortal nature, but also because of what is embodied in that temporal nature, precisely that *nothing that has happened can ever be changed,* that the past's effect on us cannot be wished away, erased, rewritten, or simply ignored. And inasmuch as there are always inevitably things that have happened in the past that have engendered things in our present lives that we should prefer to eliminate, it is the most difficult of human tasks to learn how to live with that about which nothing can be done. Saying Yes to life in its strangest and hardest problems requires us therefore to reconceive our relationship to our selves, to our past, and to the authority out of which they have been constituted.

As for the danger of such a tragic philosophy, we need to

stress once more that Nietzsche's own fate, his very insanity, could be construed as the result of his attempts to embrace life beyond all terror and pity. His breakdown could be constituted as the horrifying mark of failure that is a necessary consequence for anyone who tries to see the world whole and who seeks to embrace his fate with love in spite of that within it which can never be overcome. The very egomania we see so rampant in *Ecce Homo* could be interpreted as the unconscious formation of one who was totally incapable of living through what had happened to him, whether we choose to focus on his eye problems and digestive difficulties or on the cruel facts surrounding the reception of his work—Nietzsche's life and the revaluation of values that comes out of it, we might think, demonstrate the total inability of humans to measure up to the standards established by the aesthetic vision of existence. The difficulties of life that finally drove Nietzsche mad could be said thus to stem directly from his attempt to embrace his fate even as unconsciously he was totally incapable of facing the neglect and silence and physiological debilities that were connected to the unfolding of his life *and* his thought. That danger remains, as it always will, and it remains as a testimony of the great profundity of the work and as a potential measure of its limitations.

We can also take a more positive view toward the work and its authority, though, and see the revaluation of values not as an impossibility but rather as that which will allow us to understand and embrace our lives fully for the first time. To the extent that we become capable of this, we would have to attribute our success to Nietzsche's work, even if he himself was neither holy man nor buffoon. Again, his own appraisal may well in the end be an accurate one, even if he was off by a century or more in his estimation of the length of time it would take for his tragic vision to thread its way constructively into our lives:

> Let us look ahead a century; let us suppose that my attempt to assassinate two millennia of antinature and desecration of man were to succeed. That new

> party of life which would tackle the greatest of all tasks, the attempt to raise humanity higher, including the relentless destruction of everything that was degenerating and parasitical, would again make possible that excess of life on earth from which the Dionysian state, too, would have to awaken again. I promise a tragic age: the highest art in saying Yes to life, tragedy, will be reborn when humanity has weathered the consciousness of the hardest but most necessary wars *without suffering from it.* (p. 274)

Few people would be willing to argue that this tragic age is upon us yet, but there is no reason to think that it is not possible, particularly to the degree to which people come to understand just what Nietzsche meant by the word "tragic," particularly when one assumes that his "attempt to assassinate two millennia of antinature and desecration of man" has in some respects already begun.

The increasingly ecological focus of many humans would suggest a move away from a perspective that is hostile to nature, and the very notion of ecology assumes our essential connection to the processes of nature in a way that the previous perspectives did not. If humans are still desecrated for all sorts of political and philosophical reasons, there are some indications of positive change, and in the West at least there is also a growing awareness of the importance of acknowledging the values of the body itself. None of these changes is necessarily directly to be attributed to Nietzsche himself, though surely his own work helped to pave the way for them. In this respect *who* gets credit in the end is less important than that the changes themselves seem gradually to be occurring. Perhaps the West at least will learn to cultivate the highest art of saying Yes to life and will thus embrace the tragic age that Nietzsche himself prefigured even in his early work. At the very least it would be foolish at this near distance to Nietzsche's life to write his work off as hopelessly dangerous and finally the mark of a lunatic or one who was overrun by his own egomania. The egomania is unquestionably present and the self-aggrandizement unfortunate, but the event itself that goes by the name of "Nietzsche" might well accomplish precisely what he suggests it will do.

❦

If a work like *Ecce Homo* has an aesthetic authority in spite of the self-aggrandizing, self-interested motivations of parts of the text, and if it commands our attention at least as much as any of Nietzsche's more sober-minded assessments of his life and work, it is the overarching perspective itself, the tragic Yes-saying spirit, that provides it with that authority. What we have yet to see fully, though, is how that Yes-saying is connected to what in some respects is the most fundamental insight of Nietzsche, the argument against *ressentiment*. *Ecce Homo* is again a fitting forum for such an investigation because Nietzsche seems to be driven quite powerfully by his own resentments, thereby undercutting his very remarks throughout. The degree to which he does this is an open question, but no amount of apologizing and explaining can take away from the major resentments Nietzsche expresses in the book. Kaufmann tries to make the best of a bad case when he tells us that "In *Ecce Homo* Nietzsche embodies this attitude, this triumph over *ressentiment*. Instead of bearing a grudge toward the world that treated him so cruelly, instead of succumbing to the rancor of sickness, he relates the story of his life and work in a spirit of gratitude—and goes out of his way to pay his respects to Paul Rée and Lou Salomé, with whom he had fallen out" (p. 206, 207). Whether or not *Ecce Homo* as a whole truly embodies a triumph over *ressentiment* is something we shall have to investigate, but here at least Kaufmann is giving Nietzsche far too much credit for his noble spirit. True, he does make some respectful remarks to Paul Rée and Lou Salomé, and he pays his respects to Wagner as well, praising him, in effect, for being a worthy competitor who rivals Nietzsche in importance: "I think I know better than anyone else of what tremendous things Wagner is capable—the fifty worlds of alien ecstasies for which no one besides him had wings; and given the way I am, strong enough to turn even what is most questionable and dangerous to my advantage and thus to become stronger, I call Wagner the great benefactor of my life. That in which we are related—that we have suffered more profoundly, also from each other, than men of this century are capable of suffering—will link our names again and again, eternally. . . " (p. 250, 51). There is no resentment to be found here but rather an eloquent form of praise. When it comes to particular individuals in *Ecce Homo,* at least those who are mentioned, it would seem that Nietzsche was indeed above rancor.

Kaufmann also concedes that at times Nietzsche is hung by his own failings when it comes to resentment, as when he tells us that ". . . Nietzsche's indictments [of the Germans] are sometimes stained by his own wounds: in more than one passage he falls short of his own standards, and resentment clings to him like a leech" (p. 208). But to suggest that Nietzsche only shows resentment when it comes to the Germans—and that resentment is present quite regularly *throughout* the text—is grossly to underestimate the degree to which the text itself is driven by resentments both obvious and displaced. If no one understood better than Nietzsche why resentment was such a grave human problem, that was obviously because he was never able to cure himself of the disease. When he is listing some of the difficulties he has faced in his life and work, he discusses what he calls the rancor of what is great—in effect the notion that every great deed somehow finally turns against the person who accomplished it—and then quickly mentions that another obstacle is "the absurd sensitivity of the skin to small stings, a kind of helplessness against everything small" (p. 303), and one can only assume that Nietzsche has petty resentments particularly in mind here. Indeed, he suggests that they were a considerable obstacle to his work, diminishing his force and undermining his ability to do what he wanted to do. He admits quite frankly to "helplessness" in the face of "everything small," concedes that he cannot deal with the endless small stings that life metes out to one as a matter of course. He knows full well, we can assume, the absurdity of being weighed down by these petty forms of indignity, yet he cannot get away from them for all that. His honesty here suggests that there is probably more resentment in *Ecce Homo* than Kaufmann wants to see.

Without turning to a psychological investigation of the Nietzsche we find in the book, I would point out only the more obvious symptoms of potential resentment. Most pertinently, we have seen again and again how Nietzsche's persona in the text lets loose with self-aggrandizing statements that even he would have sublimated in some way in earlier works. These remarks are ready signs of one who has elaborated his defensive gestures of pomposity in the face of the stolid rejection of the world. They may not be simple signs of resentment, but their very necessity for a man so capable of plumbing the depths of the human psyche demonstrates how thoroughly wounded he was by the *large* stings of the world, the one thing that keeps coming up again and again even as he brushes it off. Nietzsche will tell us, for example, that he feels "no curiosity at all about reviews of my books, especially in the newspapers," and that his "friends and [his] publishers know this and do not speak to [him] about such things" (p. 262), but it is a logical assumption that he shows no curiosity about such reviews because he can't bear the thought of being destroyed in print yet again. The stings of such reviews remain with him, even if the only way he has found of dealing with them at this point in his life is to suggest that they affect him not at all because he has lost interest in them.

From another angle the same phenomenon appears in a different guise. After Nietzsche has recounted his beliefs about the effects of climate, posture, nutrition, and the like on individuals, he reflects on the seeming strangeness of the account and states: "One will ask me why on earth I've been relating all these small things which are generally considered matters of complete indifference: I only harm myself, the more so if I am destined to represent great tasks. Answer: these small things—nutrition, place, climate, recreation, the whole casuistry of selfishness—are inconceivably more important than everything one has taken to be important so far.

Precisely here one must begin to *relearn*" (p. 256). The point Nietzsche is making here is, we know, an important one for his thought, for it is based on the contexts through which everything comes to be, grounded in the world of which we are always a part and the body that attaches us to that world, and the things large and small that therefore affect that body and that context in which we always find ourselves. In this sense he is the philosopher of the small things that are generally considered matters of complete indifference only because in the traditional view the things of this world are not to be thought of as anything more than obstacles to our potential life in the next world. If we live only *here*, only *now*, then the small things take on great magnitude in the scheme of things. From an aesthetic perspective, the small things become the measure of one's location and the means through which one assesses one's life.

Outside of the odd reference to thin skin and the helplessness in the face of small stings, though, we see no lengthy discussion of these small stings and their effects on Nietzsche and other humans. One might think this demonstrates the degree to which Nietzsche has overcome his *ressentiment*, but it seems more likely that his silence on this score reflects rather his almost complete inability to deal with even the slightest of stings, to say nothing for the much larger one of *simply being ignored by the world*. No, if Nietzsche thought—quite rightly in my estimation—that the overcoming of resentment was the bridge to the overman and the only way truly to say Yes to life in the midst of its terror, he arrived at that thought because his greatest failing was his (all too understandable) *ressentiment* against the world for what it had unfairly done to him. Only because he burns with resentment is he so silent on the subject here, so willing to praise Wagner and be nice to the others who have done him harm in his own eyes; only because he cannot begin to face the seething nature of subconscious hatreds does he seek to present us with the persona of one who has gotten beyond such serious human problems.

The most compelling way in which the problem of resentment focuses itself in *Ecce Homo* is to be found in Nietzsche's repeated remarks about hygiene and the like. Here he shows just what is necessary for him to get by in the world; he demonstrates the great effort it takes him to survive without quite phrasing the matter that way. Anyone who frankly admits that "*Nausea* over man, over the 'rabble,' was always my greatest danger" (p. 234) leaves one with the suspicion that he is making a big deal out of something little. Why, after all, should Nietzsche feel nausea in the face of the rabble? What are they to him? They have little to do with his personal problems, even less to do with his publishing difficulties. If he faces strife in the world, little of it is to be attributed to the rabble over which he feels great nausea.

So the answer is obvious: Nietzsche feels great nausea over the rabble because they remind him all too much of himself. He must keep away from them because his greatest danger is to submit to the nausea that would force him to see that he was no different from the rabble in most human respects. Above all, that would compel Nietzsche to admit that the one thing he shared most with the rabble was that he was driven by *ressentiment regardless of his acute knowledge of the destructiveness of it.* And because Nietzsche is always close to this nausea within himself *over himself,* over the fact that the endless small stings infect him, the great wise man, as much as they do the riffraff all around him, he can do no more than displace his resentment back onto the rabble, thereby momentarily hiding from it and yet guaranteeing its more powerful return in his life as the guilt from his failure to get past his own resentments comes back to haunt him. The deeply instinctive reaction of nausea, and the great candor with which Nietzsche admits this weakness, never quite covers over the thing he most wants to hide: the fellow-feeling of resentment he shares with those whom he most despises because they are so like him.

Hence the need for cleanliness: "As has always been my wont—extreme cleanliness in relation to me is the presupposition of my existence; I perish under unclean conditions—I constantly swim and bathe and splash, as it were, in water—in some perfectly transparent and resplendent element. Hence association with people imposes no mean test on my patience: my humanity does *not* consist in feeling with men how they are, but in *enduring* that I feel with them" (p. 233). The *need* for constant purification through swimming and bathing and splashing suggests that Nietzsche is not quite as comfortable in his body as he would lead us to believe, would suggest further that in trying to scrub off of himself the common air he shares with the rabble, he is trying to wash away his mortality. The linkage between the need to wash and the difficulties he has in even being *around* general humanity cannot be mistaken, and the nausea is just beneath the surface here.

Yet curiously, the very next line in the text is "My humanity is a constant self-overcoming." Nietzsche cannot quite come out and say either to himself or to us that he loathes himself and he loathes the body that stinks of mortality and he loathes the resentments that one accumulates as a result of being a temporal creature, so he asserts that cleanliness is an important matter to him and the only thing that allows him to endure the presence of other people. And then he turns right around and says that the ritual cleanliness is a reflection of the fact that his "humanity is a constant self-overcoming." So he tells us without telling us that self-loathing and resentment demand constant rituals of purification, and even then the "extreme" cleanliness he requires only barely allows him to acknowledge that "my humanity does *not* consist in feeling with men how they are, but in *enduring* that I feel with them." That man be delivered from revenge, Nietzsche asserted in *Thus Spake Zarathustra,* was his highest hope and the bridge to the overman, but that bridge remained quite far away from Nietzsche here near the end of his working life.

The final ritual of purgation upon which Nietzsche relies, of course, is the splendid air of the Engadine and environs and the solitude that comes with it, as he tells us in effect in the lines directly following his assertion that his humanity is a constant self-overcoming: "But I need *solitude*—which is to say, recovery, return to myself, the breath of a free, light, playful air" (p. 233). Nietzsche requires the chilly solitude and the thin air to make himself feel *cleaner*—that is, less human, that is, less full of rancor and the touch of temporality—and cannot do without it. If the mountain solitude is also something that he resents, he remains dependent on it for his sense of self. If the "gruesome silence" provides a solitude that "has seven skins" that "nothing penetrates" anymore, that is precisely what Nietzsche needs to keep away the small stings that quickly infect the "*absurd* sensitivity of the skin" he inhabits. He needs it but resents the need, he declares his self-overcoming at the very site of his failure to overcome the self. He aggrandizes himself throughout even as he abases himself continually through his confessions.

The energy required to keep these forces somewhat at bay within him was clearly beginning to tax Nietzsche by the time he wrote *Ecce Homo,* but that by no means suggests that he wasn't at some level aware of what was going on and what the stakes were: he is worried *about being overwhelmed by the world, concerned that he will be poisoned to death by the endless stings of rancor that come from within.* So his work and his life require the careful maintenance of bathing and solitude and chill air, but those in turn always reveal the deeper problem within:

> Not to see many things, not to hear many things, not to permit many things to come close—first imperative of prudence, first proof that one is no mere accident but a necessity. The usual word for this instinct of self-defense is *taste.* It commands us not only to say No when Yes would be "selfless" but also to say *No as rarely as possible.* To detach oneself, to separate oneself from anything that would make it necessary to keep saying No. The reason in this is that when defensive expenditures, be they ever so small, become the rule and a habit, they entail an extraordinary and entirely superfluous impoverishment. Our *great* expenses are composed of the most frequent small ones. (p. 252)

How marvelously well Nietzsche understands his own sad situation, how clearly he tells us of his problem, of the "extraordinary and entirely superfluous impoverishment" of his life that has come about because he has not been able to detach himself from what the master of psychology recognizes to be nothing more than "defensive expenditures" that have become the rule and habit of his own life even as the expenditures and the structures—the self-aggrandizement, the careful cleaning, the consciously cultivated elitism, the projection onto the rabble of his own seething resentments—have become almost unmanageable. They are manageable enough for him to create yet another brilliant work, but not so pliable as to be carefully put away. The dogs are not chained in this book, though Nietzsche is trying hard. The master of the wisdom of the tragic poet, the one who knows full well that the only future for the human species lies in its triumph over *ressentiment,* is at the edge of his own possibilities because he can no longer triumph over his resentments, because the defensive expenditures he has invested in to keep them at bay have not only not worked but have grown ever-larger, as they inevitably will, and there is little left to keep them in play.

*Taste* has become obsession, the No's have grown so many that the Yes's are harder and harder to find. The very real necessity of Nietzsche's life, that fate that drove him to understand the human condition better than anyone else in Western culture, has forced him to the edge of his own humanity. And at that edge, taste is no longer what is in question, for Nietzsche has had to exclude so much in order to maintain his defensive strategies that nothing much at all is left: just that baggy and fictitious monster of a self that he keeps building up more and more throughout the pages of *Ecce Homo* and the great achievement of Nietzsche's work that cannot for whatever reason really mean what it should to him. His self-defense has been necessary, but it has cost him everything as he approaches the end of his difficulties.

Given the fierce intensity of Nietzsche's struggles and their sad end, we need once again to remind ourselves that the tragic view of life may be dangerous, may indeed be life threatening. I myself do not see it that way, and obviously Nietzsche didn't either, but one cannot deny the possibility that his very knowledge of human existence and his great desire to overcome his resentment forced him through endless displacements and defensive structures to alienate himself more and more from himself. Anyone who characterizes the "first imperative of prudence" as the need "Not to see many things, not to hear many things, not to permit many things to come close" is one who is most of all perhaps hiding from the many things within himself that he hears and sees and is all too close to. There is therefore unquestionably the possibility that Nietzsche's very ideas are sufficient to drive him insane, and by implication destructive enough to drive anyone else insane who follows them to their endpoint. This possibility cannot be excluded, *should* not be excluded, if we are to give Nietzsche's work the serious consideration it deserves and if we are to recognize what it cost Nietzsche the human to create it in the first place. Our estimation of him—and the authority of the work itself—depends on our awareness of this as one possible fate to be derived from the aesthetic event we call "Nietzsche" or "tragic philosophy."

We have yet, however, to give Nietzsche's account of the great problem of *ressentiment* as it is found in *Ecce Homo,* and our understanding of the text would not be complete without his very precise formulation of the danger of resentment. The account above of the defensive expenditures that Nietzsche was increasingly forced to employ in order "to say *No as rarely as possible*" gives us an idea of what is at stake in resentment, at least in psychological terms, but there is far more to the problem than that, as we see in the following statement: "Freedom from *ressentiment,* enlightenment about *ressentiment*—who knows how much I am ultimately indebted, in this respect also, to my protracted sickness! This problem is far from simple: one must have experienced it from strength as well as from weakness. If anything at all must be adduced against being sick and being weak, it is that man's really remedial instinct, his *fighting instinct,* wears out. One cannot get rid of anything, one cannot get over anything, one cannot repel anything—everything hurts. Men and things obtrude too closely; experiences strike one too deeply; memory becomes a festering wound. Sickness itself *is* a kind of *ressentiment*" (p. 229, 30). Here Nietzsche suggests that *ressentiment* is a function of closeness; if men and things "obtrude too closely" to give one the distance that is necessary to repel them, they overwhelm the individual and wear his "fighting instinct" out. The late reference in the text to the absurd sensitivity of the skin to small stings is here written larger still, embracing the festering wound that memory becomes when it cannot forget what has happened to it in time, when the weakness of thinking about the stings that have come one's way keeps one from concentrating on one's place in the present moment. Nietzsche goes so far as to characterize sickness itself as a form of *ressentiment*, the body presumably turning against the individual who is not capable of tossing off his complaints against the world and what it has done to him.

The consequences of *ressentiment* are powerful indeed, and they are capable of overtaking the entire person, as Nietzsche with all his maladies could well attest, as he with his acknowledged thin skin would know as well as anyone: "Nothing burns one up faster than the affects of *ressentiment*. Anger, pathological vulnerability, impotent lust for revenge, thirst for revenge, poison-mixing in any sense—no reaction could be more disadvantageous for the exhausted: such affects involve a rapid consumption of nervous energy, a pathological increase of harmful excretions—for example, of the gall bladder into the stomach" (p. 230). Inasmuch as *ressentiment* is finally always a function of our revulsion against our temporal and mortal natures, it results in pragmatic contexts in attempts to deal with the intractable elements of our fate, whether they be things that cause us frustration and anger in the moment or the slights that have come from another individual or the unfair way in which the course of life has meted out this or that event to us and thereby altered the choices available to us forever. Inasmuch as the things that happen to us in time can *never* be overcome, all self-overcoming, all attempts to abjure the fever of resentment, must be based on our willingness to accept and embrace everything that has happened to us, including those things that have debilitated and limited us in ways we should prefer not to be.[2] Yet humans have so far been incapable of overcoming their resentments for very long, as Nietzsche well knew from his own experience and from his perception of others' experience. Again, one does not declare the bridge to the overman to be deliverance from revenge unless one perceives *ressentiment* to be *the* human problem, to be the one obstacle that must be overcome if we are ever to learn to live equably on the planet.

If Nietzsche has provided more elegant definitions of *ressentiment* in other works, notably in *Zarathustra* and in the *Genealogy of Morals,* he is at his best in *Ecce Homo* in describing its effects in the most graphic way. The simple statement that "Anger, pathological vulnerability, impotent lust for revenge, thirst for revenge, poison-mixing in any sense" are reflections of resentment demonstrates both Nietzsche's mastery of prose and his inability to control himself in the face of his own troubles, which presumably include precisely this list that stops short of completion, to be followed by "no reaction could be more disadvantageous for the exhausted." Here is a man who has experienced these poisons fully himself and knows the exhaustion that comes from dealing with the utterly pointless arguments from within that *ressentiment* generates. The anger, the pathological vulnerability, the impotent lust for revenge are truly *all* forms of human impotence and self-destruction, and they all burn one up far too fast to no real effect. Nothing good ever comes of one's resentment or one's desire for revenge, and no wishing the world or the circumstances within it to be different can change anything at all. One is better off forgetting the slights and unpalatabilities that happen along the way as soon as they are gone. This is indeed Nietzsche's definition of strength. The description of the effects of resentment here indicates just how close to them Nietzsche had become, just how much his strength had been sapped in spite of his great wisdom about the need to overcome the resentment within in order to accept one's place in the world.

*Ressentiment,* as Nietzsche well knew, is nothing more than a reflection of our unwillingness to accept the circumstances of our lives. Our nausea always ultimately comes from this inability and from our impotent rage in the face of it. The desire for revenge is thus the opposite of Nietzsche's ideal, the human who embraces fully his or her fate: "My formula for greatness in a human being is *amor fati:* that one wants nothing to be different, not forward, not backward, not in all eternity. Not merely bear what is necessary, still less conceal it—all idealism is mendaciousness in the face of what is necessary—but *love* it" (p. 258). If Nietzsche had done nothing more than define *ressentiment* as the human revulsion against his temporal nature and provided the antidote in *amor fati,* his work would have been complete and completely revolutionary, for from these two concepts comes the entire aesthetic perspective that we now recognize to be an argument for a different kind of human vision and a new form of human being.

If humans are capable of the "greatness" of *amor fati,* if they can embrace their lives as they are and wish nothing to be different, not hoping for something from the past to be erased or something in the future to disappear, and not simply bearing what has happened to them in the past and will happen to them in the future but rather loving it and joyfully accepting everything life has to bring, then the species truly would undergo a revolution the likes of which it has never yet seen. Resentment would no longer be our defining characteristic, and instead we would come to say Yes to the world in all of its strangeness and terror. And Nietzsche's understanding of the relation between resentment and the need to love one's fate is the most profound of anyone within the entire history of the West. He is right in this sense to declare that "all idealism is mendaciousness in the face of what is necessary," for idealism is devoted to an articulation of the world without at least one of its fundamental features and thus is a tissue of lies devoted to covering over our revulsion in the face of what is necessary. And he is right to argue again and again that the history of the West has been generated out of the resentments of its "great people" and the idealisms that have come from those resentments.

When Nietzsche asserts that "All the problems of politics, of social organization, and of education have been falsified through and through because one mistook the most harmful men for great men—because one learned to despise 'little' things, which means the basic concerns for life" (p. 256), he has hit upon a way of formulating precisely the problems that have come from those who despise the little in whatever form. This statement occurs right after Nietzsche explains to us why he has devoted so much time to the so-called little things like nutrition and climate, but we need also to add to those "little" things the small stings of petty resentment he refers to on and off throughout the text. Both the best and the worst of the human encounter with the world come finally from the small things we face every day, from the basic concerns for life that we must deal with in order to constitute ourselves and our lives as best as possible. And Nietzsche is right to think that the political, social, and educational organizations we have developed are fundamentally flawed precisely to the extent that they despise the little things and set their sights on bigger goals. Whether or not the structures of a culture can be improved by "great" humans of the opposite definition—that is, by humans who love and embrace their fate—is something about which we know little inasmuch as such figures are hard to find in our history. But we do know that a world in which humans do not love their fates but are rather revulsed by them is one in which the destructive potential within humans consumes their own lives and the lives of others as well. All of one's energy can be quickly used up by the fires of resentment, and to the extent that we devote ourselves to the goal of denying rather than overcoming ourselves, we shall consume our limited resources on futile and impotent actions.

❦

If the life of Nietzsche gets too much tangled up in the threads of *Ecce Homo*, then, the book itself nevertheless conveys precisely what Nietzsche would want it to articulate about his most important idea: that we must learn to love our fates in order to overcome our resentment at being human.

Nietzsche surely didn't intend his own life to serve so much as a negative example. He didn't realize how thoroughly his discourse in this text was saturated with his own resentments, and his revulsion against the Germans in this sense is both the smallest and the most obvious of them, for this too is a clear reflection of his nausea at himself. The traditional form of argument at this point would suggest that Nietzsche's theory is thoroughly flawed, particularly in *Ecce Homo,* because Nietzsche himself is so obviously driven by *ressentiment.* Unable to stem the great tides of his own vengeful furies, the argument would run, Nietzsche demonstrates in turn how absurd his notion of *amor fati* finally is, for even he could not escape from continual rancor. This is to use the man to flog the work, and even if it may appear that that is what I too have been doing, my intentions have been the opposite. There is no doubt that Nietzsche failed to live up to his own ideal of *amor fati,* and we can find evidence of this failure in all the weaknesses of the text itself, from the self-aggrandizing tendencies to the resentments that seethe just beneath the surface.

But just as we can see the probity of Nietzsche's arguments as they apply to a way of thinking or living, so too we can see how the flaws in his own life that we find in the text reveal the great force of his arguments. That he himself didn't live up to his highest goal is no condemnation of the goal itself but simply a reflection of the great difficulty in doing so. That he himself was so consumed by resentment that it finally—perhaps—broke down the bridge of his sanity is no reflection on the authority of the perspective that we find in the texts. For if it can be argued that Nietzsche's work is dangerous because its very essence is such that it could drive one mad, it can also be argued that its real danger lies elsewhere, in our failure to heed its message. The real threat may come from our complete refusal to understand how the furies of rancor continue to overrun the world with the poisons of the human species, from our consistent unwillingness to appreciate properly the great richness of our lives and to embrace them in all their complexity. If there is danger, it is that we deny even the great cautionary tale of Nietzsche's life right along with his profound and revolutionary work. And if we are so heedless as to think that there is a *safer* perspective to be found in the mendaciousness of the idealisms that Nietzsche so rightly attacked, then we have run straight away from the danger of the work and into the arms of our own never-ending resentment toward life.

However much we recognize the degree to which Nietzsche and *Ecce Homo* are consumed by resentment, though, we can also see how the opposite is true, paradoxical and impossible as that may seem. For if there is *great* rancor in the text, there is also precisely what Kaufmann finds there, "triumph over *ressentiment*" and gratitude for Nietzsche's good fortune in life. If there is resentment, there is also just as clearly Nietzsche's love of his fate, and we can no more ignore that than we can hide from the marks on his absurdly thin skin. If Nietzsche most desperately does not want to be mistaken for someone else, that is because he realizes that the portraits of others are always inevitably done in the oils of resentment rather than the pastels of *amor faiti.* Inasmuch as the vision of the great human tends to be filtered through the lens of personal resentment, the picture we get of such a person may indeed reflect the "older" form of greatness, but not the one Nietzsche has in mind for himself.

Nietzsche explains the difference for us on several occasions, most notably here: "When I now compare myself with the men who have so far been honored as the *first*, the difference is palpable. I do not even count these so-called 'first' men among men in general: for me they are the refuse of humanity, monsters of sickness and vengeful instincts; they are inhuman, disastrous, at bottom incurable, and revenge themselves on life" (p. 256, 57). There is, to be sure, hyperbole in this statement, but the general rule is also clear: the traditional model for the "great" life is one that is driven by rancor and the vengeful instincts, in which the triumph is not a self-overcoming but a self-denying. In this sense the traditional great are indeed "worse" than the ordinary run of humans because they are more driven by rancor than average individuals. Nietzsche's greatness lies not in his rancor toward life—though we have seen that he is hardly lacking in that—but rather in his willingness to embrace the greatest of all human tasks: to accept himself and the world for what they are. Given the great difference between the goals and the ease with which they can be misconstrued, Nietzsche has more than enough reason to worry about being mistaken for someone else, to be concerned that he too will end up on the list of those who are defined by *ressentiment.*

If Nietzsche had great *ressentiment,* he is not to be defined by it but rather by the love of his fate. If his work carries the authority it has, that is because he truly does embrace life as much as any human ever has and is grateful for the rich life he has had. Take, for example, this slightly skewed vision of the way his life and ideas came upon him:

> The whole surface of consciousness—consciousness *is* a surface—must be kept clear of all great imperatives. Beware even of every great word, every great pose! So many dangers that the instinct comes too soon to "understand itself"—. Meanwhile the organizing "idea" that is destined to rule keeps growing deep down—it begins to command; slowly it leads us *back* from side roads and wrong roads; it prepares *single* qualities and fitnesses that will one day prove to be indispensable as means toward a whole—one by one, it trains all *subservient* capacities before giving any hint of the dominant task, "goal," "aim," or "meaning."
>
> Considered in this way, my life is simply wonderful. For the task of a *revaluation of all values* more capacities may have been needed than have ever dwelt together in a single individual—above all, even contrary capacities that had to be kept from disturbing, destroying one another. An order of rank among these capacities; distance; the art of separating without setting against one another; to mix nothing, to "reconcile" nothing; a tremendous variety that is nevertheless the opposite of chaos—this was the precondition, the long, secret work and artistry of my instinct. Its *higher protection* manifested itself to such a

> high degree that I never even suspected what was growing in me—and one day all my capacities, suddenly ripe, *leaped forth* in their ultimate perfection. I cannot remember that I ever tried hard—no trace of *struggle* can be demonstrated in my life; I am the opposite of a heroic nature. "Willing" something, "striving" for something, envisaging a "purpose," a "wish"—I know none of this from experience. At this very moment I still look upon my future—an *ample* future!—as upon calm seas: there is no ripple of desire. I do not want in the least that anything should become different than it is; I myself do not want to become different. (p. 254, 55)

Nietzsche here recognizes retrospectively all the things that could in effect have gone wrong, that would have made him *other than he was,* and he is truly grateful that they all went right for him instead. The dangers to be found even in the "great word" or the "great pose" can distract one and can take one off the track. Then there is the possibility that "the instinct comes too soon to 'understand itself'" and thus lacks the complexity of background to make full use of that which it has come to understand. The individual needs time for the "organizing 'idea'" to grow unconsciously before he can make full use of it, and when it is grown "it begins to command; slowly it leads us *back* from side roads and wrong roads." Given the opportunity unconsciously to develop into a full human, the individual comes to find himself in control of who he is, full of the knowledge of precisely what roads to take and what ones to stay away from. So the whole of the person comes together in the full expression of his fate.

But the way this happens remains mysterious, and Nietzsche no more understands how and why it occurs than we do; what he does recognize is that this all takes place below the "surface of consciousness" and that the consciousness "must be kept clear of all great imperatives" until the unconscious depths have had a chance to develop into what the human will become. Inasmuch as one therefore acknowledges one's inability to control the basic process of development itself or the way in which it manifests itself within one, how can one not be grateful for one's life if things turn out well? And Nietzsche is: "Considered in this way, my life is simply wonderful." This doesn't mean that there hasn't been rancor, for it has been with Nietzsche throughout his life; nor does it imply that the path has always been smooth. But if one looks at what happens given one's ignorance of *how* it happens, gratefulness for the happy eventualities of one's life can be the only viable response.

Nietzsche also has considerable insight into why he writes such great books, as he will put it later, and that is because "the task of a *revaluation of all values*" needed a person with great—"above all, even contrary"—capacities, and Nietzsche was nothing if not a man with hugely contrary capacities, most generally in his love of his fate and in his monstrous resentments. That the tremendous variety of his capacities should come together to engender the life and the work they do is amazing to Nietzsche, as it should be, again particularly inasmuch as these things all seemed to *happen* to him rather than being in his control. His great and opposed capacities were the "precondition, the long, secret work and artistry of [his] instinct," and through them he came to understand the full nature of his tragic vision. Again, all this happened without any real knowledge of the processes on his part: "Its *higher protection* manifested itself to such a high degree that I never even suspected what was growing in me."

And then the final act of magic begins to take place: "one day all my capacities, suddenly ripe, *leaped forth* in their ultimate perfection." Indeed, Nietzsche tells us, "I cannot remember that I ever tried hard—no trace of *struggle* can be demonstrated in my life; I am the opposite of a heroic nature." Whatever there is of heroism in Nietzsche, it didn't reflect itself in the way his capacities manifested themselves, for they simply sprang out of him in all their full-blown perfection. He has not had to strive for what he has accomplished, for it all came to him very easily. He has no "purpose," no "wish" that he has been trying to fulfill. Indeed, he tells us, "At this very moment I still look upon my future . . . as upon calm seas: there is no ripple of desire." Nietzsche unquestionably loves his fate and is most grateful for it: "I do not want in the least that anything should become different than it is; I myself do not want to become different." If ever there were a description of a man who embraced his fate, this would be it, and we have no reason to doubt Nietzsche in the least. If his gratefulness for his life resides next to the rancors that trouble him as well, it is not for us to choose which of the two is paramount. If he declares his *amor fati* to be that which defines him, there is no reason why this cannot be so in spite of the fact that he is also full of rancor. He is human and not a god, so it would be impossible for him in his circumstances not to have contrary capacities, and only we who suppose that a truly great person should have all his instincts reconciled want to think otherwise. That Nietzsche's love of his fate is not something he feels all the time is no argument against it as his defining characteristic.

Nietzsche repeatedly returns to the great good fortune of his life, and each expression of it is as sincere as can be: "Life was easy for me—easiest when it made the hardest demands on me. Whoever saw me during the seventy days this fall when, without interruption, I did several things of the first rank the like of which nobody will do after me—or impose on me—with a responsibility for all millennia after me, will not have noticed any trace of tension in me; but rather an overflowing freshness and cheerfulness. I never ate with more pleasant feelings; I never slept better" (p. 257). As a description of a particular state of mind over a particular period of time, this declares Nietzsche's happiness quite well and carries the conviction we would look for because he concedes the very easiness of his life, acknowledges indeed that life was easiest for him when it demanded most of him, as when he wrote five books in such a short period of time. That these statements might also be construed as carrying with them a tinge of mania, the edges yet again of incipient insanity, should not keep us from recognizing that the aesthetic states to which Nietzsche refers here are not necessarily related to insanity. Any aesthetic event has the feeling of "overflowing freshness and cheerfulness" and makes one feel that life is as easy as it can possibly be. Such events also carry with them the conviction that something important has occurred; if Nietzsche erroneously chooses to characterize that importance in self-aggrandizing terms here, that is only a mistake of interpretation that he himself should know better about, precisely because he recognizes how little he had to work for it and how much it was a matter of chance, of what fate has brought to him.

Indeed, Nietzsche is wise enough to draw the rule from his own good feelings about his life and work when he states: "I do not know any other way of associating with great tasks than *play:* as a sign of greatness, this is an essential presupposition. The least compulsion, a gloomy mien, or any harsh tone in the throat are all objections to a man; how much more against his work!—One must not have any nerves" (p. 258). That which he characterizes as play is the aesthetic state, that context through which life indeed always plays itself out, that location of charismatic authority through which we gauge the productions of our lives and cultures, and Nietzsche is right to assert that playfulness is a sign of greatness and that this is an essential presupposition of his entire work. The love of one's fate, after all, is predicated on one's willingness to adopt a playful, aesthetic attitude to the unfolding of events in one's life, and from such an attitude comes the great productions of any culture. Nietzsche was the one who most fully understood this within our own culture and who based his life and work on the proposition. His work derived from his aesthetic perspective and did not come from his rancor or his desire to escape from his life. It issued from his willingness to embrace fully that which he was.

Perhaps the best expression of Nietzsche's love of his fate comes early on in *Ecce Homo* when he declares the context for the production of his autobiographical speculations: "On this perfect day, when everything is ripening and not only the grape turns brown, the eye of the sun just fell upon my life: I looked back, I looked forward, and never saw so many and such good things at once. It was not for nothing that I buried my forty-fourth year today; I have the *right* to bury it; whatever was life in it has been saved, is immortal. The first book of the *Revaluation of All Values,* the *Songs of Zarathustra,* the *Twilight of the Idols,* my attempt to philosophize with a hammer—all presents of this year, indeed of its last quarter! *How could I fail to be grateful to my whole life?*—and so I tell my life to myself" (p. 221). If there is pathos in this utterance because Nietzsche has no one to tell his life to but himself, the main point is clearly not that but rather the feelings of joy Nietzsche exudes as he assesses the forty-four years of his life. Again, one might be inclined to see in this statement the mania of incipient madness, and it may well be there, but these feelings—and the assessment upon which they are based—are also as real, and as sober and as genuine, as they can be. How could Nietzsche *not* be grateful for his life? Or for the perfect day on which he began *Ecce Homo?* Inasmuch as he sees how "everything is ripening" and recognizes his own maturity within these physical processes in the midst of which he finds himself, he is unquestionably at ease.

In considering his place within the whole, looking forward to what he can anticipate, looking backward to what has already come from him, Nietzsche can state that he "never saw so many and such good things at once." Such an embrace of life, we might say, is the product of a rare moment, one of those ecstatic states that momentarily makes us see everything whole and prompts us through its powerful feelings to love our own fate as well, at least for that moment. But there is nothing to suggest that Nietzsche only embraced his life for a moment, or that he only loved his fate when he was feeling good about things. On the contrary, he recognizes full well that it is not enough to celebrate one's life when one is feeling good about the direction of one's fate, for that is the tendency that leads inevitably to the mendacious idealizing Nietzsche so opposes, the hidden desire that tries to transform life as a whole into a permanent ecstatic state.

No, Nietzsche knows that his good feelings about his life depend on the awful things he has suffered as well. Indeed, he recognizes the relative unimportance of the good feelings and happiness of life in the overall scheme of things: "In the great economy of the whole, the terrible aspects of reality (in affects, in desires, in the will to power) are to an incalculable degree more necessary than that form of petty happiness which people call 'goodness'; one actually has to be quite lenient to accord the latter any place at all, considering that it presupposes an instinctive mendaciousness" (p. 329). Nietzsche's "petty happiness" here is connected not to the good feelings he has at the end of his forty-fourth year but rather to the kind of happiness that comes from moral goodness of the kind he most opposes. But the point remains the same: the terrible aspects of reality are far more necessary than any momentary feelings of happiness one experiences, regardless of whether they come from practicing a mendacious form of morality or from experiencing fully the intensity of a beautiful morning. Nietzsche declared that the deepest insight into reality is simply that "Nothing in existence may be subtracted, nothing is dispensable" (p. 272). He asserted unequivocally that "Pain is *not* considered an objection to life" (p. 297), and we need to read the fragile moments of joy in the context of these statements because Nietzsche himself surely would.

❦

Given the contradictory fact that *Ecce Homo* is a supreme reflection of Nietzsche's love of his fate even as it is filled with great rancor, we would have to go back and reread all the reflections of rancor and self-aggrandizement we have seen if we were properly to appreciate everything that is at stake in them. Likewise, we would have to recognize the self-aggrandizing tendencies as distortions of Nietzsche's gratitude that reflect his anxieties and deflect his assertions from their proper orientation. Take, for example, a statement like this:

> Those who can breathe the air of my writings know that it is an air of the heights, a *strong* air. One must be made for it. Otherwise there is no small danger

> that one may catch cold in it. The ice is near, the solitude tremendous—but how calmly all things lie in the light! How freely one breathes! How much one feels *beneath* oneself!
>
> Philosophy, as I have so far understood and lived it, means living voluntarily among ice and high mountains—seeking out everything strange and questionable in existence, everything so far placed under a ban by morality. (p. 218)

From the most obvious angle, we can see these remarks as a reflection of Nietzsche's growing isolation and his increasing self-aggrandizing tendencies. He takes pride in the fact that he is so little read by establishing the fact that the air of his writing is a "*strong* air," one not to be trifled with or to be picked up out of mere curiosity. The danger that one might catch cold in these icy heights is a reflection of the fact that "One must be made for it." The nearness of the ice and the tremendous solitude thus project the rarity of the work, the necessity of Nietzsche's solitude, the very real loneliness he nevertheless feels, and yet again the gratitude he has for being able to create work that is turbulent yet allows one a perspective that prompts him to exclaim: "but how calmly all things lie in the light! How freely one breathes! How much one feels *beneath* oneself!" The ecstatic heights are such that their privileged viewpoint can only make one feel both proud and grateful at the same time.

For Nietzsche philosophy does indeed mean "seeking out everything strange and questionable in existence, everything so far placed under a ban by morality," and that means that he will inevitably spend most of his time by himself, for most people subscribe to the prevailing morality that he has called into question. But if one is fated to seek out the strange and questionable, this doesn't matter in the overall scheme of things. If one is "made for" the kind of inquiry Nietzsche undertook and the heights to which it takes one, then one is doing precisely what one ought to be doing. Everything is just as it should be, including the great strength one derives from breathing the fresh air and the gruesome silence that accompanies it. The warning of the passage is not really a serious one, however, for it is designed more to make the work seem special than it is to make people wary. As Nietzsche well knows, there is no reason to make people suspicious of his work, for they recognize its threatening nature without any prompting from him. So he hides his ego here under the danger of the high mountain air. Even so, he also seeks to celebrate the work and its effects and express a very real joy he must feel in the face of what he has accomplished, and thus is at one with his fate, just as the prose itself protects through its pose of danger and rarefied heights.

The juxtaposition of a love of fate with a perpetually resentful body is similarly articulated in remarks we have already seen about Nietzsche's solitude and his commitment to it: "The energy to choose absolute solitude and leave the life to which I had become accustomed; the insistence on not allowing myself any longer to be cared for, waited on, and *doctored*—that betrayed an absolute instinctive certainty about *what* was needed above all at that time. I took myself in hand, I made myself healthy again: the condition for this—every physiologist would admit that—is *that one be healthy at bottom.* A typically morbid being cannot become healthy, much less make itself healthy. For a typically healthy person, conversely, being sick can even become an energetic *stimulus* for life, for living *more*" (p. 224). Given what we are told later about the origin of sickness in *ressentiment,* we can see here how the two states of the Yes to life and the No of resentment have always been struggling within Nietzsche, even as they are while he writes *Ecce Homo.* He tells us that he had sufficient "energy" to choose "absolute solitude," thereby reflecting fully the kind of commitment that is necessary to embrace such a position in the world, and he sees this choice in the context of a reaction against *ressentiment.*

Still, it was a choice he could make only because he was *"healthy at bottom"*; that is the condition that is required if one is to be able to overcome one's perpetual bouts of resentment, whether they come in the form of sickness or as the small stings on the flesh that one gets within the social world. Inasmuch as Nietzsche himself was basically healthy in *attitude*—because he was born to say Yes to life—even his resentments come to be "an energetic *stimulus* for life, for living *more.*" So Nietzsche acknowledges the continuing conflict within himself even as he declares his fundamental healthiness to be the original condition of his being that allows him always to overcome the poisons of resentment that are the major form of sickness he experiences.

Nietzsche's love of solitude, then, is indeed a genuine love of seclusion, even as it is that state which allows him to do the work he needs to do, even as it is also an enforced condition imposed upon him as a result of who he is and what he seeks to question, even, that is, as it is a cause for resentment as well. He loves his solitude and insists that he chose it, but he also hates the enforced seclusion he has no choice in because of who he has become and what his interests are. It is not sufficient to see only the gruesome nature of his solitude and to imagine the chilly air as a reflection of a certain sterility that generates resentment within him, though that is certainly present. The solitude is also his great joy, the calm that allows him truly to experience life most fully and to affirm it in all of its clarity as revealed in the mountaintop air. The two conditions exist side by side in Nietzsche until the end, and it would be wrong to see him from only one of the two states.

The near-inseparability of these two conditions at war within Nietzsche also emphasizes another trait that remains hidden in his work as long as one focusses on the degree to which the prose develops a pose through which he can try to hide his very real resentments. Nietzsche's regimen of mountain air and lonely solitudes has seemed in places to be the life of an ascetic, that species of human with whom Nietzsche would least like his name associated. He sees his state from a different angle, though, one that recognizes the great self-discipline that was involved in responding to and developing the energy within in order to create the great affirmations of his life. His description of how we recognize one who has turned out well exemplifies this:

> What is it, fundamentally, that allows us to recognize *who has turned out well?* That a well-turned-out person

> pleases our senses, that he is carved from wood that is hard, delicate, and at the same time smells good. He has a taste only for what is good for him; his pleasure, his delight cease where the measure of what is good for him is transgressed. He guesses what remedies avail against what is harmful; he exploits bad accidents to his advantage; what does not kill him makes him stronger. Instinctively, he collects from everything he sees, hears, lives through, *his* sum: he is a principle of selection, he discards much. He is always in his own company, whether he associates with books, human beings, or landscapes: he honors by *choosing,* by *admitting,* by *trusting.* (p. 225)

As with later statements that Nietzsche makes, we can construe this as a reflection of a man who has sustained himself through a continuing process of exclusions whereby more and more was cut out of his life so that he could bear what was left. The man cannot stand the odor of everyday life, so he removes himself through perfumes, poses, and general distance. How could any such person truly be said to embrace life with an unequivocal Yes?

And yet his definition can also be understood as a fitting reflection of one who has discovered how to become what one is, how one learns to take the great potential that grew in one beneath one's surface consciousness and transmute it into a fulfilled existence. One does in that case indeed appear to be "carved from wood that is hard, delicate, and at the same time smells good." Such a self-disciplined individual "has a taste only for what is good for him; his pleasure, his delight cease where the measure of what is good for him is transgressed." Surely one who has unfolded in the marvelous way Nietzsche feels that he himself has developed would recognize that once one knows who one is, one also has a taste only for that which is good and fitting to who one is, and one knows how to avoid transgressing the boundaries of that which appeals. These are the acts of a mature sensibility at the peak of its powers, knowing full well what will suit at any given time, knowing how to avoid what will either be unappealing or less than satisfying. These are not the choices of one who wants to cut himself off from the world but rather the preferences of one who knows most fully how to integrate who he is into the contexts that are available to him.

In short, only one who truly loves his fate and knows what it is could have employed the self-discipline that was necessary to arrive at a sufficient understanding of himself to be so fully formed. And only such an individual would be capable of instinctively guessing what "remedies avail against what is harmful" and would know how to exploit "bad accidents to his advantage." These things do not come *naturally* to an individual; they have to be developed through great effort and careful attention to the way the self unfolds in the midst of the world. And in order to be able to achieve such attention and self-discipline, one also has to be able instinctively to collect "from everything he sees, hears, lives through, *his* sum"; he has to both *be* an acute "principle of selection" and realize just what that principle of selection is in his particular case. Whether or not such an individual "honors by *choosing,* by *admitting,* by *trusting*" is perhaps a different question, one that concerns yet another swerve off into the attitude that the world itself ought to be grateful for the attention of such individuals, but even this line can be construed in generous terms to reflect the degree to which this fully-formed individual loves and acts out his fate precisely through the acts of choosing, admitting, and trusting with great insight. This displaced picture of Nietzsche reflects one who truly loves his fate as much as any other statement in the book, but it remains only a shadow away from other depictions that reflect a nearly sterile life that has developed that way in response to the stings of resentment and the inability of the individual to forget them.

The great conflict within Nietzsche needs to be dealt with in one more way before we can fully understand the authority of *Ecce Homo,* though, for yet another of the repeated statements of the work suggests a different kind of problem: "At this point the real answer to the question, *how one becomes what one is,* can no longer be avoided. And thus I touch on the masterpiece of the art of self-preservation—of *selfish-*

*ness*" (p. 253). Selfishness as the means through which one becomes what one is would seem to be a problematic notion within this revaluation of values. True, the linkages between the love of one's fate and the need to overcome one's *ressentiment* are in evident opposition to the "mendaciousness" of the selfless "Christian" view that is Nietzsche's main target throughout his life. As Nietzsche puts it: "The loss of the center of gravity, resistance to the natural instincts—in one word, 'selflessness'—that is what was hitherto called *morality.*—With the *Dawn* I first took up the fight against the morality that would unself man" (p. 292). Given his commitment to overcome the values that had "unselved" humans for millennia, Nietzsche would clearly not be inclined to uphold the virtue of selflessness, an essentially nihilistic state from his perspective. The question that remains is whether the only alternative to selflessness is selfishness, whether one can only become what one is through a crude assertion of self-interest in the world or whether there is another possibility. This is one way of talking about the uncertain oscillations throughout the text, veering at times toward the completely self-aggrandizing and rancor-filled utterances of a deeply troubled man, steering at other times toward the full acceptance of life in all its complexity.

Any serious reader of Nietzsche knows that if the oscillation between these two points of view is more intense in *Ecce Homo* than in other books, it is to be found throughout his work, best encapsulated in the dual and contradictory definitions of the will to power as a pure expression of self-interest on the one hand and as expression of the overflowing abundance of life within one on the other. Will to power, that is, can be either a mark of resentment, a reflection of one who asserts his power in the world to the fullest in order to deny the encumbrances of the past and to guarantee a better place for one in the future; or it can be a reflection of the joy one experiences within life as a result of a love of one's fate, in which case it is not self-interested in the nihilistic way of the other definition. And this distinction in turn depends on yet another crucial point: the Nietzschean assumption that the world is first and foremost an aesthetic place where our interests are part of the overall play of life rather than separable and subjectively self-interested. The aesthetic self, if you will, is a marker within the flow of life or the flow of discourse, a measure of where one is within it and a guide for where one should go within what one perceives to be the drift of its flows. The subjective self is a fiction that seeks to essentialize the self and its interests above or beyond or before the flows that always constrain (and make possible) its activity. Each self is self-interested in a way, but the latter self has as its main goal the impossible one of removing itself from the flows of life all around it whereas the aesthetic self seeks ways to unfold what it is within them and within a joyous acceptance of where it is within them.

The problem is that the word "selfishness" to a certain extent covers both situations, for both selves are "interested" to the extent that they seek to measure the world from the location within the flows in which they find themselves, and they are also "interested" to the extent that they hope to maintain and develop their place in the world. What is in question is *how* they seek to do that, by accepting the flows of which they are a part or by seeking to end the play of the flows in order to overcome the limitations they impose on the self. As with Weber's charismatic context for authority, the self that locates its interests within the flows of life and discourse has in a specific way renounced the centrality of the self in the very acceptance of its place within the flows. It is in this respect both disinterested and self-interested at the same time. It is not necessarily "selfless" at all in Nietzsche's sense of the term, for to be selfless is to lose one's location within the flows, to drop out of them altogether.

So Nietzsche was right to be scornful of the selfless and to see that arguments for selflessness are based on the mendacious logic of those who fundamentally abhor life and everything within it that flows. But instead of articulating more fully just what the aesthetic self is like, by resorting so easily to that term which opposes "selflessness," Nietzsche undermined his arguments and undercut his own aesthetic vision by suggesting that there was little to separate the self-interests of one who embraces the authority of the aesthetic event and one who carefully cultivates self-interest in the most self-serving and nihilistic of ways.

The text does not resolve this problem of definition because Nietzsche himself never did in his own life. And some critics locate the danger of the text here in the blatant assertion of pure selfishness: if this is to be the rule in the post-Nietzschean world, the argument runs, then we truly are in for an endless sea of nihilistic furies, for if self-interest is the only arbiter of our choices, the socius is bound eventually totally to self-destruct. Indeed, many people associate precisely this kind of nihilism with Nietzsche's name, notwithstanding the fact that his revaluation of values was his attempt to overcome the kind of self that would be committed to nothing other than nihilistic self-interest. More than any other accusation that has been leveled at Nietzsche, this one of self-interest sticks most often, and in part this is because he failed adequately to address the issue in an intelligent way. Here and too often elsewhere he is content with the equivalent of name-calling, for he obviously relishes the opportunity to create scandal by declaring himself to be committed to pure selfishness. This reflects his own lack of discipline, the tendency to want to bait the opposition that was another of his less than useful traits. But even in the midst of such baiting—and there is more than enough of it in *Ecce Homo*—it is hard to lose sight of the fact that Nietzsche remains committed to something other than nihilism and describes the manner in which one's fate unfolds in ways that are antithetical to the ordinary definition of the selfish life.

The final demonstration of Nietzsche's affirmative view, a statement that shows quite clearly the way in which the bombast about selfishness was wide of the mark, comes near the end of *Ecce Homo* when Nietzsche quotes Zarathustra and interprets him for us in order to establish yet again the basis of his vision and its aesthetic authority:

> "You highest men whom my eyes have seen, this is my doubt about you and my secret laughter: I guess that you would call my overman—devil."
>
> "What is great is so alien to your souls that the overman would be terrifying to you in his goodness."
>
> It is here and nowhere else that one must make a start to comprehend what Zarathustra wants: this type of man that he conceives, conceives reality *as it is,* being strong enough to do so; this type is not estranged or removed from reality but is reality itself and exemplifies all that is terrible and questionable in it—*only in that way can man attain greatness.* (p. 331)

Quite clearly in his own way Nietzsche *was* a moralist whose main goal was to become one of the "improvers of mankind." If he rejected such titles, he did so for good reason, for they were tainted by those who had spent millennia turning humans away from the great richness of the reality all around them. In order not to be misunderstood or mistaken for someone else, Nietzsche must therefore abjure the goal of improving humans and settle instead for a mere description of human possibility.

And here is his definition of human greatness: one who is willing to conceive reality *as it is,* one who is not estranged from the real or in flight from its terrors but who embraces all that is mysterious in it. If humans could overcome their revulsion against their own natures and see reality as it truly is, they would as a matter of definition both abjure the endless bouts of resentment that determine their lives so thoroughly at present and also love their fates with all the intensity they could muster. In the world we have allowed to come to be, this is indeed the only way left for humans to achieve greatness, for pure self-interest cannot engender the nobility of purpose or the moral courage that this goal has, and the idealisms of the past no longer suffice as a description of what we are or what the real is: we know them to be illusions that have allowed us to keep from seeing reality as it is.

Nietzsche's work as a whole achieves its authority both by offering us this measure for life and work and by going some distance toward measuring up to its difficulties. His perspective's aesthetic power comes as close to conceiving reality as it is in all its terrible and questionable aspects as the work of any human who contributed to the development of our culture, and we have learned from him both what our goal as a species ought to be and what the measure of our individual lives must be: to see things as they are and to say Yes to them in all their complexity. When we evaluate Nietzsche's work at the distance of a century, we can see the great coherence of his aesthetic vision even as we begin to recognize the way all authority first inheres in the playful contexts Nietzsche articulates from *The Birth of Tragedy* to *Ecce Homo*. And if a work like *Ecce Homo* is clearly tinged with quite a bit of self-aggrandizing rancor, we can understand according to Nietzsche's own standards that those elements of the text provide part of the mixture that was Nietzsche, human, all too human, but they constitute impediments to the vision of self-overcoming to which he himself was devoted. We should not as a result condemn his work as a failed experiment because he didn't live up to his own ideals and didn't therefore achieve the greatness he hypostatized for humans in general; after all, Nietzsche himself was fully aware of the huge difficulties that lay in the way of his hopes for humanity and knew what kind of courage is required of a human to face reality as it is. That he, the first one seriously to attempt to weigh the values of the world in these terms, did not completely succeed is less a reflection of how much he failed than it is a mark of how much he attained through the attempt he made to love his fate and overcome his resentment at being human. Neither holy man nor buffoon, not a role model nor a devil, Nietzsche provided through his work a model of the human toward which we can, and should, all aspire, in spite of the dangers and the difficulty and *because of them* as well.

And then there is this, no more fitting an end to a discussion of the authority of Nietzsche's works than a statement he cut out of an earlier draft of *Ecce Homo* that takes us back to one of our points of origin: "Finally, I speak only of what I have lived through; the opposition of thinking and life is lacking in my case. My 'theory' grows from my 'practice'—oh, from a practice that is not by any means harmless or unproblematic!" (p. 340). Foucault and Weber exist for us as they do because Nietzsche reconnected his own experiences to his work. He spoke only of what he had lived through and broke down the fictive border between thinking and life. If it always does—and always *will*—matter who's speaking, that is because thinking and life are not separable in the way we would like them to be. Nietzsche's authority inheres in the contexts through which he was able to articulate his powerful vision of the world, but he was a primary agent in the establishment of the authority that resides in those texts. It matters that he spoke, just as it matters what was spoken, and no one's work makes this clearer because Nietzsche's theory—which did indeed grow from his practice—was unquestionably a "practice that is not by any means harmless or unproblematic." In opening up the space of the aesthetic world of joy and terror for us, Nietzsche did what he could to live to the fullest his theory in all of its strange and terrible and questionable aspects, and his courage in attempting such a life provides an added measure of conviction to his writing that it would not otherwise possess.

Nietzsche's work quite clearly does not articulate a utopian vision, even if the goal it sets for humanity could be construed as an impossible one, for humans would not sacrifice their lives for the goal but would rather live their lives more fully with more love for them through the attempt to overcome the resentments that have driven the moral systems of the past. And the work is by no means harmless, as we have seen throughout. It is *dangerous,* even hypothetically *fatal,* as Nietzsche's own madness might suggest. Even if it does not induce insanity—a rather silly argument from hysterics who are unwilling to abandon their own mendaciousness and the false authority they derive from it—it does place one within the dangers of living one's life as fully as possible outside of the blinders of illusion, whether those illusions come from a religious dogma or from psychological strategies of displacement, projection, repression, and the like. It takes great courage to seek to affirm life as Nietzsche would have us do, and there is no doubt that the authority for any attempt on our part to do so does *not* come from Nietzsche—it comes from the work that was articulated through precisely such an attempt to live and wholly affirm one's fate within the world and to love it without condition.

We cannot take up the authority of Nietzsche's works and simply transport it to our own works or lives, for the authority of the aesthetic event can only be established through the contexts within life through which it is put into practice. Our courage in facing our own lives and articulating our own affirmations through the experiences that life has thrown our way is the only measure of authority Nietzsche's texts could offer us, and at that they do no more than provide a support for our own convictions and an added spur to our hopes. This is not the location where we had expected to find authority, for it is not so easily translatable from one place to another and comes with no easy tips for living or practices that would guarantee "goodness" or a fitting life. But it is the only context of authority we have ever had, and if it took a couple of millennia and Nietzsche's work for us to recognize this, we have perhaps at long last begun to discern how our civilization becomes what it is and have found just what its fate is: to be the first civilization on the planet that seeks to love its fate and affirm the world in spite of its own mendacious history. If we always need authority to assess our lives, and if we have found all previous forms of authority to be incomplete and artificial expressions of one kind of self-interest or another, there is no more appropriate gauge for our future aspirations than this most Nietzschean of goals to love our fate, to see reality as it is and recognize it as home.

# Chapter Three

# The Way of Heaven

One of the difficulties that has always faced us in our attempts to discern the origins and value of authority in our lives is that in its aesthetic or charismatic form it inevitably remains elusive. Attached to a particular context and to the statements that come from it, it cannot be separated from the specifics of its articulation, leaving us with no general rules we can establish about it. It can be routinized, as Weber demonstrated, but it becomes traditional authority in the process, and so leaves behind that which we most want to discover, the fundamental principles of its original assertion. Another problem we encounter is that most forms of charismatic authority have been associated with religious belief, and it is difficult as a result to separate the authority from religious visions to which we give no credence. We can see this most apparently in locations not quite so near to us as the Judeo-Christian tradition that has done so much to make us what we are, and so a brief investigation of two other contexts for aesthetic authority, the Chinese world of Confucius and the Greek world of Homer, will help us to discern the general patterns that Foucault, Weber and Nietzsche have already done much to establish. Our very difference from these sites of authority will allow us more clearly to determine precisely what is at stake in all forms of authority.

Confucius has always been something of a mystery to the West, in part because his culture itself is "inscrutable" and resists our modes of questioning, in part because his authority rests on a highly conservative base with a reverence for the past and its command over us that we have not generally subscribed to, and in part because that aspect of his authority that doesn't derive from his deeply traditional ways carries with it the same enigmatic character as the words of a writer like Nietzsche. We can read translations of his work, and they appear to be straightforward enough, but they seem *too* straightforward. Confucius seems to be saying everything and nothing at the same time. His remarks strike us as so totally obvious as to be completely banal, or so mysterious as to be unfathomable. I would assert that all aesthetic authority bears these features, that indeed they are among its distinguishing features. *Amor fati,* after all, can be seen as a statement of great profundity or of total banality—*of course* one should love one's fate; why would one want to *hate* one's fate? *Ressentiment* as Nietzsche uses it can either be a defining characteristic of the human species that is so profound as to be capable of accounting for the majority of our behavior, or it can be so nebulous in its generality as to have no value whatsoever. When I assert that aesthetic authority always inheres in a particular context, when I state that no easily formulable general conclusions can be derived from it, this is precisely what I am referring to. If one grants such utterances authority, they have great profundity; if one fails to recognize their power, they seem banal at best and dangerous at worst—dangerous because their very nebulousness can be used to advantage, stirring up people with empty words that carry no real "meaning" beyond the emotional force they convey.

Confucius's work certainly has the same enigmatic flavor to it, and it is that upon which I wish to concentrate, though I also want to discern as far as possible whether or not there is any inevitable relationship between Confucius's cryptic utterances and the highly traditional and conservative form of authority he also sought to embody. Are these two forms of authority, the charismatic and the traditional, inseparable in Confucius? Or did he simply graft his charismatic authority onto the traditional authority that preceded his own vision of things? Although I don't think there are definitive answers to these questions, we need to ask them because they affect the way we look at Confucius's utterances. If most of the important work that has been done in our own culture in the past century has been devoted to an ongoing critique of the lures of traditional forms of authority, we can hardly grant as much credence to Confucius's aesthetic authority if we conclude that it is of a piece with the tradition he believed in but we are deeply suspicious of. But we shall look at this problem through the nature of Confucius's enigmatic utterances rather than the other way around.

One of the most famous of Confucius's statements was given considerable currency early in our century by Ezra Pound, among others, and it certainly bears all the earmarks of an enigmatic aesthetic statement:

> The ancients who wished to preserve the fresh or clear character of the people of the world, would first set about ordering their national life. Those who wished to order their national life, would first set about regulating their family life. Those who wished to regulate their family life would set about cultivating their personal life. Those who wished to cultivate their personal lives, would first set about setting their hearts right. Those who wished to set their hearts right would first set about making their wills sincere. Those who wished to make their wills sincere would first set about achieving true knowledge. The achieving of true knowledge depended upon the investigation of things. When things are investigated, then true knowledge is achieved; when true knowledge is achieved, then the will becomes sincere; when the will is sincere, then the heart is set right (or then the mind sees right); when the heart is set right, then the personal life is cultivated, then the family life is regulated, then the national life is orderly; and when the national life is orderly, then there is peace in this world. From the emperor down to the common men, all must regard the cultivation of the personal life as the root or foundation. There is never an orderly upshoot or superstructure when the root or foundation is disorderly. There is never yet a tree whose trunk is

> slim and slender and whose top branches are thick and heavy. This is called "to know the root or foundation of things."[1]

Fresh from a discussion of Nietzsche's work and the problem of selfishness and self-discipline, one might be inclined to argue that Nietzsche would have been closer to establishing his point in opposition to the selflessness of the Judeo-Christian tradition if he had argued instead that "all must regard the cultivation of the personal life as the root or foundation." Surely this is most, if not all, of what Nietzsche means by selfishness, the need through self-discipline to cultivate the self in such a way that it is in harmony with its surroundings. This is the locus of aesthetic authority in Nietzsche, and Confucius here argues the same thing in a simple yet comprehensive series of statements.

The basic argument of Confucius's remarks is fairly straightforward. Those who wanted to preserve the fresh character of the people of the world would have to begin by ordering the lives of the individuals in their own nation. In order to do that, they would first have to order the family lives of the people of the nation. In order to do that, they would have to bring order to their personal lives. To do that, they would have to set their hearts right, which would in turn depend on their ability to make their wills sincere, which would finally allow them to achieve true knowledge. But in order to achieve true knowledge, they would have to be able to investigate the nature of things. If they were able to do that, then they would achieve true knowledge, the will would be sincere, the heart would be set right, the personal life would be well cultivated, the family life would be well ordered, the nation's life would be regulated, and there would be a world in harmony with itself. The careful interlocking of these steps and the mirror image they present going down and coming up reflect the supreme simplicity of Confucius's own knowledge of the way things are, and in some respects what he has articulated here is so clear that nothing further need or should be said.

The same can be remarked about the nature of Confucius's conclusions. It is true that there has never been "an orderly upshoot or superstructure when the root or foundation is disorderly." This is true for the tree, and it is true for the great human tree as well. If we want "to know the root or foundation of things," Confucius has here told us everything we need to know and has provided us with his own fitting measure of our efforts to live meaningful lives. He gives us a set of goals that will keep us busy until the day we die, he has supplied a structure through which those goals make sense and at the same time also play into larger and larger fields and have larger and larger effects. In a few short sentences he establishes his own route to self-overcoming, and in many respects it bears striking similarities to Nietzsche's views.

To be sure, Nietzsche was the last individual to pay obeisance to the family or the nation, or even the species as a whole, but he did more than simply diagnose the confusion of the root, even if he did that supremely well too. Nietzsche does not follow the tree structure from the investigation of things on up to world harmony in quite the way Confucius does, but there can be little doubt that he saw both his life and his theory in terms of the same root. His notion of the overman is such that it implies all the other orders Confucius so carefully lists. First, the overman must be able to investigate things so he can know what is and learn to accept it for what it is; if he cannot do that, no overman is possible. The fundamental step, the first mark of order, is the simple willingness to investigate things. Yet, as Nietzsche's own work makes so clear, that is precisely the first problem for most people, for the last thing they want to do is to investigate the nature of things. To do so would be to remind them of the reality from which they are in flight. If Nietzsche's time was a decadent one of nihilism and anarchy, that was because the socius was based on an almost complete denial of reality and the refusal to investigate the way things are. The root was in confusion, as Nietzsche saw, because everything that was supposed to be a truth turned out to be "the most harmful, subterranean form of lie," because those who sought to improve humanity by bringing order to the root instead used the improvement of the species as a "ruse for sucking the blood of life itself. Morality as vampirism" (p. 334).

If it is easy enough to begin with such a simple statement—order depends on one's ability to investigate the nature of things—it is most difficult to address the world in that manner, and whereas Nietzsche is far more insistent about the decadence of his times than Confucius is, that by no means implies that the times were any better for Confucius. He too, after all, never really found a safe home within the bureaucratic structure of the ruling elite; he too, in effect, became a wanderer of mountain paths and a breather of the chill air, even if, unlike Nietzsche, he did indeed have disciples. Confucius's statement and his life confirm what Nietzsche repeatedly argued millennia later: the societies we have constructed are based on a hatred of life and a revulsion against our own being, and, so constructed, they keep us from beginning with the investigation of things that would lead to the order we all desire. And the pathway to that investigation is within reach of us all; we only need to agree to investigate things as best we can without the ruse of self-interest or the illusions that keep the horrors of the world hidden from view.

Confucius does not paint a picture of decadence and terror in his work because there was no real need to do so given his tradition. The tightly woven structure he asserts is rather a quieter version of the same thing, for if each of the steps he mentions is straightforward in itself, each is also almost, if not altogether, impossibly difficult to achieve. The amount of human energy that would have to be put toward the self-discipline that would be required to effect the necessary changes at every level of Confucius's simple chain suggests by omission what is to be found outside of that incredible self-discipline: decadence and terror, both of human make and of natural character as well. Confucius is also perhaps more sanguine about the chances for order at the root than Nietzsche could afford to be. This may simply be a result of different temperaments, or it could reflect the extra thousands of years that Nietzsche could investigate for evidence of the human willingness to look at things and see them squarely.

Quite clearly Nietzsche would like to effect his goals and seeks to do so in precisely the way Confucius suggests: he will bring order to himself first through an investigation of things, and that order, in connection with the theory of the overman that reflects it, will lead to a diminution of confusion on up the line until humans have indeed achieved greatness. But Nietzsche's times were not such that they would give him much hope for a revolution of this sort, and if it was unfair and rancorous of him to blame most of the world's ills on the Germans, he clearly used them as a metaphor for the decadent nature of the times in general even as he reflected his knowledge of his own shortcomings by attacking his own heritage. It may be true that at a conscious level he could escape his connection to the Germans through his imagined Polish heritage, but surely he knew as well as anyone that he was as much a German as Wagner was. And if the Germans had no order and were decadent at heart, Nietzsche too could not bring order to himself, try as he might. Nevertheless, we might say that he came closer to bringing order to his life through the investigation of things than did most other people in the course of our history.

Confucius genuinely believes, it would seem, that the simple steps he outlines can be accomplished by all. Indeed, at times it seems that he thinks that he only needs the ears of the powerful to implement the plan. Given his faith in the great value of traditional authority, he thinks that if he can get the leaders to promulgate his views and to live through them themselves, it will only be a matter of time before the necessary linkages are made to fill out the tree and lead to harmony throughout the world. We may be inclined at this distance to think therefore that Confucius's work is based upon incredible naiveté, for few of us would be willing to hazard any money on the chances of such harmony occurring in our lifetime. But perhaps he was not as naive as he might seem to us. Perhaps, like Nietzsche, he recognized that a good bit of the difficulty could be overcome by creating a set of circumstances wherein his orderly world would become a positive value. If he thought that the traditional bureaucratic structure would serve him in this respect, he failed to understand what Nietzsche knew, that the traditional structures are invariably mendacious in nature and hardly interested in the nature of things at all. The powers within the structure would be at risk if things were investigated, so even with an enlightened leader there would be great resistance to Confucius's ideas. He seemed not to realize this until relatively late in his life and so did not take it into account in his writings, except in his careful detailing of the linkages within the order that provide a rather imposing challenge even in the best of circumstances.

More importantly, we need to inquire into the seriousness of Confucius's statement here, for if it makes perfect sense in a way, it does indeed manifest the elusive characteristics of vatic utterances. I have, for example, assumed that the need to investigate things as stated by Confucius is equivalent to Nietzsche's assertion that humans must finally and for the first time conceive "reality *as it is,*" but there is nothing in "the investigation of things" or its original formulation that necessarily leads to conceiving reality as it is, particularly if we assume that when Nietzsche asserted this need he did so in the belief that no culture with which he was familiar had *ever* attempted to do so. How can one possibly assume that Confucius is making a similar statement here, particularly given the spare simplicity of his utterances and their own very clear order? What would lead us to surmise that he too recognized and asserted through his remark the great difficulty of what he established as necessary for our future as a species?

In a way, of course, there is no necessary linkage between Confucius's utterance and Nietzsche's statements about the need to see reality, but in another way the very connections that are made in Confucius's declaration suggest much the same thing. First, it is true that the origin of order is to be found in a simple place: the investigation of things. That Confucius even feels the need to state this implies in itself that for the most part precisely this is ignored or forgotten. He does not speak of psychological displacements and the human need for illusions, nor does he argue that it is extremely difficult to see the way things are. But if his entire order depends on nothing more exotic than seeing things as they are, and if his order had yet to be implemented within a highly sophisticated culture, then of necessity there would have to be obstacles to the investigation of things.

Confucius doesn't bother to tell us what those obstacles are in particular, whereas Nietzsche does. But he doesn't have to explain what they are; he only needs to acknowledge them implicitly, as he does by revealing the opposite, the simple center that they always attempt to displace. He may well think that people have failed to see this precisely because it is too simple to be believed—humans tend to expect more exotic solutions to their problems than this and so cast their eyes over a larger surface. And the structure of the passage suggests that this is indeed the primary obstacle for Confucius, for after all, the ancients began with the largest of contexts first: they wanted to preserve the clear character of the people of the world. They didn't start with the need to investigate things but rather had to work down to it as they came to realize that each of the larger orders was dependent on a smaller order for its own harmonies. Their obvious assumption would thus be that one wouldn't look to the investigation of things to preserve the order of the people of the world any more than one would look to the need to cultivate the personal life. Like us, they would doubtless see some of these orders as more or less autonomous from the others and would therefore fail to note the essential feature of Confucius's order: everything is interconnected, the smallest dependent on the largest, the largest dependent on the smallest. Without this knowledge above all, harmony is not possible, authority is not possible, understanding is not possible, personal cultivation is not possible, and so forth. Small steps, but giant difficulties along the way precisely because the linkages are so strong.

Still, there is nothing definitive in Confucius's statement that would allow us with certitude to connect his remarks to Nietzsche's. If I choose to make the point that they are related, I must rely upon the elusiveness of the texts I am employing (Nietzsche, after all, never really explained what he meant by conceiving reality as it is either, and his prose is filled with baggy words like "joy" and "terror" that could cover all sorts of terrain that may or may not have been intended). This is to say yet again that the authority of the text is an aesthetic one and is dependent on relations that are established across cultures and millennia on the basis of a vision of order that cannot escape from a tacit acceptance of its values. Either one agrees that the point Confucius makes is related to the one Nietzsche asserted many years later in considerably different cultural circumstances, or one can find any number of historical, linguistic, and cultural differences to argue against the proposition that at some fundamental level Confucius and Nietzsche are talking about the same kind of aesthetic order and are basing the authority of their utterances upon just that perspective.

❦

If this is less than satisfying as a conclusion, it is one of the conclusions we must inevitably draw. But there are other possibilities as well, one of which would suggest yet again that a fundamentally aesthetic vision of reality has certain similar features regardless of the culture or the epoch in which it is found. It reflects a displacement of the self back into the world out of which it originally emerged but to which it was always attached even without its knowledge, yet at the same time that self must also be able to practice the art of "personal cultivation" or self-discipline in order to understand the nature of what is. If we assume that one cannot see what is without personal cultivation and cannot cultivate the self without seeing what is, the interdependence between these two is deep and irretrievable. The cultivation of the self depends on something outside of it, the investigation of things, that leads to a kind of knowledge, that leads to a kind of sincerity of will, that leads to a kind of fitting heart, that leads to the well-cultivated life, the well-ordered family, the well-regulated nation, and the harmonious world. If nothing else, Confucius is clearly *not* articulating a Western, self-centered vision of the universe.

Indeed, the assumption that the investigation of things

leads to the achievement of knowledge that leads to the sincere will suggests that the more likely human context is for there to be an *insincere* will, what Nietzsche means when he refers to the form of will to power that is driven exclusively by self-interest. What else would an insincere will be? The pure will, without self-interest, reflects an aesthetic perception of the way things are, and if we more often find the will functioning insincerely, that is because the individual has centered the world around himself and removed himself from the aesthetic flows that would provide him with the necessary knowledge to put his will on the true path of personal cultivation.

If we assume that in a general way Confucius uses the will here to refer to that aspect of our being through which we make choices and decisions about our lives, and the heart to refer to the affective context through which we construe our relations with the rest of the world, human and nonhuman, we can imagine easily enough how both the heart and the will would be set straight through a proper understanding of the world. If one saw things correctly, one would know how to act in the world, one would know how to choose, and one would also therefore know how to order one's emotional investment in the contexts and choices of which one is a part. What else would personal cultivation be? And what else is the aesthetic event than a context that makes all these linkages perfectly clear, even if elusive, and which provides us with the authority to continue to seek to order our lives in the fashion that Confucius argues for in this very brief passage?

To know the way things are is to have an understanding of the flows of the world and our placement within them, to recognize both the flows and the locations through which humans measure them; with that kind of knowledge our will makes choices in the world from an affirmative rather than a nihilistic perspective, and everything in turn follows from that. If we think for a moment of one of Nietzsche's famous aesthetic definitions in *The Gay Science,* we can understand Confucius's point more fully: "Regarding all aesthetic values I now avail myself of this main distinction: I ask in every instance, 'is it hunger or superabundance that has here become creative?' "[2] The will that is driven by hunger is lacking in sincerity because self-interest is its main preoccupation, whereas the will that has been made sincere would realize that choices ought to be made on the basis of superabundance rather than hunger, out of love of what is rather than resentment over what one doesn't have but thinks one needs. Part of the superabundance through which the sincerity of the will is developed comes from the knowledge of things in general, for that knowledge is such that it prompts one to want to continue to see and embrace things as they are rather than as the ego would like them to be. Again, the training of the eye and the mind to investigate things leads to the kind of knowledge that affirms the value of what is, that inclines the will toward the sincerity of choice of which aesthetic authority is the mark.

The powerful feelings of the heart are thus trained as well to manifest themselves coherently as a reflection of the exuberant, overabundant joy of life. Instead of being dispersed into the random events that come to us as they will, being driven in such cases at least as much by the poisons of *ressentiment* as by the pleasures of affirming our connections to others and to the world in general, the sincere will's choices focus the expressions of the heart so that they are right and fitting for the event in the midst of which one finds oneself. The heart achieves clarity of expression and greater power through this focussing, and the result is yet a further reflection of the superabundance that is to be found in the nature of things. If we think of Confucius's statement as suggesting that the mind *sees* right rather than the heart is set right, the same general description applies, only here the emphasis would be on the need to perceive the world aesthetically rather than on the affects that accompany such perception. To be in the midst of the aesthetic flows of the world and to perceive one's place within them is both to see the order of the root without which all lives are in confusion and to feel the powerful emotion of joy in the midst of the harmony we all instinctively assume is to be found in the world. To set the heart right is to emphasize the emotions that attend an aesthetic event; to prompt the mind to see right is to stress the need for a particular mode of perception, one that has displaced self-interest for the flows of the aesthetic.

Either way one chooses to look at the changes that are induced by the sincere will, the result is the same: the personal life is cultivated in a fruitful way that brings order to one's life. The root is no longer in confusion. This personal cultivation of the self is not an act of self-aggrandizement or pure self-interest, at least in the way we think of purely selfish acts that serve no one but the interested party, for Confucius's statement makes clear that the rest of the order of the world depends on the harmony to be found through personal cultivation. But in our own social and philosophical context we would have to emphasize that personal cultivation also doesn't mean a *lack* of self-interest either, any more than the overman is devoid of self-interest for Nietzsche. Humans cannot function without self-interest, which is, in any case, in some respects nothing more than the obvious necessity of measuring the effects of the flows in the midst of which one finds oneself in order to assess one's needs and direction in terms of them.

The absence of self-interest is a non-category in this sense, as Nietzsche suggests through his endless railing about selfless people. A selfless person cannot in strict terms exist in any other location than a mental hospital, for such an individual would be thoroughly incapable of personal cultivation at even the most general level, that of the care and feeding of the body. Although our culture has at times suggested otherwise, true selflessness is indeed a mendacious category of human possibility. The only question is whether self-interest is paramount and the will to power is all, or whether self-interest has been displaced to the periphery for the greater understanding of the individual location's place within the flows of life and discourse. There must still be an individual within those flows who measures and attends to the needs of that location—even the most "selfless" of individuals must devote part of his day to thinking about how to manage the existence within the body that he has—

but the degree to which the world is construed through that perspective is minimized even as one comes to see the greater power of and value in construing our locations as part of the endless productions of the flows around us rather than as manipulators of the flows purely for our own benefit.

Given the sense of the steps leading up to personal cultivation—which in a way, it should be stressed, are also not really steps at all but rather different ways of expressing the same aesthetic perspective from the angle of things, of knowledge, of the will, the heart, the individual, and so on—the logic that would extend the order of the individual to the family, then to the nation and the world as a whole, makes perfect sense and is the easiest part of Confucius's statement to understand, if also the most difficult to enact. For if one's personal life is in order, one will understand the nature of the flows around one and the ways in which one's location plays into and out of them, and if one knows that, one can make perfect sense out of the family life of which one is a part as well, for it too manifests the same structure of forces within flows through which the play of the field produces whatever effects it is going to have. Further, the *example* of the one who has cultivated himself would provide for the others in the family the sense of order that they would need to follow and thus offer a fitting gauge for the activities of the group as a whole. No doubt Confucius intended this personal authority of the example to be paramount, given his belief in the great value of the paternal tradition of which he is a part, and perhaps he put more credence in the usefulness of example per se than the reality of human existence would bear out, but even if we were to construe the relationship between personal and familial order in this way, based on hierarchy and patriarchy rather than on the dynamic flow of forces within the structure, we could also argue that Confucius's conception here could be understood better through a less hierarchical, less patriarchal, mode of order.

Although the general assumptions of our own culture would argue otherwise, and although even many of those who have devoted so much of their lives to attacking the current social hierarchies in the end also remain committed to hierarchies of a different nature, I would assert that aesthetic authority and hierarchy are antithetical to one another, that personal cultivation, based on a displacement of self-interest to the periphery, cannot lead to a family order in which the paternal figure is central and the others measure themselves in terms of his example. If the order one achieves through personal cultivation creates the sincerity of will that makes one recognize one's subordinate place within the flows of discourse, then the same pattern must manifest itself in the family as well. And if the authority to be found within personal cultivation comes from the aesthetic event and not the agent one chooses normally to focus on, then the authority within the family cannot rest exclusively within the paternal agent but must rather derive from the ongoing event the family structure unfolds through its cultivation of self. I have no doubt that Confucius himself would take issue with this point, for hierarchy is so ingrained in his thought that he would not imagine another mode of order to be possible, just as is more or less true of those who espouse a different order today. For the most part their order differs only in the agents who will be at the top of the hierarchy, not in the conception of order that would make authority inhere first and foremost in the event itself and only secondarily in the agents who participated in it to a greater or lesser degree.

It is worth pursuing this point of hierarchy a bit more because both the order of Confucius and the order of the West are based on the idea that the alternative to hierarchy is chaos, that if there were not strictly delimited structures of superiority and inferiority, no order would be possible. Yet at the same time we realize that any hierarchical structure is in itself based on a falsely frozen and static conception of the flows of force and power: it tacitly assumes that they will always manifest themselves in the same way. Given our current understanding of things, we can really only maintain our commitment to hierarchy as long as we imagine it taking place through what we might see as an endless series of snapshots: at point one, A occupies the top spot, B the second, C the third, D the fourth, and so on; at point two, A may still occupy the top spot, but perhaps C has moved into the second spot over B, while D remains in the fourth spot; at point three, things may have either changed again in some way, displacing A from the top or reinforcing his position, with further changes to be noted only when we get to point ten or even further down the line. This way of conceiving of the flows of power makes no sense precisely because it cannot account for their *flow.* It can only show them as they exist at any particular moment and thus misses the main point in the end, the dynamic process through which the flows of force, or power if you will, are *endlessly* measured out in new ways.

Within any field of activity there are unquestionably sites of greater and lesser power; all is *not* chaos by any means. Some locations have a greater ability to shape the flows of the fields than others, and to a great extent their power derives from their ability to understand the way the field flows in the first place. The more they recognize the dynamic nature of all energy flows, the more they can find ways of putting their energy to productive use within the field, and the more they do that, the more "powerful" their location within the flows will be. But *no* location remains in the same position within the flows, for by definition everything is flowing; at any given moment the effectiveness or forcefulness of one's location within a field is either growing or diminishing both relative to what it was in itself and relative to the other locations within the field that constitute the nature of its flows. Only this dynamic way of conceiving of effectiveness, or power, or authority, makes any sense from an aesthetic perspective, and if neither Nietzsche nor Confucius was able to see that the move from things to knowledge to the sincere will forces one to have a different, nonhierarchical conception of order, that was because the investments in hierarchy have been so unequivocal and complete in both cultures that no other alternative seemed possible.

In any case, Confucius's order is dependent on a contradiction that manifests itself at the level of the family structure. Up to that point order is built on the subordination of self-interest to the nature of what is, and the sincerity of the will derived from a willingness to choose on the basis of the larger order one perceived oneself a part of, but once the individual has cultivated himself he presumably becomes a central model for the family, which in turn would become a model for the nation, which in turn would become a model for the harmony of the world. But if Confucius saw the remaining orders as contingent on a paternalistic and hierarchical order, there is no reason why we have to follow him down that road. It is just as easy for us to allow the nature of things to be reflected in the family and national order as well and thereby to arrive at a world order that is both orderly *and* nonhierarchical. Indeed, in itself Confucius's statement leaves more than enough latitude for us to do precisely that. Only our knowledge of his deep commitment to the traditional structures of his time persuades us that he doubtless meant his depiction of human order to be a patriarchal one.

If we assume that personal cultivation leads to an understanding of the individual's subordinate place in the overall scheme of things, and if we perceive the overall scheme of things to be based on flows within fields rather than on rigid hierarchies within eternal and unchanging structures, then it makes perfect sense for us to see the order of family life to be based on its own flows and to manifest itself in the way those flows are played out. Within this context there will inevitably be greater and lesser degrees of power, but those forces are always changing, and indeed they change most specifically in terms of the degree to which each of the members of the family has sufficiently cultivated him- or herself to be able to recognize the order within the field as a function of flows within it that are measured through the respective locations the various members of the family occupy. At that point, we have arrived at a dynamic understanding of the flows of the family that is both harmonious and yet ever-changing, one that acknowledges the greater force and effectiveness of some of the locations within the field and still recognizes that those relations of force are always in the process of changing. In this way the authority of the family, and the authority *for* the family, does not reside within one person, the great father whose example is the measure of the group, but rather in the overall way the family itself is construed as a result of the dynamics within it.

As always, there are greater and lesser agents within that flow, and thus greater and lesser loci of power, and thus greater and lesser placements of responsibility, for we need always to keep in mind that the generalizing of authority to an event in the midst of a flow does not mean that humans cease to have responsibility for their actions within the flows. On the contrary, they have in some respects even greater responsibility because we can see the way that individual actions do not simply affect oneself or even other individuals but also and more importantly *the entire flow of the field*. Given that, the effects of one's choices are not so easily located and contained and responsibility becomes greater than it does when one must only account for one's actions in terms of a specific result. So authority and responsibility have *not* been taken away from humans within this structure but rather given back to them in a more meaningful way. Nevertheless, because the agents within the flows derive their authority from the event and not the other way around, there can be no centralizing of one agent over the others. To construe this authority on the basis of hierarchical structures is to lose sight of its inevitable attachments to the context through which it is established in the first place. If we recognize this, there is no reason whatsoever why we must think of the family order as one that is based on hierarchy and patriarchy.

If we can agree that there are alternative ways of construing both order and authority that are preferable given our investigation of things, we can just as easily see how the order of the family provides a perfect example for the order of the nation as a whole. Again, if Confucius made clear in other ways that both family and nation depended on paternalistic figures of authority at the top, we can also within the play of his statement about the order of the root construe the national order in terms of our altered vision of family life. Just as the authority within the family comes from the play of forces among locations that generates the events within the field, so too within the national context the authority does not inhere in an agent at the top but rather is played out through the dynamics of the various forces within the nation as a whole. If authority manifests itself through the events that are generated within and by the nation, then although we must carefully assess the responsibility each agent within it must take up, we acknowledge that the event itself is never exclusively dependent on the presumed person at the top, that authority is always dispersed into the flows and can never be so localized within a particular site as to be permanently in place and unquestionably in control.

Confucius's hierarchical conception of power is at variance with the order of things we have found in the lesser orders and contrary to the sense of the overall order we have as well and therefore can no longer be seriously countenanced. Just as we today do not confer on Confucius's words the value they have (in the West, anyway) because they are Confucius's words but rather because they create a context for understanding that has great value, so too we cannot confer on *any* agent, national, familial, or personal, that kind of reified authority. Confucius is a historical, cultural, and religious figure of great importance because of the context his words worked through and helped to create, and their authority is always to be found in that context, even if they are always also justifiably associated with his name.

If, as Heraclitus suggested, the way up and the way down are the same, if the larger orders and the smaller orders are one and the same, then we can see in Confucius's brief articulation of the foundation of things a way of construing the world in aesthetic terms that makes perfect sense to us today, that indeed may make more sense to us today than it has in previous generations. The order of the root—whether the root be the entire order of the world or the little shoot that springs forth as the individual seeks to investigate the nature of things—is manifest throughout the orders we as humans perceive. And if Confucius's way of construing the aesthetic nature of authority has a different character to it than Nietzsche's does, they are still linked at their most fundamental level, the level of the event and the authority that derives from it. If Confucius does not expatiate at length about the all-consuming dangers of *ressentiment*, that is because his own mode of articulation covers the same broad ground with the phrase "sincere will." If he feels no necessity to go on at length about the need to affirm the world in all its joy and terror, he covers the same terrain with his emphasis on the need to investigate things. And if he misconstrues the relation of his aesthetic order to hierarchy, Nietzsche also thinks that his perspective depends on elitism and hierarchy. In this respect too the writers are linked in ways we might not have imagined. That their views are related, however, is less important in the end than any contribution that linkage might bring to our investigation of things, that which we must always concentrate on above all other things inasmuch as everything follows from our willingness to investigate the nature of things and the way in which we set about doing so.

❦

Another approach Confucius makes to the same question of order and authority is perfectly encapsulated in his vision of the individual who has achieved the life toward which we all aspire:

> He who is naturally true to himself is one who without effort, hits upon what is right, and without thinking understands what he wants to know, whose life is easily and naturally in harmony with the moral law. Such a one is what we call a saint or a man of divine nature. He who learns to be his true self is one who finds out what is good and holds fast to it.
>
> In order to learn to be one's true self, it is necessary to obtain a wide and extensive knowledge of what has been said and done in the world; critically to inquire into it; carefully to ponder over it; clearly to sift it; and earnestly to carry it out. (p. 122, 23)

Here again we find the same simplicity of utterance that we discerned in the earlier passage and the same elusiveness as well. One either acknowledges the probity of the remarks Confucius has made or else decides that they mean nothing at all.

What, we might ask, would it mean to be "naturally true to oneself"? And what on earth could it mean to "hit upon what is right"? The words flow by so smoothly that we are almost willing to confer value on them without thought, yet a moment's reflection suggests that we may well not have any real idea of what it is Confucius is talking about. How do we decide that these remarks are highly profound? It is easy enough to conclude that they are gibberish, for we can see from a purely rational context that to be naturally true to oneself makes no sense, both because the word "natural" is suspect and because the word "true" is perpetually in question. Confucius's utterances are a function of a circularity of language: we confer value on these statements by assuming we know what he means by "true" and "naturally" (and "self" as well), when in fact we are the ones who read into those words exactly what we want to find there. A skeptic would want to argue that there is little that differentiates this kind of prose from that to be found in advertising slogans, a language so devoid of specific meaning that it allows the reader to see just what he wants to see and nothing more. Its appeal from this context would be one of deceit: Confucius presumes to offer us great truths, but in effect what he provides is merely a series of hollow formulae that are so thoroughly dependent on our interpretation of their key words as to be virtually meaningless in themselves.

On the other hand, we might also argue that to the extent that this is true, it is true of *all* human utterances, and that even if it is true that Confucius's words are broad and vague enough to be defined in any number of ways, they are also self-limiting in that the overall context of his remarks constrains our definitions and keeps them from exceeding the boundaries of what he intends by them. Such a passage is in this respect a perfect reflection of the hermeneutic circle as Heidegger imagined it: the words themselves are loose and broad enough that their meaning inevitably comes from our understanding of the whole context in which they are to be found, yet our understanding of that whole is contingent upon our ability to define specifically these very baggy words. Is this a vicious circle or a virtuous circle? Is something profound conveyed in this aesthetic context, or is it a region of nebulous affects whose goal can only be momentary self-satisfaction? As with all aesthetic (*and* religious) discourse, the value of Confucius's remarks is clearly contingent on our own sincerity when we read them and on our willingness to work within the context he establishes to arrive at a larger sense of the way things are. A skeptical and distanced form of reading can find nothing of value in what Confucius has to say, but one certainly doesn't need to be an Eastern mystic to recognize the great profundity of his statements and the simple order that Confucius must have had within himself to be able to articulate in so few words the ideal order of an individual human life.

Confucius's description of the man of divine nature bears some striking resemblances to the assertions by Nietzsche we saw earlier through which he construed his own life:

> Considered in this way, my life is simply wonderful. For the task of a *revaluation of all values* more capacities may have been needed than have ever dwelt together in a single individual—above all, even contrary capacities that had to be kept from disturbing, destroying one another. An order of rank among these capacities; distance; the art of separating without setting against one another; to mix nothing, to "reconcile" nothing; a tremendous variety that is nevertheless the opposite of chaos—this was the precondition, the long, secret work and artistry of my instinct. Its *higher protection* manifested itself to such a high degree that I never even suspected what was growing in me—and one day all my capacities, suddenly ripe, *leaped forth* in their ultimate perfection. I cannot remember that I ever tried hard—no trace of *struggle* can be demonstrated in my life; I am the opposite of a heroic nature. "Willing" something, "striving" for something, envisaging a "purpose," a "wish"—I know none of this from experience. At this very moment I still look upon my future—an *ample* future!—as upon calm seas: there is no ripple of desire. I do

> not want in the least that anything should become different than it is; I myself do not want to become different. (p. 254, 55)

Although we might begin by stating that what Nietzsche says here also demonstrates that he is not quite the man of divine nature that Confucius has in mind—as he himself would be the first to acknowledge because he concedes that he is far too much preoccupied with resentments of many kinds—and although we can see that clearly in the self-aggrandizing way Nietzsche describes his attitude toward his life and work and their great ease, we can also notice that his remarks have much in common with Confucius's and suggest yet again a similar orientation to the world.

Nietzsche asserts that "no trace of *struggle*" is to be found in his life, and Confucius stresses the way in which one hits upon what is right "without effort." Nietzsche claims that he knows nothing of willing or striving and has had no desires that have pushed him forward. And not only has he never tried hard, but he has no worries about what may happen to him in the future either, which he looks upon as one looks upon "calm seas." If Confucius wishes to stress that the distinguished individual is one who "without thinking understands what he wants to know," Nietzsche tells us that his capacities simply grew within him and then "suddenly ripe, *leaped forth* in their ultimate perfection," allowing him to perceive the world in accord with who he was. And if the moral law is something Nietzsche has problems with because of its association with mendaciousness, his conception of the overman as the bridge to a better human is unquestionably the mark of another moral law and another system of values that is as rigorous in its own way as the Judeo-Christian one with which he takes issue.

Nietzsche emphasizes again and again that one must love one's fate and embrace what one has become, and Confucius concurs in asserting that "He who learns to be his true self is one who finds out what is good and holds fast to it." What he calls "personal cultivation" is closely related to the discipline Nietzsche describes that is necessary if we are to learn how to embrace who we are, and the relationship between the good and the cultivation of that self is emphasized in both Nietzsche and Confucius. That such cultivation requires "a wide and extensive knowledge of what has been said and done in the world" goes without saying, though in Nietzsche's case this knowledge may have more of a negative value than it does for Confucius, suggesting the range and depth of the mendaciousness of Western thinkers. Nevertheless, both great knowledge and a large capacity are required for the one who is to be true to himself, and both thinkers recognize this.

Nietzsche's true self is based more extensively on conflicting capacities whereas Confucius chooses to emphasize the harmonious relationship among the various aspects of the self, but Nietzsche mentions his conflicting capacities to demonstrate the range of phenomena he understands in his life—he has not encountered only one side of it but the other as well—and to suggest the need for the "true" self to be able to keep these capacities unreconciled and yet still realize the way the self itself can be in harmony in spite of its mixed nature. In emphasizing the mixed capacities of the human, Nietzsche reflects a different sense of the self than Confucius, as he clearly does in speaking of these characteristics through a self-description rather than abstractly as Confucius does, and the self-aggrandizing nature of the description does indeed demonstrate that Nietzsche had not kept all his capacities sufficiently disciplined in his prose here, as Confucius so clearly has. But the fact remains that both writers are speaking about the nature of aesthetic authority as it is to be cultivated from the perspective of the individual person.

Of course Confucius's statement is hardly designed to provide a checklist for personal cultivation any more than it is supposed to gratify the ego of one who thinks he has achieved such a fate. Nor is it inclined to justify itself. Confucius does not tell us why, for example, the one who is true to himself manages without effort to hit upon what is right, but then neither does Nietzsche. In part both are simply describing one of the effects of the aesthetic event: it happens seemingly "naturally" and requires no great effort or anxiety. One who knows who he is will without effort be able to discern what is the case in a given situation and will thus know how to act. The locus of aesthetic authority is to be found in precisely this situation where the cultivated individual, the one who is naturally true to himself, hits what is right without any agonizing or any struggle whatever. The authority that derives from the aesthetic context comes from the conviction that such easeful choices reflect. One who has developed the capacity to be true to himself will as a matter of course understand what he wants to know in any given situation and set about acquiring the necessary knowledge. It is as simple as that, or so Confucius would have us think.

The individual who is capable of hitting upon what is right without effort is also therefore one "whose life is easily and naturally in harmony with the moral law." This is the kind of statement of which we are most suspicious in the late twentieth century, once again because of the weight the abstract words carry without filling out the context sufficiently. The very notion of hitting what is "right" presupposes what that right is; the repeated assertions about what is natural presuppose a definition of nature that we might well find not to be natural at all; the idea that one can naturally be in harmony with the moral law is something we might be inclined to take issue with, asserting on the contrary that one has to be trained by those who regulate the flows of discourse to *think* our lives are in harmony with a moral law that comes naturally to us when in fact it is imposed upon us by those in whose interests it is to make us think the law itself is an outgrowth of nature. And there can be no doubt that Confucius's statement is susceptible to such a critique, and would doubtless be more susceptible still to such an assessment if he had gone so far as to provide particulars here, for they would have revealed to us the ways in which his ideas of what was natural and what was moral were contingent upon his own personal and cultural values. The only question that remains is whether or not his statement has great value in spite of this danger, regardless of the fact that the words are loose enough to allow abusive powers to coerce us through assertions of natural harmony with the moral law.

If Confucius stresses that the distinguished individual manages without effort to hit what is "right," and if he argues that such a person has a life that is "easily and naturally in harmony with the moral law," we need to understand the linkages between these statements and the implications of their language. What does it mean to be able to hit upon what is "right," and what does that have to do with the moral law? In some respects it would seem that the rightness to which Confucius refers is broader in conception than the moral law, for what is right might simply be a question of completing a task in a certain way. The *right* way to build a fire is thus and so, or the right way to hold the brush when one is painting is *this* way—these kinds of rightness seem to have nothing to do with morality but are rather a function of skills one acquires on the basis of one's understanding of one's body and its relationship to the world of which it is a part. If one learns properly how to build a fire, that means that one has integrated one's bodily skills into the environment that calls for the action of building a fire. If one learns how to hold the paintbrush in a way that is fitting for what one is painting, that means one has learned how to adapt the body to a set of physical articulations that will allow it to accomplish its goals.

Such means of hitting upon what is right might extend to any number of domains. Certainly, for example, a great baseball player, a "natural," is one who has a body that is supremely adapted to the functions that are required of one who wishes to hit a small ball with a bat, but he is also one who has disciplined those "natural" skills in such a way as to know what is "right," to know what the proper swing *feels like* so that he can put it into effect and hit the ball with force and direction. There is a sense of rightness to any good swing that is dependent on the careful cultivation of the body's capabilities and the particular series of movements that must be brought in play to hit the ball where one wants it to go. Confucius's sense of hitting upon what is right suggests these kinds of rightness, to me at least, rather than any specifically moral kind of rightness. Indeed, I might never even think of morality in this context if it weren't for Confucius's next statement and its assertion that such rightnesses have something to do with one who is in harmony with the moral law.

Another reflection of the rightnesses one might ordinarily think of that have no obvious relation to morality is the rightness that occurs when an idea just comes to one. If Nietzsche spoke of the way his capacities one day *leaped forth* in all their fullness, this too is the way in which many ideas come into being. They are suddenly just there, though sometimes the effort that precedes them is much greater than Confucius would allow for. One could have been working without success for weeks on the resolution of a problem and then suddenly the answer just comes to one. This "rightness" strikes one as inevitably the case, the situation resolves itself, and nothing further needs to be considered. But again, this kind of rightness, the appropriateness of a resolution to a context, seems no more moral than the appropriateness of the techniques whereby the stroke of a great hitter manages to do the "right" thing to the ball. In the English language, this sense of rightness is distinguished from the sense of rightness that has to do with being a morally good person.

If we assume that Confucius includes such forms of rightness in his description of aesthetic authority, that context wherein one achieves what is right without effort and thus reflects the manner in which one is naturally true to oneself and one's place in the world, then we need to think a bit differently about morality and the good. If we assume that Confucius makes no essential distinction between the right and the good that come from performing a specific act in accordance with its possibilities or arriving at the resolution of a problem with a spontaneous sense of what to do, and the right and good that come from adhering to specific moral laws, we begin to get a sense of the true profundity of his remarks. We know that Eastern cultures through the millennia have been far more interested in cultivating the personal life through disciplines that are physical and yet deeply spiritual at the same time, whether they be forms of painting or martial arts, so we recognize that they have as a matter of course found the regulation of the body through such activities to be an intrinsic part of the good. Without such bodily discipline, as manifested through whatever form of human activity, the other kinds of good to which the human must attend could not possibly be fitting. We in the West have cultivated different notions of these two kinds of right and have separated the one into a field in which morality doesn't really come into play and the other into the religious dogmas through which we have constructed the rules of our societies. True, the early Greeks connected the rightness of these two fields in a way that bears resemblance to the Eastern way of thinking, but that knowledge has for the most part been unexplored within our own tradition for millennia.

Nietzsche's return to our embodied status within the world, however, has placed us back into a context where we must think once again about the relationship between these two forms of right. If Nietzsche makes a big deal out of the so-called little things like nutrition and climate and walking and sitting, that is because in his mind there is an irretrievable relationship between the physical discipline through which one acted in the world and the mental discipline through which one began to imagine the overman as the mark of the greatest human potential. If he sees himself as one who has had to work to overcome the prevailing morality, that is because the morality he opposes is one that negates the bodily world and turns it into the locus of evil rather than into one of the essential sites for rightness that all humans possess. If Nietzsche finds all forms of morality to be mendacious, that is because they deny the very real ground of all their codes in the cultivation of the body. And if Nietzsche doesn't want the word "morality" associated with his writing, that is *not* because he doesn't posit a very clear morality with a specific perspective through which it can be articulated in anyone's life, for his goal is to do precisely that; it is rather that he recognizes the way in which the word "morality" is opposed historically in the West to the kinds of bodily rightness upon which it depends. In order to begin where one must, with the bodily rightnesses out of which the moral law itself emerges, one has no choice but to renounce a word that has sought to deny precisely those origins. For Nietzsche, to love one's fate is nothing more or less than to appreciate in every way the rightness of who one is and *where* one is, and it thus reflects the larger sense of rightness and moral law that Confucius asserts in connecting the two.

Nevertheless, we have yet to understand completely what the two forms of rightness could have in common. We might assume that Confucius's emphasis on the word "naturally" in this context also plays itself out in two ways, on the one hand emphasizing that the sense of right always comes from our recognition of our place within the natural world and on the other suggesting simply that which comes easily. For him the two are parts of the same process, for if one truly understands one's place in the world, one will have no choice but to love his fate and to be "naturally true to himself." And if one is naturally true to himself and to his place in the world, then his actions will come to him naturally, with ease, and he will hit upon what is right seemingly without effort. That one needs great self-discipline in order to be able to understand one's place in the world and to be at ease with who one is goes without saying. If we must first investigate things—and thereby acquire true knowledge, and thereby discipline the will and make it sincere, and thereby set the heart right, and thereby achieve cultivation—the "ease" with which an individual "naturally" comes upon what is right is obviously something that involves a rigorous discipline from top to bottom. If that were not the case, everyone would have long ago come to Confucius's knowledge without needing Confucius, and the world would be a radically different place. After all, Confucius tells us that "Such a one is what we call a saint or a man of divine nature," so what he is describing through the ease of rightness is not something that comes easily to all, or even most, or even a very few of us. It is the rarest of human embodiments, a model through which to measure our own lives that has the same value inherent in it as Nietzsche's gauge of the overman.

If the rightness of the body and its knowledge is not simply *related to* the rightness of the moral law but rather is an essential part of it, as seems to be the case for Confucius, then one does indeed end up with a different moral law than the one the West has developed. And if the rightness of the body is in some crucial respects not to be distinguished from the other forms of rightness in the human world, then we must assert yet again what inevitably follows from Confucius's statement: all knowledge is finally *aesthetic* in nature, all truths are first and foremost aesthetic truths, and all *authority* is therefore to be found within an aesthetic event, for authority can only be legitimately derived from a fitting assessment of the nature of what is, and such an assessment is only possible from within a context in which one is naturally true to oneself, in which one hits upon what is right without effort because one has cultivated oneself sufficiently so as to have developed a *sincere* will, one that instinctively chooses what is good, whether that "good" be a physical action, as in making a stroke with a brush, or a more obviously "moral" action, as in doing the right thing in a difficult situation with apparently conflicting moral choices.

He who has properly cultivated the self understands the fundamentally aesthetic nature of the world, and he who has done that can thereby fathom the complexity of a situation fully and thus know how to act within it. In turn the authority of the individual who has properly cultivated the self is derived from an aesthetic context, one in which self-interest has been displaced for the more comprehensive understanding of one's actions in a situation as they apply to the flow of the field as a whole. And again, such authority does not really inhere in, say, *Confucius* per se, even if it is through his own personal cultivation that he has arrived at his understanding of things and thereby achieved great authority; rather, the authority inheres in the situation in which Confucius at any given moment finds himself—his ability to hit upon what is right in such a context is no more than a reflection of an aesthetic understanding of just what that situation involves.

Another problem we have with what Confucius is saying, though, is that he does indeed emphasize the need for personal cultivation and knowledge of the self, yet what he establishes finally articulates a region in which that self-knowledge is in a real way *location*-knowledge. The self that knows itself is in a sense nothing more than a self that knows fully its place in the world and understands how to measures its real and potential effects within the flows of the fields of which it is a part, so self-cultivation in Confucius leads to a forgetfulness of the self as we know it, or at the very least to a context in which one no longer needs to think about the self in particular. If one hits upon what is right without effort, then one doesn't have to inquire into the needs and values of the self or to isolate it as a separable datum within the field of the problem; it is just *there,* a part of a field that has called for a response, an action, that will move the play of the field into another direction.

So on the one hand Confucius calls for an unquestionably intense and rigorous cultivation of the self—only through great self-discipline can one hope to be naturally true to oneself—and on the other the great self-discipline brings one so fully into the context in the midst of which that self is always found that it ceases to be something to which one has to devote attention anymore. This statement is akin to the other seeming paradox of Confucius's utterance, which is that on the one hand the saint is one who simply does what comes naturally to him, but on the other hand he first requires the greatest of self-discipline in order to be able to discern what truly *does* come naturally to him. He begins "unnaturally," if you will, within the illusions of culture perhaps, and must bring the most intense form of concentration to bear on his life before he can achieve the point where he is able to act with ease and in harmony with the moral law.

One needs to stress the obvious at this point: what Confucius means by personal cultivation—what *Nietzsche* means by learning to love one's fate—bears little resemblance to the current forms of personal cultivation we find all around us. If Foucault was both right and wrong to ask what matter who's speaking, that is because he was right to demonstrate how skewed our fetishizations of the self are, how far they take us away from any proper understanding of our own lives or the world of which we are a part; he was wrong to argue that as a result it doesn't matter who's speaking in a world where the self has been (to his mind properly) dissolved, for the authority upon which we depend always manifests itself within a particular context in a particular situation and therefore always is associated with agents as well as events. But our current fetishization of the self bears no resemblance whatsoever to Confucius's personal cultivation, and this needs to be emphasized both so the two are not mistaken and so we can recognize the ways in which our current self-images in all their self-absorption are misinterpretations of the Nietzschean context on which they rely.

If Nietzsche brought us back to a full awareness of our bodily—that is temporal—natures, if he did more than anyone else in modern history to demonstrate the mendaciousness of those who would turn us away from our embodied existence and would prompt us to deny the value of the present world, he also established the consequent necessity for a *standard,* for an order through which our understanding of the body and its place within the world can be gauged, and this, the most difficult part of Nietzsche, naturally enough, is that which has been ignored. If the path to the overman requires supreme self-discipline—that is, a specific form of intense concentration on the self—yet that form of self-discipline and the image of the self that derives from it are radically different from the self-images that are to be found in the current world of fetishizations we find ourselves in. And if the cultivation of the self requires a standard, as it most assuredly does, it is not an artificially derived gauge to be imposed on our conduct from some external forces whose interests are chiefly the perpetuation of their own power any more than it is a utopian measure that would sway us away from a commitment to the world we have right here; it is rather the standard that derives inevitably from investigating things, an *aesthetic* measure that comes "naturally" from any sincere attempt to understand one's place in the overall flows of the fields in which we are to be found.

The current sense of self is based on the necessity of *poses,* to use Nietzsche's term, on the need to create an artificialized self through a "life-style" or through a series of consciously cultivated ruses through which we can lure others into an interest in who we are, even if that "who" is in fact nothing more than a pose. This fetishization is based not on an *understanding* of the self and its position in the world but rather on a *flight from* understanding the self and its position in the world. It creates nothing more than a different form of mendaciousness, the form indeed, against which the Judeo-Christian world established its own order. What has happened is that one form of mendaciousness has been replaced by another, "self-sacrifice" has been transformed into total self-absorption, one form of denial transmuted into another, perhaps even more desperate form of self-loathing and world-denial.

Personal cultivation as Confucius intends it is the highest of human arts, and all human orders—we might say today a good bit of the *natural* order as well, given our relatively destructive potential—depend on it. And Confucius's art of personal cultivation is based on the premise that what is "right" extends from the most simple of appropriate physical actions in a particular context to the "fitting" response in the most difficult of moral situations. For him there is no distinction to be drawn between these two forms of human rightness, nor is the one derived from the other. It is not that one first learns a bodily kind of rightness and then extends it to the moral world; bodily rightness *is* moral rightness, and moral rightness *is* bodily rightness. The sincere will expresses itself equally and at the same time through the body and through all one's other actions as well. Even so, we have yet fully to comprehend the full import of the good that the sincere will relates to and need therefore to devote a bit more attention to just what Confucius's good might be said to be.

If the sincere will is that will which, as a result of its knowledge of the way things are, naturally and without effort hits upon what is right, what kind of good can we associate with it? Is it the same general good to which we have subscribed as a result of our traditions, or does it change considerably once we connect it to the bodily world and to the tradition that comes from Confucius? In one respect, the answer to this question must be the same as the answer to the question of authority in general: the good, like aesthetic authority, depends on the flows of the fields out of which it emerges, and if that means it is always determined through its presence within a context, that doesn't necessarily suggest that the moral law would look greatly different in many respects than the one to which Western cultures have subscribed.

If we assume that the good is determined by the flows of the fields and our place within them, that only an assessment of the world that is based on a decentered self can generate aesthetic authority, there is every reason to believe that most of the tenets to which Western and most other cultures subscribe would continue to be applicable. One would find proscriptions of murder and other violent acts as a result of their deleterious effects on the flows as a whole, disrupting not only the context of the particular individuals involved but also the larger regions that surround them. If most societies have some belief in a "golden rule" of reciprocity, that is doubtless because the flows of the fields are inherently based upon reciprocal interchanges without end, and inasmuch as they are without end—inasmuch as one's business is never necessarily done with any of the locations within a field (even after one is dead in some respects, given the memory of others, the possibilities for good thoughts and guilt alike)—surely an awareness of reciprocity and the need to put oneself in the place of others within the flows is an essential ingredient of any moral law.

Beyond such general tenets, one must recognize the ways in which the good of a given culture is always filtered through the historical situations it has already faced and so acknowledge that the specifics of each context would inevitably remain dependent on past visions of self, world and human purpose. In this respect, not much changes in the moral law when considered in its basics. It is only when one begins to think seriously about that law as it manifests itself through traditional and rational authority that the major reappraisals begin, but such assessments need to be made on the basis of an aesthetic authority rather than on the grounds of only another form of traditional authority, or else they will end up with the same problems of artificial hierarchies and the same values that reflect the will to power as an expression of self-interest rather than a declaration of the overabundance of life.

The specifics of any moral system are always dependent on the practices that get worked out in everyday life, as we know just from the major changes that have come about in the past generation or so in our views of the body, sexuality, race, gender, and age. As the experience of a society moves in new directions, these things are inevitably defined through the altered contexts through which they are mediated. The only question then has to do with the degree to which they are intelligently mediated through the flows of the fields. Confucius's description of the human of divine nature, after all, ends with the assertion that "In order to learn to be one's true self, it is necessary to obtain a wide and extensive knowledge of what has been said and done in the world; critically to inquire into it; carefully to ponder over it; clearly to sift it, and earnestly to carry it out." Only through such a rigorous process can the will be made sincere and its choices lead to the cultivated self that is at ease with its choices and the manner of its choosing. And if we might be inclined to think that Confucius himself would give more weight to what has been said and done in the world than we ourselves would inasmuch as he is more committed to the value of traditional authority, again his statement is broad, yet precise enough for us to be able to see that the degree to which one's understanding of what has been said and done in the world ends up reinforcing the traditions that have been generated out of it depends on the critical nature of one's inquiry into it. Given Confucius's own emphasis on the need for such questioning, the assertion does not mean that we must in the end go along with what traditional authority has already established.

Our more skeptical relationship to our traditions might make us less likely to discern through a rigorous and extensive investigation into what has been said and done the positive values of a good part of those traditions. Certainly the ongoing critique of the past century would suggest that our critical appraisal has found much in our values to be wanting, and if there hasn't been a great deal of careful pondering of the cultural situation in which we find ourselves, if the sifting process has not been as clear as it should be, the earnestness with which our reappraisals have been put into effect has not always been as fitting or effective as it should have been. Our impatience has kept us from working through our critique of the values of the past in the way that Confucius suggests, and no doubt this is a result of the fact that there are few humans of divine nature to carry out this enterprise, and even fewer who would listen to such humans when they are to be found.

Even if we take Nietzsche as a "divine nature," something of an exaggeration of the term that would doubtless make both Confucius and Nietzsche uncomfortable, we can see how few people have bothered seriously to understand the entire context of his work. His conflicting capacities may have contributed to this problem, with each writer in turn playing off of those aspects of Nietzsche's work that most suit his or her own, but it is also true that, as with most such figures, Nietzsche's writing has been much abused by those who want to do little more than exert power through his words. That there have been few who have carefully explored the possibility of Nietzsche's revaluation of values and many who have embraced his critique of culture may reflect the difficulty of the very notion of a revaluation of values and its attendant machinery like *amor fati* and the eternal return and the overman; or it may reflect the conservative tendencies within culture that are uncomfortable with the very idea of a new system of values; or it may be the result of the self-interested exploitation of Nietzsche's thought for personal ends. But whatever the reason, the result has been that few have bothered seriously to sift the work and carefully to ponder it while far too many have been willing earnestly to carry out their very limited visions of the consequences of Nietzsche's work.

At this juncture of our own history we might also be inclined to say that the kind of assessment of what has been said and done in the world that Confucius has in mind is not really possible, that the contingencies of interpretation are such that any assessment of what has been said and done will inevitably be partial. One might argue that in Nietzsche's case, for example, it is not that few people have seen his work in all its complexity but rather that, as is always the case, individuals have simply grafted onto his work at those locations within it through which their own ideas can find fitting expression, and this is as natural as it is inevitable. From this vantage point, it could be better done only from the older, metaphysical conceptions of interpretation through which it could be argued that there was indeed an "objective" way to assess Nietzsche's work in its entirety. Inasmuch as we no longer believe in such objectivity, recognizing the ways in which all the flows of discourse are filtered through the contexts we find them in, we should hardly expect the kind of valuation Confucius discusses.

But there is nothing in Confucius's remarks that would fail to take account of a complex and contextualized interpretational system; on the contrary, Confucius's statements suggest precisely that vision of interpretation, for otherwise there would be no need for the "wide and extensive knowledge" upon which the entire system is predicated. If the principles of interpretation were simple and straightforward, or if the moral values of a culture were obvious to everyone, there would be no need for the extensive personal cultivation to which Confucius is devoted. It is only because all our values—and all our interpretations, which are always reflections of those values—are to be worked out through the mixture and complexity of everyday life that the road to an orderly life is so difficult. So our own conflicts with the past and our overly-historicized sense of the world is not the obstacle to personal cultivation that we might like to think it is.

One might also argue that Confucius's viewpoint portrays the ideal of the saint or divine human and thus could not be applicable to the way that critical history actually proceeds. Inasmuch as there are many individuals who participate in the critical assessment of culture and very few who even come close to the ideal embodied in the human who is true to himself, how could we ever hope to have an ongoing relationship with the aesthetic authority through which our values are articulated that would properly reflect the order inherent in it? Since there are few who have the knowledge Confucius demands and even fewer with the patience to sift and criticize and ponder this knowledge, how could we hope for people who both had knowledge and the wills that would be necessary earnestly to carry out the results of their inquiries? That there is a great deal of truth underlying these questions does not take away from the fact that our own inquiries have hardly been models of careful thought.

Likewise, that Confucius establishes a useful ideal in terms of which we should measure our own lives rather than articulating the possibilities for the typical human situation no more undermines the value of what he says than does the possibility in Nietzsche's case that the overman is an impossible ideal as well, that humans don't have the capacity to love their fates and abjure their resentments. Neither the overman nor the divine human can be a model for us in the sense that we should seek out actual humans who come close to embodying these conditions and then emulate them. That may well have been a part of what Confucius had in mind, but in our own time and culture such modes of emulation are not effective. And even for Confucius the *idea* of the divine human that we cultivate within ourselves is more important than any individual we might know who could approximate its values. There is no need for a perfect master in Confucius's thought any more than there is in Nietzsche's. And there is likewise no possibility that the species as a whole is likely to become transformed into one full of divine humans or overmen. Thus, our ongoing critique and our revaluations of values will always take place in circumstances that are less than ideal, but this is no reason to downplay the need to make them as wise and as comprehensive as possible in order to compensate for the earnestness that is too often attached to far too slim a knowledge of what has been said and done in the world.

Confucius also has a few specific human characteristics he attaches to aesthetic authority, though, features that are a reflection of the human who has learned how to be true to himself and has therefore arrived at the point where he hits upon what is right without effort. These moral qualities are the base of the entire system of valuation, the root without which the foundation will always be in confusion:

> Wisdom, compassion and courage—these are the three universally recognized moral qualities of man. It matters not in what way men come to the exercise of these moral qualities, the result is one and the same.
>
> Some men are born with the knowledge of these moral qualities; some acquire it as the result of education; some acquire it as the result of hard experience. But when the knowledge is acquired, it comes to one and the same thing. Some exercise these moral qualities naturally and easily; some because they find it advantageous to do so; some with effort and difficulty. But when the achievement is made it comes to one and the same thing. . . .
>
> Love of knowledge is akin to wisdom. Strenuous attention to conduct is akin to compassion. Sensitiveness to shame is akin to courage.

> When a man understands the nature and use of these three moral qualities, he will then understand how to put in order his personal conduct and character. When a man understands how to put in order his personal conduct and character, he will understand how to govern men. When a man understands how to govern men, he will then understand how to govern nations and empires. (p. 118, 19)

As always with Confucius, we see here how everything is interrelated, how the largest phenomena are contingent on the smallest, how the greatest ideas are based on the simplest of conceptions, how the largest of human possibilities are related to three qualities with which we are all familiar, wisdom, compassion, and courage. We might note that Nietzsche placed a high value on wisdom and courage but seemed contemptuous of compassion, a mark of pity, he might argue against Confucius, a value that is a sign of "weakness" because it reflects the worst of human possibilities rather than the best.

But Nietzsche would have no problem with Confucius's definition of compassion as "Strenuous attention to conduct." Indeed, we might recall these words from *Ecce Homo:* "To this day I still have the same affability for everyone; I even treat with special respect those who are lowliest: in all of this there is not one grain of arrogance or secret contempt. If I despise a man, he *guesses* that I despise him: by my mere existence I outrage everything that has bad blood in its veins" (p. 258). Although we cannot know to what extent Nietzsche's assertion here is true—it does have the aura of insanity about it—we can if we take it seriously recognize the degree to which he has his own strenuous rules of conduct. There is surely a conflict within him between that which the "rabble" signifies for him—largely his own incapacities and inability to deal with his *ressentiment,* in my estimation—and "those who are lowliest" here, for he is more than willing to treat them with special respect. Even if Nietzsche repeatedly attacks the "rabble" in the abstract, for the most part those whom he really wishes to attack are rabble only in the sense that their ideas are base, and these are usually far from the lowest rungs of society. So we might think that Nietzsche's conduct toward the lowliest is indeed exemplary, and that he saves his scorn for the self-pitying types of the bourgeoisie whose values are so decadent. Even so, the difference between the two writers here might well be significant.

What is most striking about Confucius's statement is that it demonstrates both that there are various ways through which one can acquire the three moral qualities that humans need and that none of the ways is superior to the others. If Confucius chooses to emphasize that it doesn't matter "in what way men come to the exercise of these moral qualities," that is clearly because most of us think that it *does* matter, that some ways of acquiring virtue are better than others. Confucius rightly perceives that, on the contrary, the endpoint of wisdom, compassion, and courage is all that matters, not the road there. If one is born with a knowledge of these capacities, so much the better, but there is nothing in such an individual that is superior to the one who acquires this knowledge through education or hard experience. However one comes to the proper understanding of these qualities, "it is one and the same thing," and it is so because regardless of how one achieves wisdom, the discipline one has had to employ to achieve it is one and the same. The rigor is not more or less if one is born with it or if one gets it through a difficult life. There are no hierarchies through which to construe the achievement of wisdom, compassion and courage; they in themselves are sufficiently beyond hierarchy as to make it meaningless as a way of measuring relative wisdom, compassion or courage.

More strikingly, Confucius asserts that "Some exercise these moral qualities naturally and easily; some because they find it advantageous to do so; [and] some with effort and difficulty," and we might wonder how this could be so. It is easy enough for us to imagine that some people manage to exercise these best of human capacities with effort and difficulty and some do so naturally and easily, but how can one exercise them with effort and difficulty when Confucius has also told us that the one who naturally understands himself hits what is right without effort? We might hypothesize that there is the way to wisdom, compassion and courage, and then there is the state of possessing them, and Confucius is referring here to the process whereby one arrives at final wisdom, compassion and courage, but inasmuch as he refers to the exercising of these qualities, we would have to think that this way of looking at the matter doesn't quite work. How can one exercise wisdom before one actually possesses it? Inasmuch as that makes no sense, we cannot readily construe Confucius in this way. So we might be inclined to speak about relative degrees of wisdom, compassion and courage, but this too seems to go against the grain of his work, though perhaps to a lesser extent. It may be that Confucius imagines a situation in which there are few truly "divine humans" who possess the full capacity for wisdom, compassion and courage but that us lesser humans are still nonetheless capable of acquiring wisdom, compassion and courage, only in less perfect form—that is, only in a form that makes their exercise contingent on our abilities to assess the context in which we find them. This is a possible way of interpreting Confucius here, but it too seems to cover less of the terrain than it should.

When we look at the same difficulty from another angle, we can ask ourselves how it could be possible for one to exercise these virtues because one finds it advantageous to do so? Advantage, and the desire *for* advantage, would seem to be a function of an opposing form of valuation, one that is self-interested rather than aesthetic in nature, and so we would need to know how one could both have these great qualities and yet at the same time be able to exercise them to one's advantage. The easy way out of this dilemma would be to construe advantage in a liberal way, meaning simply anything that is advantageous to one, for from Confucius's perspective there can be no doubt that it is to our advantage to have these moral qualities. But "advantage" clearly implies "social" advantage here and is thus associated with hierarchical privileges, so the easy out doesn't suffice. We can only assume that Confucius is imagining a context in which a leader would actually find it to his advantage to possess and exercise the values of wisdom, compassion and courage, and that the exercise of these values would be perceived by those beneath him as a reflection of his own advantageous situation.

That we find this harder to believe than Confucius may have to do with our more extensive historical understanding, and it may have to do with our knowledge of his own life as well. If Confucius wanted to believe that he could find a leader who would see the importance of exercising these values, he also assumed that he could find a leader who would give him a position as the equivalent of master of these virtues, and inasmuch as he himself never found any such position with any government, and therefore obviously never found any leader who embodied these virtues from a position of advantage, his later life—or the life as a whole—would suggest that perhaps his own wisdom didn't extend far enough to recognize the incompatibility of the moral qualities and advantage. So it would seem at this distance in any case, where we would have to assert that the linkage between advantage and these moral qualities has until now been little more than an ideal, and one that is almost always ignored by those in advantageous positions.

Still, Confucius's emphasis on the fact that the three great moral qualities *could* be exercised in any number of contexts is in itself an essential and important point, for it demonstrates that these virtues should not be incompatible with the various situations in which they are to be found. Just as some people seem to learn mathematics quite easily—it comes "naturally" to them—while others must work hard to acquire that knowledge; just as some find it advantageous to possess a knowledge of mathematics; so too we could say that the exercise of wisdom, compassion and courage could take place in any of these contexts. In an important respect, after all, it is true that a wise person like Confucius clearly does exercise his moral qualities from an advantageous position, even as it could be said that he profits from these qualities. If he becomes known as the possessor of such wisdom, he comes to make his way in the world on the basis of this reputation. There is nothing wrong with this "advantage," and it is not necessarily in conflict with the moral qualities in themselves, though again, when Confucius in his later life gives up any hope of gaining a meaningful position in the court life of his time, he in effect to some degree decides that in order to preserve the moral qualities he exercises he must abjure his advantage within the social system. Even so, in theory there is no reason why advantage and the moral qualities couldn't go together, and in the world Confucius strives for, the world of order that begins at the root and moves up through the individual to the family to the nation to the world, there is no reason to think that advantage and virtue cannot go together. Likewise, there is no reason why the striving person who through hard experience achieves these virtues is in any way inferior to one who comes by them easily.

What stands out most in Confucius's discussion of the moral qualities, though, is his simple definitions of them. It may be conventional enough to think of wisdom as a love of knowledge, for we have associated the two for millennia, but to construe compassion as strenuous attention to conduct and courage as sensitiveness to shame is astonishing and a mark of Confucius's genius. Even the most straightforward assertion—that wisdom is the love of knowledge—strikes from an unconventional angle, for we would ordinarily think of one who has wisdom as one who *possesses* knowledge rather than as one who possesses a *love* of knowledge. To be wise is to know, not to love, knowledge, though we would concede that one who loves knowledge might well achieve wisdom through the pursuit of it. In focussing on the love of knowledge rather than on the possession of it, Confucius defines the characteristic through which wisdom is achieved rather than emphasizing the state of possessing knowledge in itself. Because one loves knowledge, one seeks it out, and if one seeks it out, wisdom is possible; therefore, one who has wisdom is inevitably one who loves knowledge. By displacing the notion of *possession* in favor of *love,* Confucius reorients our understanding of the wise individual, for in doing so, he connects wisdom to a human state that has affects as well as intellectual content. "Love" is a word possessed of powerful emotions if nothing else, so a lover of knowledge is one who is passionately driven to know—only such a person, Confucius suggests, is capable of achieving true wisdom. And in this respect mere knowledge is not enough, for it lacks the passion that would transmute the knowledge into wisdom.

Wisdom in turn, we might think, is linked to compassion and courage, for it is not likely that one would have Confucian compassion or courage without first possessing Confucian wisdom. One has to have obtained that wide and extensive knowledge of what has been said and done (and one needs both what has been said *and* done because what is said and what is done are clearly not always even remotely related) in order to be compassionate because for Confucius compassion is nothing more than strenuous attention to conduct, and that rests on the personal cultivation that derives from the knowledge of what is. We might think it strange of Confucius to construe compassion in such a way, for our more traditional definition would suggest sympathy with or for others rather than strenuous attention to conduct, and it would be easy enough to argue that in effect this is precisely the direction in which Confucius's own definition points, for strenuous attention to conduct could be understood as working to preserve the delicate relations that exist between people, gauging them carefully in order to discern just how to react to the particular problems of the individuals in one's life. Our sympathy in this respect would be measured by the degree to which our conduct evinced empathy for those who compelled such a response.

Even if we should wish to construe Confucius's comment in this way, though, we would be better off thinking more along the lines of Nietzsche's overman and reflecting on the nature of what makes us most human, for that is the chief direction of the statement that strenuous attention is akin to compassion. Confucius's basic argument is that one needs to cultivate the self in order to become more wholly human, and the more wholly human one becomes, the more one shares with all humanity what it means to be alive. If "compassion" is not quite the word that would suit the context in any ordinary way, yet it seems appropriate given the larger concerns of Confucius's boxlike structure, where personal cultivation leads to a regulated family, which leads to an orderly nation, which leads to an harmonious world. In this context, one is doing the most one possibly can for humanity in devoting strenuous attention to one's own conduct, for only by bringing order to the root can one hope to cultivate humanity as a whole. One's compassion, then, resides in the image of humanity one seeks to effect by the way in which one's self-discipline allows one to come to be. It is a function that relates to Nietzsche's love of fate in that both allow the best aspects of human being to flourish, and both can only be achieved by great self-discipline, by the rigorous and never-ending attempt to put out of one's mind that which comes from the resentful aspects of one's humanity. And in striving to eliminate the resentment and its effects from one's life, one creates in turn a sympathetic image of the human and allows that image to govern one's conduct.

The final link in the chain of the three great moral qualities has to do with one's sensitiveness to shame, and once again we can see how an attentiveness to this has to do with courage and self-discipline, most pertinently because people tend to want to hide from their own shamefulness and deny that it exists; in so doing, they tend to project it onto others who are more obviously shameful in a public way. As I have argued elsewhere, the relationship between shame and beauty could be conceived of as the fundamental one out of which all our values grow, and it is certainly the one out of which Nietzsche's aesthetic vision developed; but the great knowledge to be derived from an understanding of the relationship between shame and beauty requires that we be willing to attend to our own shamefulness, something we in the West in particular are loath to do.[3] It takes great courage to be able to face up to all that one is and not to run from what one finds within oneself, and this courage is necessary if we are to be able to address who we are in all our complexity and thereby overcome the simplistic visions of human behavior upon which our traditional forms of authority are based.

Our more likely inclination when we consider courage as a great virtue is to think of strength in battle or the willingness to resist temptations of one kind or another, and doubtless these too reflect an individual's relative courage. But Confucius refuses to define the word so easily, insisting instead that the true definition is "sensitiveness to shame." And as with the strenuous attention to conduct, we can see how a sensitiveness to shame requires both great discipline *and* leads to the kind of personal cultivation that allows a better prospect for humanity to emerge. Courage in the face of one's shamefulness—or in the face of others' shamefulness—is not merely a personal characteristic that has no value for the whole. On the contrary, courage is to be praised because it provides positive effects for the socius in general and allows its flows to be regulated in a more harmonious way. Baldly phrased, we might argue that if everyone were willing to face fully his or her own shame, there would be no need for the endless projections and displacements of that shame, projections and displacements that lead to everything from unfair discrimination of many kinds to wars that decimate entire populations. And if we were to connect our shame to that about which we feel resentment, an argument could be made that most—if not all—of our *ressentiment* stems from our unwillingness to consider carefully what it means to be an embodied, temporal creature. Those things about which we feel shame are inevitably tied to our bodies and our temporal natures, and inasmuch as the embodied world of which we are a part and the things it inflicts on us within time are the source of our resentments, they are always in some shape or form connected to our sense of shame and our willingness or unwillingness to deal with it.

I want to emphasize the linkage between courage and sensitiveness to shame not because Confucius is careful to make it; the very connection is striking and profound on its own, and in one sense needs no further commentary—one either recognizes the courage that is necessary in facing shame (one's own or another's)—or else there seems to be a misplaced definition here or a mistranslation. But if one recognizes how fundamental a sensitiveness to shame is in the cultivation of the self and the growth of the orderly root, one also knows the great difficultly in disciplining the self both to address the shame that is part of our existence and consequently to bring an order to the life that keeps one's shamefulness from poisoning one's own life or the lives of others. If one fails to see how the wisdom and discipline of the self are dependent on a full awareness of who one is and therefore a recognition of one's full shamefulness, then one has deliberately sheared off an essential part of that self. It is worth emphasizing that Confucius is speaking here of moral traits he asserts are to be found in the humans of divine nature, doubtless including himself at least tacitly. We tend to assume that people of divine nature are without shame because they have nothing to be shameful of whereas Confucius makes it clear that all humans have something to be shameful of simply because that is part of their nature. It cannot be *eliminated,* but it can be *disciplined* with courage, and that is what one needs to do to achieve the most wholly human of possibilities.

When we think of the moral qualities of wisdom, compassion, and courage as Confucius understands them, we need to remember the way in which his description of the person who is naturally true to himself defines in effect one who is "naturally in harmony with the moral law." The aesthetic authority upon which the wise person's well-cultivated self rests can also be recognized through our awareness of the presence of wisdom, compassion and courage in the individual. If in one respect aesthetic authority is always an elusive concept that resists our attempts at any final formulation, yet it can easily be located, if not defined, in the presence of one who exercises the three great moral qualities. And if the authority inherent in such a situation derives neither from the individual nor from the exercise of the three moral qualities, yet they are a mark of the individual's attachment to an aesthetic context through which his qualities and his self-discipline allow an assertion of what is to come to be. In effect, then, Confucius has provided us with the necessary, if oblique, means through which we can gauge the presence of aesthetic authority within any particular flow. First, there must be a human agent located somewhere within that flow, even if that agent is ourselves rather than someone of whom we take note; second, that agent must be aware of the flows of the field *and* his fitting place within them; third, the agent therefore knows how to make choices within the flows upon which he, and perhaps others, can depend. Or we can start from the simple recognition of traits within the very best of humans, and if they clearly possess the wisdom, compassion and courage Confucius finds at the heart of the person who has properly cultivated his life, then we can assume an agent whose knowledge of the flows and his location within them will confer an authority on his assessments of that particular flow.

It goes without saying that saints and divine natures are rare to come by, so even these oblique ways of evaluating aesthetic authority are less than perfect. We might assume, for example, that a person of divine nature would be capable of assessing the flows of all the fields in which he might find himself, and so his authority would be broad indeed. But we are more likely to encounter humans who at best have through their own personal cultivation discerned acutely the flows of maybe only one or two fields, and who therefore have a less comprehensive form of aesthetic authority. More to the point still, there is almost an inverse relationship between the degree of personal cultivation one possesses and the degree to which one is willing to make claims on the basis of any form of authority, aesthetic or otherwise. Confucius is willing to make specific statements about how to achieve the wisdom that is necessary to be a complete human being, yet his utterances are seldom as prescriptive as they might seem, and even more infrequently as prescriptive as we would like them to be. Their specificity is broad and inclusive because it must cover the infinite variety of contexts through which humans gauge their lives, and even if the flows of the fields of which we are a part are regular in many respects, yet every event within every flow is a different one that calls for a unique response. Given this, the best Confucius or any other truly divine nature can do is to provide pointers for the necessary self-discipline that will allow one to achieve wisdom, compassion, and courage, and thus aesthetic authority.

The specificity of Confucius's assertions manages to cover the infinite range of human possibility because Confucius understands that any rules for personal cultivation have to be effected in particular ways, just as every new situation is by definition a new situation. If, for example, Nietzsche acknowledged that he was a man who had greatly conflicting capacities and was more than willing to let us know that fact—in the face of our own desire for an image of the self that is unified, coherent and essential—he was also capable of seeing that those conflicting capacities were needed given the very mixed nature of the world of which we are a part. In a similar way, Confucius is quite aware of the need to see each context and what it demands of one on its own terms, as when he tells us that "When a country is in order, it is a shame to be a poor and common man. When a country is in chaos, it is a shame to be rich and an official" (p. 180). Here is an example of why one must have a sensitiveness to shame, for it always depends on the context in which it is found. If a country truly is in order, it is shameful to be poor and common because the country itself has provided one with the order that should be a stimulus to one's desire for personal order and has given one the best possible circumstances through which to have a good life that is well cultivated. But if a country lacks order, it is shameful to be rich and/or an official because those who are in charge of the wealth and government of the country ought to expend their energies on bringing order to themselves and to the country as a whole. If they have power and authority and chaos reigns, by definition they are decadent, expending their energies on self-indulgent acts rather than disciplining the self in order to create an order through which everyone's life can be made more meaningful.

Given a world in which all authority resides in contexts,

and all contexts are by definition the products of unique events, and given a world in which there are few humans of divine nature, one is forced to put one's wisdom and self-discipline to even greater tests, for one has to act on the basis of aesthetic events in a world that is not driven exclusively—and in the human domain hardly at all—by aesthetic authority. One's choices, therefore, are inevitably going to be weighed in a context that is relative, but not relativistic. Confucius, for example, was given to making distinctions of the following sort: "The people who live extravagantly are apt to be snobbish (or conceited), and the people who live simply are apt to be vulgar. I prefer the vulgar people to the snobs" (p. 180). The implication of this statement is that neither the vulgar people nor the snobs are self-cultivated, and thus one would hope to find neither of them existing as they do. Inasmuch as both do exist in the present world, though, one's values are reflected in one's preference for one of the two groups. And if Confucius would choose the vulgar people over the snobs, that doubtless relates to his belief that in a chaotic world it is a shameful to live extravagantly. The choices one makes do not occur in a vacuum, and thus if aesthetic authority is to have any value for the individual, it must reflect the usefulness of making decisions in a world that remains unconcerned with personal cultivation.

Inasmuch as both Confucius and Nietzsche posit potential types of humans—the divine nature and the overman—one might be inclined to think they are practicing their own forms of idealism, or at the very least that their writing cannot be effective if few people construe the world through their terms. But both Confucius and Nietzsche make it clear that to aspire toward a divine nature or toward the overman is not to create an otherworldly ideal that distracts one from life in this world and makes one vulnerable to the self-interests that dominate it. On the contrary, both models of existence are based on the necessity for acute interpretation of what is, including the wide-ranging nihilism that drives so many of the social flows of which one is inevitably a part. Aesthetic authority cannot in itself overcome the force of self-interested will to power, and in that respect doesn't have much to say about how to live within a society whose authority is traditional. But both Confucius and Nietzsche show that one can indeed live responsibly within such a world and make choices in spite of the relative lack of good possibilities. If one is forced to choose between the vulgar and the snobs, preferring the vulgar is something that effects at least minor change in the socius to the degree that it reflects a viewpoint toward the snobs. That will doubtless not change the snobs' attitude toward their own behavior or toward the choices of one like Confucius, but it does at least call into question the value of their mode of being and thus slightly alters the flows. This is the best anyone can do in situations where one's values are not in accord with the prevailing system, and in some respects the self-discipline both Confucius and Nietzsche demand through the divine nature and the overman must be as intensely cultivated as it is because the socius is never driven by the aesthetics of the world. If it were, personal cultivation would be much easier than it is, the value inherent in an aesthetic event would be easier to determine, and the charismatic voices one heard could be assessed with greater certitude than they can be in a world where the poses of self-interest dominate almost everything.

But if the self-interested drives of the socius compel greater discipline in personal cultivation, that is no reason to imagine that either Confucius's or Nietzsche's aesthetic vision is flawed. Both seek to revalue the values of their society and yet recognize the difficulty inherent in such practices. And both realize that for the most part their own authority will be measured by less than divine natures who aspire toward a better sense of themselves or less than overmen who hope more fully to learn how to love their fates and abjure *ressentiment*. The fact that there are as yet no overmen and few divine natures does not make these aesthetic systems idealistic or mendacious in the least, for their disciplines do not depend on perfection any more than they rely upon a perfect world. And because both disciplines force the individual to cultivate the self *and* the moment—*this* moment, right now, when one is in the midst of the flows of the fields—they are not mendacious in the sense of providing one with a tissue of lies to cover up the horrors of this world. They focus one's attention supremely on this world and don't direct it elsewhere, as most other aesthetic, religious, and political perspectives do. And by forcing one to cultivate one's life as it is in the moment even as their discipline of focussing on the moment prompts one to embrace life fully without question, they have offered us an argument for a revaluation of our own values that ought to be most compelling. At the very least they provide an alternative to the purely self-interested version of authority one confronts every day from the moment one wakes up until one falls asleep at night.

❦

One final way of articulating the sense of aesthetic judgment at the heart of Confucius's work concerns yet again the problem of valuation, the ongoing need for choices in our lives that either measure up to our vision of what humans are capable of or that perpetuate an entirely self-interested sense of the species. One who has properly cultivated his nature will invariably construe the world in different ways, and in some basic respects that change in viewpoint has striking consequences, as Confucius points out via the more normal perspective: "People usually lose their sense of judgment toward those whom they love, toward those whom they despise or dislike, toward those whom they fear, toward those whom they pity and toward those whom they pamper or are proud of. Therefore, there are few people in this world who can see the bad in those whom they like and see the good in those whom they dislike. Hence the saying that 'People do not know their own children's faults, as they do not know the imperceptible growth of the rice plants in their fields.' That is why it is said that those who do not cultivate their personal life cannot regulate their home life" (p. 144, 45). Aesthetic authority, we know, depends on an orientation toward the world that displaces one's self-interest from its usual centrality. That in turn means that one construes the values of the world in different ways and measures events in purely aesthetic terms, gauging their value and their authority in terms of a standard that doesn't bend to suit the convenience of the ordinary interests of the self.

One is thus capable of recognizing the degree to which one tends to shape one's viewpoints in accord with one's established priorities. One values one's family, so one tends to overlook the weaknesses of those within it. One does not know one's children's faults because they are reflections of oneself that encourage one to find in them that which flatters one's self-image. So one hides their faults, buries them or places them onto others. Likewise, one consequently tends to construe the behavior of those whom one dislikes in purely negative terms, finding nothing of redeeming value in the way they act. If it is in one's interests to find only the good in those whom one loves, it is also in one's interests to find only the bad in those whom one despises, for both modes of evaluation make choice much easier, reducing the context to a simple palette of colors that leaves no doubt about what to do.

Confucius is careful to pick out those human relations that most strenuously put to the test our aesthetic vision of things, those to be found in people whom we love, dislike, fear, pity, pamper, and are proud of. Each of these kinds of individuals sways us from an aesthetic perspective for various self-interested reasons. If it is easy for us to see how we are inclined to construe favorably the actions of those we love, pamper, and are proud of, it is also easy to recognize why it is in our self-interest to devalue everything one whom we dislike might do. To recognize flaws in those to whom we are devoted and strengths in those whom we dislike is to call into question our own selves, for the flaw in the one we love might well be a flaw we too possess, and a strength in one whom we dislike might well be a strength that we do not possess, suggesting that the relative value of our own selves and that of the one whom we dislike is less obvious than it appears to us on the basis of our instinctive reactions to the person. Finding strengths in those whom we dislike and weaknesses in those whom we love makes it harder to create a pose for ourselves, forces us to be more rigorous in our evaluations of the sincerity of our will and its effects. And this makes the self-discipline of aesthetic authority much harder to cultivate than it would be if the values to be articulated were invariably clear-cut and transparent.

Equally important is our attitude toward those whom we fear and pity, for these contexts provide still different forces that work against an aesthetic perspective. Quite clearly it is not in our traditional interests to judge properly the acts of one whom we fear, for that is to make such a person more human and to bring him closer to our own selves, something we are loath to do. Likewise, any careful judgment of one whom we fear runs the risk of making the person more fearful still. Out of our own psychic needs we are more apt either to diminish or to increase the person's potential power over us in order to deal with it more predictably, by making it so awesome that it is beyond our control or by so diminishing it that we can almost convince ourselves that there is nothing to fear. When a gap in values and force emerges between our sense of self and our sense of another, we seek to confront that hierarchical difference in self-serving ways to preserve the relative harmony of our psychic lives.

The same is true in the face of those whom we might pity. As Nietzsche never tired of reminding us, pity is in some respects the worst of human emotions, for it makes us less than we could be even as it makes the one we pity less than he or she could be as well. It is a degrading emotion in the sense that its inherent condescension quietly aggrandizes the self while the self-satisfaction of feeling sorry for another diminishes them. Again, the scale of difference tends to be magnified, enhancing our own sense of value and diminishing the value of the other. Confucius's entire point in one respect is that there is little enough difference between the qualitative values of those whom we love and those whom we dislike, between those whom we fear and those whom we pity. Most humans are more or less human in the same sorts of ways with the same decidedly mixed natures and the same inevitably mixed record of choices and values.

And yet out of our own self-interest and need for a convenient nomenclature, we tend as a matter of course to demonize and lionize individuals in order to make the scale of value more straightforward and easier to deal with. If courage is indeed sensitiveness to shame, that is because it is extremely difficult to see honestly the full complexity of human beings who move us strongly one way or the other, and as such these kinds of individuals are a fitting test for the degree to which our authority is dependent on the traditions of self-interest in the midst of which we always find ourselves, or rather on the aesthetic authority that measures the full force and value of any location in terms of the flows of the field rather than construes them through the lens of self-preservation. In this respect, the maturity of one's judgment is always best assessed through these kinds of human relations, for they test the degree to which one is committed to investigating the way things are and the degree to which one is compelled to see what aggrandizes and preserves the central self.

When one thinks through the nature of aesthetic authority, one returns inevitably to one of the terms that links Confucius and Nietzsche, the word "will." Confucius's practice is devoted to the development of the sincere will—though the will's sincerity can be phrased in other ways as well, as the ability to govern oneself or to investigate things or the degree to which one possesses knowledge, and so forth—and Nietzsche's is devoted to the development of the form of will to power that expresses an overabundance of life in the face of the will to power that exudes pure self-interest. Both the Confucian and the Nietzschean will are trained to show us only what is, and the great self-discipline needed to engender the sincere will is necessary only because of the powerful human desire to see things in self-interested ways. If the power within the flows of discourse we participate in is almost always regulated to some degree by those whose interests compel them to shape the flow of language in self-serving ways, that is only to be expected given the great human desire for pose and illusion, given the tendency of the species to prefer mendacious lies to the shameful truths. If our societies are constructed the way they are, that is because this has been the most convenient way of constituting them, at least from the perspective of those who had the power to assert authority over those who must submit. But we tend to ignore how much those who have submitted have also agreed to participate in the game of power in self-serving ways, even if their position forces them into subordination rather than into a position of superiority. We exaggerate the characteristics of both elements in any flow of power and thereby turn the assessment into a morality play that reflects our own interests.

It is extremely difficult for humans to discipline themselves to see what is, to have a sincere will that expresses the overabundance of life that is potentially to be found within all of us. It might seem as though that abundance of life would flow naturally from us, as it indeed does to a great extent in early childhood, but in fact our strengths and our forms of discourse have developed in such a way as to incline us otherwise, to sway us away from our potential as humans who find themselves in the midst of aesthetic flows that are beautiful yet terrifying. Our sense of judgment tends to be clouded by our unwillingness to face the terrors of this planet, to confront the shameful aspects of being human, and so we devote our wills to an equally intense exercise, the shaping of the world in terms of a series of self-interests that engenders specific poses for us and that articulates a world of clear-cut values and demonized and lionized human possibilities. So one form of traditional authority after another perpetuates the same all too self-interested viewpoint through somewhat different individuals, while the aesthetic authority upon which all sincere visions of what is depends remains in scant evidence in our everyday lives.

What we fail to recognize is to be found in an implicit premise in both Confucius's and Nietzsche's work: we do indeed have to devote *great* effort and *great* self-discipline to get the facts of the world to adhere to the vision of ourselves that we seek to will. It requires major effort to create the poses that cover up the uncomfortable facts, the shameful aspects of our being and the terrifying aspects of the flows themselves. And we fail to recognize the great amount of training that goes into the disciplines that prompt us to construe the world in purely self-interested ways. Our mendaciousness is so complete that we fail to see it as mendaciousness, and our societies are so driven by the same mendaciousness that it is easy to assume that one's will hasn't had to expend great energy in fabricating the tissue of lies through which the world can be reduced to one's self-interest. The number of centuries that pass between Confucius and Nietzsche are more than enough to convince us that these human circumstances are hardly new and that our own age is scarcely different in this respect, and probably not any worse than any other era, although its instruments of power may have greater destructiveness. The training of our wills toward self-interest, doubtless an inevitable part of our natures from the beginning, has been going on for so long that by now it seems completely natural, so natural that we have people like Freud who can detail the strategies through which we make the world seem to submit to our desires for it.

If our tendencies toward mendaciousness and self-interest are in some senses "natural," or at least the outgrowth of the very real fears and concerns that any conscious creature would have, our tendencies toward sincerity and toward the investigation of things are also "natural" in the same way, for our species is truly a curious one that seeks things out not merely to preserve itself but also just to see what there is to see. We are born with an interest in *life* as well as a *self*-interest, and there is no inherent reason why we cannot find ways of developing our wills to further the interests of life itself, assuming that thereby we also serve our own interests. That is precisely the authority that is to be found within the aesthetic event, and this form of authority is at the heart of Confucius even as it is central to Nietzsche's work. Neither Confucius nor Nietzsche was an individual of divine nature or an overman, for their work too depended on misperceptions that were driven by cloudy vision and hidden self-interest, even if they came closer to an aesthetic perspective than most humans do.

Confucius was unquestionably committed to a highly conservative traditional form of authority that was pernicious in its effects and discriminatory in the worst of ways, yet he was sufficiently a person of his own time to believe deeply in the vision of authority that is inherent in the hierarchical and patriarchal traditions he sought to uphold. He himself in this respect found ways of construing this traditional authority in superior terms just as one who loves one's child tends not to see the faults in it. Confucius had the intensity of vision to perceive the aesthetic nature of the world in all its fullness, and he had the necessary self-discipline to cultivate himself thoroughly, yet he was still capable of misconstruing the virtues of the system of authority that he upheld and very much wanted to be a part of for many years. At our great cultural and temporal distance from him, we can see the ways in which his vision was indeed truly driven by an aesthetic awareness of the value of life itself and was devoted to establishing forms of discipline through which humans could fully affirm their place within the abundant life around them, but we can also see that even in the midst of one of the most comprehensive and powerful visions of human possibility that has ever been achieved, he also managed to believe in and support a form of traditional authority that was finally antithetical to the aesthetic authority upon which his own work depended.

We have already seen how Nietzsche in several respects worked against his own vision of the overman and the need to love one's fate, but this too is something he shares with Confucius. If Nietzsche is more embraced and reviled in our culture today than Confucius, that is only because Confucius is not one of our cultural measures whereas Nietzsche is. If Confucius were as central to our culture as Nietzsche or Plato is, he too would be exalted and reviled in turn as much as Nietzsche is. The excessive appraisals of both reflect their very real value to us and their very real limitations as humans. That is as it should be, and the mixed yet authoritative voices we hear in them should remind us that finally the authority of their work inheres in a larger context than the "self" to which we append the name "Confucius" or "Nietzsche": it comes from the contexts they articulate that provide us with means for living our lives more fully and affirming them with sincere wills whose sensitivity in the midst of shame and strenuous attention to their own personal conduct reflect the love of knowledge that drives them ever more rigorously to the discipline of life.

# Chapter Four

# The Wiles of Self-Discipline

Perhaps no account of the authority of the aesthetic would be complete without some discussion of at least one of the early texts of our culture, and for that purpose nothing is more suitable than the *Odyssey.* Not only is this the most famous of Western works, but it is also an event that carries great authority even today. In part that authority derives from the pride of place it has at the beginning of our civilization: we can look endlessly for the origin of this or that particular feature of the West in this work because it is there at the beginning and thus represents for us a kind of source for our way of thinking. As with all historical visions of aesthetic texts, though, this way of construing the importance of the *Odyssey* denies its aesthetic authority and puts in its place a merely temporal authority that derives its force from tradition alone rather than from the aesthetic grounds it provides for that tradition.

As with any powerful work, the *Odyssey* thoroughly depends on the values of its time, and we are in many respects far removed from the concerns that established those values. Our struggles tend to be of a different sort than the ones to which Odysseus and his men must attend, and our daily lives are measured out in radically different ways. If we are still all too attentive to the Homeric wish for wealth and creature comforts, our lives are much less uncomfortable, the demands placed upon us are of a generally lesser intensity, and the choices we make present us with much less risk than Odysseus's. On the other hand, these very real benefits also diminish the intensity of our vision and make our lives seem smaller than they are. Measured against the great accomplishments of one like Odysseus, or even of the other individuals who populate the *Odyssey,* there seems, we tell ourselves, little to do with our own energies, for we find no obvious worlds left to conquer and therefore no great goals to drive us onward during our journey through life. Even if we remind ourselves that by definition those who were named in the *Odyssey* were the exceptional humans of the time, those whose inclusion reflects the degree to which their exploits for good or ill were memorable enough to be recorded, still one could argue that if life was more risky back then, it was also more gratifying in some respects because the humans of that era lived so fully in the present and partook more completely of the delights of the world than those of us who live in the much more mediated and abstract structures of the late twentieth century.

At the same time, even a casual glance at Odysseus's exploits reminds us how much more "civilized" we have become. We need only remember that Odysseus's tag line is "man of many wiles" to recognize that in some respects he is the hero that he is chiefly because he could lie better than anyone else. True, he had other gifts, and he was looked upon most favorably by Athena, but in the end he was the man of many wiles, a man who made his long journey successfully only because he could create ruses that would befuddle almost any human. He was also very good at slaughtering other people and could do so with a truly godlike ferocity, and it would seem that his greed knew few bounds. Nor was he oblivious of the desire to achieve a high estimation in the eyes of others.

These traits certainly are not all that extravagant even today—though the ability to slaughter has generally lost its cachet—but they are also not characteristics that we tend to praise publicly. We may or may not secretly wish for the powers and capabilities of Odysseus and recognize that even today those who possess his skills tend to rise far up in the social structure, but our public values are generally in opposition to those espoused by the *Odyssey,* with the exception of Odysseus's great courage in the midst of his fate and the relative fidelity he has for Penelope. These still seem to be virtues in our public discourse, even if we construe both courage and fidelity differently. Nonetheless, unlike him though we be and different as our own values may be, Odysseus still carries an authority that is not to be denied and represents for us a kind of nobility that provides its own fitting measure for what humans can accomplish.

When we consider the authority of the *Odyssey* and of the tale of Odysseus itself, we inevitably need to ask ourselves about the relationship between the gods and the humans in the text, for we know that authority has traditionally derived from whatever gods a culture might have, and we can see throughout the poem that the humans establish their own authority and interpret the authority of others in terms of the gods who determine who shall find favor. To find favor, in this sense, is to have the authority of the gods on one's side, even if in the most obvious respect this favor and its authority come down finally to the simple fact of survival: Odysseus made it through an incredible journey and thus must have received the help of the gods and must therefore be possessed of their authority. Certainly much that is found in the poem can be construed in this manner, suggesting that the gods were first and foremost an interpretive means whereby the Greeks made sense out of the various possible outcomes to lives. Those who strove mightily and did well had special dispensations from the gods; those who did not were clearly not favored. In effect they redoubled an individual's authority by linking his acts to the dispensations of the gods.

The authority of the gods, then, comes into play as a way of accounting for the lack of balance in the fates of the humans, and it can be relied upon in this respect only after the fact to help one account for the reasons why this or that life succeeded so well or failed so miserably. Athena has a special relationship with Odysseus because he is such a godlike human, and he is a godlike human because he has a special relationship with Athena. Of course we know full well that if the relationship to Athena in one sense gives Odysseus more authority, it certainly doesn't make his life easier, for no one struggled more mightily than he did, no one had more miseries to confront. And the struggles themselves must be considered an essential part of Odysseus's authority, for the way in which he succeeded confirms his wiliness—few humans could have escaped all the snares he encountered, and so his ability to do so suggests his mastery at reading situations carefully, or as Confucius would have it, at investigating things and addressing them with a sincere will.

Even if the gods do help the Greeks to measure the respective fates of individuals, though, and thus contribute to the authority the exceptional individuals acquire, they are not a simple means whereby humans escape from responsibility for their own lives. Zeus himself makes this clear at the very beginning of the *Odyssey:*

> "Men are so quick to blame the gods: they say
> that we devise their misery. But they
> themselves—in their depravity—design
> grief greater than the griefs that fate assigns.
> So did Aegisthus act when he transgressed
> the boundaries that fate and reason set.
> He took the lawful wife of Agamemnon;
> and when the son of Atreus had come back,
> Aegisthus murdered him—although he knew
> how steep was that descent."[1]

If the gods like to intrude on the human world—"fate assigns" any number of events to an individual's life—still humans are chiefly responsible for what happens to them, and if their depravity is such that, like Aegisthus, they ignore the "boundaries that fate and reason set," then they are engendering their own descent and can hardly blame some external agent. Clearly, traditional authority is here covered by Zeus in his reference to "the boundaries that fate and reason" set; the rules through which the community establishes itself are partially a function of the fate of the particular social system and partially a result of reasoned rules to keep harmony within the socius. One cannot break these rules and expect to live without the consequences.

As was true for Confucius, traditional authority plays a major role in the lives of the archaic Greeks, first in establishing the boundaries through which lives can be lived, second in providing a clear set of expectations for the individual. There are ways to treat one's kin and one's community as a whole, there are ways to treat strangers and gods, and there are ways of trying to sway the gods or the fates in one's favor. All of these practices are regularly employed in order to effect the best life possible. And even at our distance from their system of values, the Greeks had ingenious ways of seeking to provide order. The rules of guest and host, for example, are designed to protect the safety of both in a potentially precarious situation: people do travel and need to find assistance along the way, just as they and their potential hosts need to avoid the violence that is nearby any time easy plunder might be available. What better way to deal with this situation, we might think, than to believe that any guest could potentially be a god who is checking out the host's fidelity to Zeus's decrees about the need to treat guests well? Inasmuch as the gods could and did take any number of forms, from animals to lowly and great humans, they could at any moment stop at one's door, and if one didn't care for them properly, one would have breached the rules and have lost the authority of the house.

With violence and potential victimage much more a factor of daily life in some ways for the Greeks, the uncertainties of actions and the suspiciousness that was attached to anything out of the ordinary in turn gave it a kind of authority. Indeed, the place of authority in most of the central events in the *Odyssey* manifests itself in an aesthetic context. In one respect, this is almost inevitable, for the people of the time lived much more concretely within the moment than we tend to do and were thus far more attuned to the changes in the local environment. Their lives depended to a larger degree on their ability to interpret the signals they received from others and from the context as a whole, and so the authority to which they attended and the authority they themselves established came from their abilities to mark out the significant moments in an intelligent way.

If Odysseus is known chiefly for his stratagems, and therefore for his ability to respond with authority to a situation that demands it, he should also be known for his *wariness*. Wariness and wiliness are close kin in the lives of the ancient Greeks, and for all practical purposes one is not to be found without the other. An individual tends to assume that every assertion by a human is a ruse of some sort, a pose designed to further the self-interests of the one who makes it; one assumes that the natural world's forces too have the equivalent of their own self-interests, and thus one is perpetually wary, always on guard to note the potential threat. In some respects this feature is more important to Odysseus than his ability to contrive his own ruses, though there can be no denying that his ability to tell compelling lies for his own self-interest is considerable indeed.

A wary attitude could be construed as one that is purely possessed of its own self-interests, and in a way this is true. Odysseus is constantly on the lookout for those things that might threaten his existence, and nothing could be more self-interested than that. But just as Confucius pointed out how difficult it is for us to see the bad in those whom we love and the good in those whom we despise, how our fear of an individual can bend our interpretation of his or her actions and our pity can do likewise, so too a wary *but wise* perspective cannot be overridden by one's desires for particular outcomes. It depends on seeing things as they are, on disciplining the will to note only what is there and not what one fears or hopes for. Odysseus possesses such a perspective—an aesthetic perspective—and it allows him both to assess carefully what is going on around him and to formulate choices on the basis of that assessment. The power of his stratagems, after all, can only come from his ability to know just what will work in any given context, to discern what particular strategy will lead to a positive outcome. Odysseus is ingenious enough to realize that if formulaic responses are fitting in some contexts—hecatombs to this or that god are *always* helpful—in the murky world of human affairs the unique response to the current situation is the wily one, not a generic reaction that assumes all contexts to be the same.

The gods are also connected to the abilities of one like Odysseus to read the situations in which he finds himself, even though at times the opposite is also the case. Athena, for example, places a mist around him when he arrives home in Ithaca and thus keeps him from recognizing where he is. His befuddlement is great until the mist is lifted, and while we might characterize the reasons for this mist in any number of ways—his memory is shot after all those years and trials, and he can no longer recall what his home is like; there has been considerable urban renewal and the place hardly resembles the one he left twenty years earlier—in fact most of the mists in the *Odyssey* simply suggest that human knowledge only carries a certain distance and doesn't always extend itself as far in one situation as it does in others. Odysseus, if you will, is wily and therefore capable of penetrating many of the metaphorical mists that surround events, but his powers of interpretation are not universally applicable, and at times they simply fail, sometimes for reasons that are obvious, sometimes for reasons that remain misty themselves.

One of the most intriguing things about Odysseus, after all, is the way his attention wanders and focusses itself, for wiliness and wariness are dependent on attention, and we might think, therefore, that Odysseus is one who through personal cultivation always manages to attend fully to the moment and what it presents him with. Surely his capacity to respond intelligently comes from his powerful abilities of concentration, but still, his mind wanders, his discipline flags, his senses mist over, and he makes mistakes, sometimes *huge* mistakes. Most obviously, it was not in Odysseus's interests to harass the Cyclops, as even his men recognize full well:

> "Why must you goad that savage so? Just now,
> the mass that monster cast into the sea
> drove back our ship to shore: we thought we'd reached
> our end. And if he'd heard us breathe or speak
> even the slightest word, he would have hurled
> one more rough rock and smashed our heads and hull.
> That brute has force to spare: he can throw far."
> (p. 189, 90)

Odysseus should recognize that it could be very destructive for him to let the Cyclops know who he is, but he is so taken with his own success—and so driven by resentful anger for what the Cyclops has done to his men—that he loses sight of the situation and tells him his name, thereby guaranteeing further grief for himself down the road. His attention lapses, his wiliness is overcome by the powerful emotions that accompany the success of stratagems and the release that comes from having escaped a perilous situation. And without the usual strict attention to the situation, grave mistakes are made that easily could have been avoided if only Odysseus had determined the need to see the situation clearly. The mistiness of his own mind's surging force keeps him from seeing what he should.

Likewise, Odysseus's curiosity can also be an impediment, even if we might think otherwise. Confucius did state the need to investigate the things of the world, and Odysseus has that overriding interest. Unfortunately, human as he is, he doesn't always recognize that curiosity should be overridden by cautiousness at times, as we find once again in his fatal mistake to stay around the Cyclops's den long enough to see what he is like:

> "My comrades urged
> our quick departure—though they wanted me
> to take the cheeses, above all, and then
> drive from the fold those sheep and goats and stow
> those stores on our swift ship. That done—they said—
> we should be off, to sail across the sea.
> But I ignored their counsel, though that course
> would have avoided many griefs for us.
> Instead I had to wait to see that man,
> to find out if he'd welcome me. But then
> the courtesy he showed my friends was scant."
> (p. 181)

Odysseus is curious about whether or not the Cyclops will welcome him and his crew, wants to find out if he listens to the gods or rather is unwilling to treat guests as Zeus would demand, but in waiting to discover this fact, he costs several of his crew their lives. The potential dangers of the situation should have suggested to Odysseus that this was not the place to wait to find such things out, but his curiosity gets the better of them. He desires only to see the way things are, yet in some cases fails to base his own vision on what he knows about the potential for danger.

Indeed, we would *expect* Odysseus to act differently in this situation, for we know that he *is* a wary person. One of the formulaic utterances Homer gives him reflects fully his own understanding of every new situation where strangers are encountered, as seen here just before Odysseus and Nausicaa meet:

> "What misery is mine? What mortals must
> I meet in this new land that I now touch?
> Are they unfeeling beings—wild, unjust?
> Or do they welcome strangers—does their thought
> include fear of the gods? That cry I heard,
> the cry that captured me, was tender—like
> the voice of young girls—voice of nymphs who haunt
> the steepest mountain peaks, the springs that feed
> the rivers, and the green of grazing lands.
> Can men with human speech be here—close by?
> But I must try—must see with my own eyes." (p. 121)

Odysseus is always immediately on his guard, always worried that those he is about to meet will be "unfeeling beings" with no civilized forms through which to mediate the uncertain relations between guest and host. Whether or not they welcome strangers is to him another way of asking whether or not their thought includes fear of the gods, for if it does, then they will truly welcome strangers.

Wily and full of stratagems as he is, capable of attending fully to the moment and discerning its nuances in order to determine whether there is danger or not, Odysseus seeks to gauge the degree to which a stranger possesses fear of the gods. And yet with the Cyclops it was curiosity and not wariness that drove him to wait and see if the Cyclops treated guests as Zeus had directed. We might think that because Odysseus meets Nausicaa after the encounter with the Cyclops that the wariness in the present context stems from the earlier calamity, but Odysseus knew well before he ran into the Cyclops that one should always be wary of the intentions of others. It simply seems to be the case that, adventurer that he is, he lets his curiosity get the best of him at times and pays mightily for it. Instead of attending fully to the potential of the moment, his discipline lapses, his mind metaphorically mists over, and dangers invade.

❦

We recognize this lapsing of attention or discipline in other contexts too. If in a general way one of Odysseus's best traits is his fidelity to wife and home, that faithfulness is measured in his commitment to keep them firmly in mind for twenty years when he could just as easily have been swayed to stay in any number of places. Certainly the life he had with Calypso was quite pleasing, and he could have lived forever if he had stayed with her. So we are meant to admire him because his mind arches from the past toward a future in which he returns to Penelope and his own home, and we respect him because he is willing to give up immortality for that goal. At the same time, particularly given the make-up of the ancient Greeks, we perhaps lose sight of what an amazing feat of self-discipline it was for Odysseus to be intent for so many years on the goal of returning home. Many another would have been swayed away from the goal by fatigue, to say nothing for the highly pleasing potential to be found with one like Calypso. Still others would lose their great desire to return home as their memories of it gradually faded. Given the adventures and difficulties Odysseus underwent, an entire lifetime of vivid memories, there is more than enough reason for him gradually to lose interest in returning to his place of origin. But his discipline is such that he keeps a more or less steady course in his mind, and that course leads him back to Ithaca.

The route back to the homeland, though, is not always on Odysseus's mind, and this too reflects his all too human capacity, the fact that even his attention lapses, his discipline gives way, and the goal is temporarily thwarted. Sometimes this is the result of despair, as when we find him on Calypso's island. When we first see him:

> He was seated
> along the shore; his eyes were never dry,
> and his sweet life was squandered as he wept
> for his dear home; he now took no delight
> in her: the nymph no longer pleased his sight.
> (p. 102)

Consumed by his own despair, Odysseus no longer spends his time devising stratagems, as we might think such a man would; his self-discipline gone slack, he festers in the midst of his own self-pity, obsessed by home and yet incapable of trying to devise ways to return. So "his sweet life was squandered as he wept," and he thus has been stripped of those characteristics that most distinguished him from other humans: his curiosity, his wiliness and wariness, the aesthetic authority that comes from his ability to assess situations, his becoming mien, and the commitment to cultivate the self in order to see things as they are. His attention has indeed lapsed, but the passage also makes clear a different notion of attention, for in saying that "the nymph no longer pleased his sight," Homer is telling us that Odysseus didn't mind dallying with her for a while. She satisfied his urges and his curiosity for a time, but now he has become jaded, and he takes no delight in her.

One of the things that makes Odysseus's feats of attention so striking is that the people of the *Odyssey* have a considerably different sense of temporality than we have and were quite content to spend a year or so in a strange place taking in its delights. They may or may not have been committed to returning from whence they came, but the laws of host and guest and the general flows of life were such that any serious interaction between proper guests and hosts could go on for what we today would think of as an extraordinary length of time. To be sure, the relatively great distances and difficulties of travel would prompt one to stay longer in foreign places once one arrived there, but the fact that Odysseus and his men were quite willing in some cases to spend a year or more visiting others suggests a willingness to let the context—and one's relative fatigue with it—

determine how and when one moved on. Given this, it is indeed striking that Odysseus made it all the way back to his home after all those years and their many diversions.

Odysseus has his lapses here too, though, as we find when he stays with Circe, whose delights are compelling enough for him to forget entirely about his homeland. Only his crew urges him to remember his overarching goal:

> "Day after day we stayed for one whole year:
> we ate much meat; the wine was honey-sweet.
>
> "But when the months that fill a year had passed,
> and seasons had revolved, and once again
> the long days reached their end, my comrades said:
>
> "'Wake from your trance, remember your own land,
> if fate is yet to save you, if you can
> still reach your high-walled house, your native isle.'
>
> "These were their words. And my proud heart
> agreed." (p. 210)

Quite clearly the delights that Circe and her isle provide are more than compelling, so much so that even the somewhat typical lengthy stay grows so long that Odysseus alone remains uninterested in returning home. His comrades urge him to "Wake from [his] trance," suggesting yet a different kind of mist in his mind on this occasion, one that has sapped his will to return to his homeland and swayed him away from the self-discipline that is necessary to keep that thought in his mind.

Odysseus's crewmen point out that his problem is that he has forgotten his own land, and they seek to compel him to remember it, arguing that "if fate is to save [him]," he will have to be roused from the trance that has prompted him to succumb to the local pleasures Circe can provide in abundance. Such an utterance suggests that Odysseus will be truly lost if he remains with Circe, that at the very least he will become something other than he was, the man of many wiles whose furious will insisted on a return to Ithaca, a man whose stratagems and assessments of the world were without equal. The man who reclines with ease and drinks the honey-sweet wine and eats the surfeit of meat is not the same man who attended fully to the reality in front of him and yet kept his mind on his final goal of a return home. If he lapses into self-pity and therefore into the absorbing pit of emotion with Calypso, with Circe he slips into an absorption with the delights of the moment and loses sight of his goal.

In stressing that Odysseus's greatness stems from his incredible self-discipline and his fierce ability to attend to the moment, and in showing those places where these great qualities leave him for a time and force him to be recalled to who he is by others, I want to suggest that in the end the qualities we find in Odysseus are connected to the personal cultivation of Confucius and to the full aesthetic affirmation of the world of Nietzsche. True, Odysseus is far from a saint or a divine nature, and he certainly has overcome neither his *ressentiment* nor even his own emotions. His "lapses" in this sense, the degree to which he is allowed to fall short of his own great capabilities at times, imply that he is much less than one who is a saint or who loves his fate without question.

If this is true, though, it is equally the case that Odysseus as a result is probably much more like Confucius and Nietzsche themselves than like the ideals posited in their work. His very strength as a character comes from the fact that he both possesses the qualities of greatness and yet fails always to be great. He can wallow in self-pity with the best of them, he can go literally mad with anger or be overcome by the pleasures of wine and meat and sex, and at times he needs to be called back to himself by others. He is also part of a culture that is wholly committed to vengeance, and both Confucius and Nietzsche were opposed to the endless resentments that such a commitment entails. This is a crucial difference in Odysseus that marks him as a special case, and whether we wish to attribute this difference to his uniqueness, to the relatively "primitive" nature of his cultural circumstances, or to the generally vengeful tendencies of the West itself, we cannot ignore that the viciousness with which Odysseus is capable of attending to his own desires for blood vengeance is both awesome and horrific to us and inimical to the visions of both Confucius and Nietzsche. Nevertheless, his genius resides in his aesthetic awareness and in his ability to attend fully to what is, to see only what is there and to determine what needs to be done on that basis.

When we think of the relationship between Confucian self-discipline and the aesthetic authority to which it is finally connected, we can discern another function the gods take up in the *Odyssey:* they are a way of accounting for the discipline to be found in people's lives. In this sense, Odysseus is favored by the gods because of his great attentiveness to what is, to his disciplined ability to confront what he sees; his life is charmed to the extent that he can do these things, and when he falls short of the mark, it is almost always because his attention has lapsed, because his discipline has slipped and he has fallen into self-pity or into an absorption with the delights of the moment. We find this connection between self-discipline, attention, and the gods early on in the *Odyssey* when Athena first begins to prod Telemachus down the path toward maturity. When Telemachus is inclined to use his own wariness as a strategy through which he can doubt his parentage and thereby avoid the fact that he is old enough to begin to think of ways of addressing the abominations of the suitors, Athena becomes outraged and upbraids him in the strongest terms:

> "The absent one, Odysseus, is indeed
> the man whom you, unhappy son, could use:
> he'd break the back of this marauding band. . . .
> For if Odysseus were to show himself
> among this pack of suitors with the same
> strength he showed then, they all would meet quick death
> and bitter wooing. . . . But for yourself, you must consider
> the way in which to rid the house of suitors." (p. 15)

Lest Telemachus miss the point that his shameful lack of willingness to confront the suitors is something that needs to be attended to, Athena leaves no room for doubt:

> "Forget the pastimes of a child: you are
> a boy no longer. Or have you not heard
> what fame Orestes gained when he avenged
> the murder of his father?" (p. 16)

Athena goads Telemachus with the deeds of his own father and shows how little he measures up to Odysseus—if Telemachus doubts who his father is, his own lack of resolve might indeed cause others to wonder who his father is as well—and for further incentive she insists that he is preoccupied by the "pastimes of a child" at a time when he is no longer a boy. If that is not enough, she compares his behavior unfavorably to that of famed Orestes who avenged the murder of his father and thereby took upon him the maturity that events demanded of him. Telemachus quite clearly has failed to answer the call the suitors should be prompting him to.

The result of Athena's words is one of those great changes of state that occur fairly regularly in the *Odyssey:*

> When that was said, gray-eyed Athena left,
> quick as a bird. Within his heart she'd set
> resolve and strength and memories more intense—
> more bent upon his father—than before.
> And he was pensive, marveling, aware
> that he had had some god as visitor. (p. 17)

We can choose to construe these remarks literally, as though Athena really did intervene and prod Telemachus, or we could see them as a reflection of Telemachus's own inner battles. He knows full well what he should be doing, but it is hard to make the transition from youth to adulthood, and it is even harder to move from one role to the other when one is confronting a problem of the magnitude that the suitors present him with. Recognizing what should be his duty, acutely aware of what his great father would do if he were there, Telemachus thus goads himself through the seeming prodding of a god. *Somehow* he has suddenly achieved the "resolve and strength" he needed, and that change has been fused to "memories more intense" of his father and the measure he should live up to. If he is "aware / that he had had some god as visitor," that reflects his own surprise at his change. How could he be a boy one moment and a man the next? From whence comes the change of state? Inasmuch as he couldn't find resolve on his own before, it is seemingly implausible that he should find it now. So a god must have been present, Athena must have effected the changes in him, even if he doesn't quite know that it is her.

The results of Telemachus's sudden resolve are equally striking. Once he has made his mind up that it is time for him to be a man, he wastes no time at all:

> At once he went among the suitors—he,
> a mortal like a god. The flawless bard
> was chanting still; the suitors sat in silent
> astonishment. (p. 17)

The suitors cannot believe that Telemachus could have changed so quickly, for he now is "a mortal like a god" rather than a young boy with a comely appearance but nothing to suggest godlike strength or courage. And yet Telemachus gives a speech to them that makes it clear in no uncertain terms that "within this house, I have authority" (p. 18). In part, we might think, he has authority because he has decided that he should have it and that he can uphold it; simple resolve, we know, can often accomplish a great deal. At the very least, it can change one's appearance, if not quite as drastically as the scene above suggests, and it can provide others with an immediate awareness of a change, real or contrived. And if we assume that the ancient Greeks were at their best more attuned to some kinds of changes than we are, or perhaps simply had a sufficiently different sense of the world for them to perceive great changes where we would find minor ones, there is no reason not to think that Telemachus could have had this striking effect on the suitors just because of a change in resolve. The new strength he feels brings a focus and a discipline to his actions that they previously lacked precisely because he was at odds with himself. Once he has brought unity to his mind, his mien could change considerably.

It is worth stressing that even if the resolve did more or less in one sense come from within him, Telemachus quite obviously doesn't believe in a subjective self in the way we do, so he would not see things that way; hence the presence of the god accounts for changes we might think of as a reflection of our own subjectivity, or perhaps as a moment when the superego and the ego reconcile their two visions of what the individual ought to be doing. But if Telemachus doesn't have available to him a sense of interiority that would allow him to realize the part he himself played in bringing his self-discipline finally to bear, he is nonetheless right to recognize that in a real way the change within him *did* come from outside of him, prompted by the conflict within the house that has set him deeply at odds with himself. If we are inclined to see Athena's presence here as a bit absurd, we ourselves might look equally ridiculous to one who recognized the degree to which our own ideas of subjective states are equivalent illusions in our own era.

That Telemachus addressed something outside of as well as "within" himself is reflected in the fact that both he and the suitors recognize immediately and with astonishment that he is no longer what he was. He does indeed have authority, even if he has yet to learn how to exercise it as well as he will need to. Quite clearly Antinous may have been astonished and may recognize a great change in Telemachus, but he is hardly going to change his own attitude as a result:

> "Telemachus, the gods indeed may teach
> brash blustering to you and braggart speech.
> But let us hope that they'll not intervene,
> that Cronos' son will not make you the king
> of seagirt Ithaca, whatever claim
> your birth might bring." (p. 19)

His mien charged with concentration and resolve, his words evincing a newly authoritative role, Telemachus seeks to effect immediate change in the suitors, but they are not about to take his words with authority regardless of his change of mien or nobility of speech. To them he is full of "brash blustering" and "braggart speech," words not backed up by any real measure that would be capable of truly manifesting authority. So they will come very quickly to see him as a threat, as one to be done away with if possible, and thus tacitly recognize a kind of authority he has achieved, but they will not acknowledge the power of that authority in their own lives, regardless of his upbringing, his birthright, or his change of state.

One might think that once Telemachus was rebuked in such a fashion by Antinous he would lapse into at least temporary uncertainty, but no, he has indeed been well and truly changed, and if the suitors have yet to recognize his authority in any but a negative way—by perceiving him as a threat to be eliminated—he still carries himself in a new way that reflects the kind of resolve that may have lapses but will carry him a long way. So when the next day comes, he is if anything more resplendent than he was the day before, more overwhelming in his presence, more clearly one whose authority resides within an aesthetic context in the largest of senses:

> Firstlight: when Dawn's rose fingers touched the sky,
> the dear son of Odysseus—quick to rise
> and dress—soon set within his shoulder strap
> his sharp blade; to his feet—anointed, sleek—
> he tied fine sandals. As he crossed the threshold,
> he seemed a god. At once he told his heralds—
> with voices clarion-clear—to call a council.
> The long-haired Ithacans were soon assembled.
> Then he, his lance of bronze held fast, advanced—
> but not alone: behind, two brisk hounds paced.
> On him Athena shed a deathless grace,
> and all the people marveled as he came
> to the assembly ground. He took his place:
> his father's seat. The elders all gave way. (p. 25)

Telemachus rises early and alertly, eager for the day to begin, ready to take on the challenges that come with the authority he now feels within him. He "seemed a god" as he crossed the threshold, perfect in qualities, powerful in manner, authoritative from head to foot. He gives orders for the council meeting as though he had been giving them his entire life, and "all the people marveled as he came / to the assembly ground." Again the transformation is due in part to the temporary intervention of Athena, who "shed a deathless grace" on him that would carry the true force of a godlike mien, but whatever the local and general causes, Telemachus here takes up his position as Odysseus's rightful heir and states his case with clarity.

Indeed, not only is Telemachus changed in his appearance and discourse, but he is suddenly capable of making the mature rather than the puerile argument. He doesn't whine about his stocks being depleted or the absence of his father; rather, he warns the people that they should turn away from the actions of the suitors for their own good:

> "You, too, should scorn their ways and feel the force
> of shame for what your neighbors here have wrought:
> beware—the gods, grown angry for these acts
> of malice, may assault you in their wrath." (p. 27)

This is by no means the argument of a child. On the contrary, it displays great persuasive skill in calling attention to the shamefulness of the suitors' actions and reminds the people that the gods could turn on them as well once their anger for the way in which the suitors have violated the laws urges them into action. These words are compelling and carry great force. They are authoritative in the best of senses, for they are the perfect response to the situation that confronts Telemachus. In bringing order to himself, in disciplining his mind and focussing it with resolve upon that which needs to be done, he has also developed the concomitant ability to assess and articulate what circumstances he confronts and what the best course of action is. He knows the suitors are not going to change their ways just because he is now grown up and ready to take his proper place, so his confident and careful appeal to the people as a whole is the next best strategy available to him. Telemachus has gained all sorts of new powers in no time at all, and in that respect he truly is a wonder.

Of course, Telemachus does indeed have his lapses. It won't be long before he is whining to Mentor/Athena:

"Mentor, how shall I meet, how shall I greet him [Nestor]?
I'm still unskilled at subtle turns of speech.
When one is young, he may indeed be blamed
for questioning his elder. I'm ashamed." (p. 43)

A fresh day might begin with great resolve, but new challenges still call into question his sense of his capabilities. He remembers that he was just a boy a short time ago and therefore has yet to discover a way of addressing elders from the position of an adult himself. And even though we have already seen that his speech is fine indeed, he worries about finding the proper words when he must ask about Odysseus's fate. In short, he is ashamed and self-conscious and seemingly unready for the tasks ahead of him, even though he seemed nearly invulnerable only a short time before. He has yet to develop sufficient confidence in his gifts to carry his authority into the regions into which it must go, but that, we know, is what experience does and what his own experiences will do, making him seasoned enough in his authority to be a fitting ally of his father when he returns.

If Telemachus questions his authority here and turns self-consciously to evaluate his present skills, Mentor/Athena manages to provide a wise response to his worries that applies perfectly to his situation and to the origins of authority within anyone:

"Telemachus, your mind will prompt some words;
others will come to you—a god will urge.
I do not think that you were born and raised
without the gods' attentive tutelage." (p. 43, 44)

Authority comes in part from assuming that the proper response will be forthcoming to the degree to which one attends fully to the given situation. Thus, Telemachus need only not worry about what words to use, and his "mind will prompt some words" that will suit the occasion. The urging of some god will allow others to come to him, a nobler inspiration still, making him eloquent and compelling in his speech. The site of inspiration is thus a combination of self-assured, self-disciplined confidence in one's own authority and the promptings of a god who urges the mind to say things it wouldn't on its own. Once Telemachus masters these simple lessons, he will lose his concern for the right word, and his shame will disappear.

Athena's advice makes use of phrases that are linked to the bards of the *Odyssey* as well, so what Telemachus is told reflects Homer's sense of the origin of all rhetorical inspiration. Before Demodocus begins the tale of Troy for Odysseus, for example, the moment is set with the following words: "And when a god had urged / the singer, he began" (p. 167). Master of the art of "supremely sweet" song that is "sung with style and truth" (p. 166), Demodocus's gift lies in his willingness to wait for the moment when a god urges his mouth to begin, prompts him to chant the words that will enchant his audience and reflect his mastery of self and knowledge of the world and of poetry. The truth of Demodocus's poetry is not to be distinguished from the truth that is to be found in Telemachus's rhetoric as he inquires of Nestor about his father's whereabouts. Both depend on the careful attention to the urgings of the god who will help their words to emerge. By themselves, the words would not ring true enough.

Depending on the perspective from which we construe these things today, we might be inclined to move in one of two directions when we take account of the magic of poetry. Some of us would refer to an individual's subjectivity as the origin of poetic utterance and would locate the genius of the person in the internal essence of the self. Others of more recent vintage would make reference to the endless play of signs of which we are all a part and would thus dissolve the poet into the midst of the play and thus displace linguistic genius into the interstices of language itself. Indirectly, of course, this is the result of work like Foucault's that insists it doesn't, or at least shouldn't, matter who is speaking.

Both the internalized and externalized visions of "inspiration" contrast with what Homer portrays, for to him poetic utterance seems to exist in neither the internal nor the external spaces we would tend to locate it. Poetic inspiration provokes wonder or astonishment in the humans of the *Od-*

*yssey* in much the same way as Telemachus provoked the shocking effects he had upon the suitors, and the location of the astonishment, accounted for most often through a combination of the individual himself and the presence of the gods—Telemachus's ability to provoke astonishment, that is, depends on his own appeal, but he also needs the help of Athena to be truly provocative—is neither purely in the self nor in the god. It is worth noting that figures like Telemachus and Odysseus are never *taken over* by the presence of Athena or some other god; rather, the god always performs some kind of magic upon them that transforms them into godlike creatures. The "inspiration" in this sense isn't literally breathed through them but more applied to the outside to reflect a change "within."

Raymond Prier's recent work on Homer and sight and appearance deals with the site of wonder by seeking to establish a region of experience that is similarly neither internal nor wholly external but rather what he would characterize as "intermediating." In speaking of what the wonder of the gods and the wonder that humans can induce have in common, Prier tells us that "The common point of focus of the wonder of gods and men is clearly, then, an 'amazing deed.' It is the *ergon* toward which their 'lines' of sight-wonder are directed and the purveyor or point of meaning in that place between the two, that is, in the phenomenological intermediation between 'this' and the 'other.'"[2] What Prier here characterizes as "the phenomenological intermediation between 'this' and the 'other'" is a region that is neither to be ascribed to the subjective states of the individual nor to the purely external imposition of a state upon that individual but rather something that comes to be in the midst of those internal and external states, something that mediates between the two.

A moment of wonder in this sense is a context in which the individual "this"—a word employed by Prier in part to avoid the false imposition of a word like "subjectivity," just as his use of "other/that" seeks among other things to avoid a word like "objective"—and the "that" outside of it are brought together through the lines of sight that connect them. They are no longer specifically a "this" and an "other," but are rather linked to this region of wonder that yokes them into an aesthetic experience. Prier himself does not refer to these linkages in terms of aesthetic experience, nor, doubtless, would he be comfortable with my assertion that he has located here the site of aesthetic authority, but he has characterized the relationship between sight and appearance in Homer in a way that is relatively uncontaminated by the now-traditional presuppositions of internal and external states to which we so readily refer, and thus he has gone some distance toward locating that region of "intermediation" through which all authority, that of the gods and that of humans, is established.

In a way, Prier's point about wonder is quite simple: "*Phenomenologically, wonder must have its outside instigation*" (p. 79). Wonder or astonishment does not come from within, and nothing "subjective" can provoke it; it always comes from some outside instigation that pulls the individual in turn out of his or her normal ways of conceiving of things. Another way Prier gets at this phenomenon is to suggest that it is neither this nor that: "Observing the god-given ritual of the dance, Odysseus is struck with wonder. This wonder is either produced by or produces the vision of the floor, the dancers, and the glancing 'light' movement of their feet. Odysseus marvels, it seems, at a work of geometric art" (p. 82, 83). To suggest that Odysseus's wonder is "either produced by or produces the vision of the floor" and the dance that takes place on it is to imply that in a real way we have no satisfactory means of accounting for his wonder, for we would tend to think of the site as being *either* the vision itself *or* the subjective energies that in turn allow the dance to engender wonder. Is this wonder a function of Odysseus's "subjective" creativity or a pure product of the dance's work upon his psyche? Clearly, Prier suggests, it is both and neither, or rather not really quite either one. Something is produced through the coming together of Odysseus's lines of sight and the dance, and the result is wonder, but to say what part Odysseus and what part the dance had in producing the event is to arrive in murky territory without a guide.

The important point is that such moments of wonder in the *Odyssey* prompt us to rethink our relationship to that which provokes wonder or that which engenders inspiration or that which establishes aesthetic authority, for Homer makes it clear that all three of these human phenomena are different aspects of the same event. He who has authority is he who provokes wonder through the mien he possesses or through the sweet words through which he commands those over whom he has authority; he who chants poetry provokes wonder through the aesthetic authority of his words, through their sweet truths; he who is taken up by wonder responds to an aesthetic authority to be found within the event, yet he himself is part of that event, and thus the authority also rests partially within him. Again, we lack the language adequately to delineate precisely with straightforward prose the implications of this region, as Prier's own "phenomenological" contortions demonstrate, but there is little doubt that our traditional ways of articulating the context of wonder or the location of authority fail to account for that to which we respond in such situations, and without a better understanding of this most important site of human experiences, we are forced to conclude with Foucault that it doesn't matter who's speaking and turn to the equally traditional forms of self-interest we have been much more adept at developing.

It is true, as Prier argues, that Homer accounts for this region of sight and wonder in similar ways when he is talking about phenomena we would keep quite separate. The very linkages I made above between the poet and Telemachus would not generally be countenanced in our usual ways of thinking about authority, for we believe that the authority of someone like Telemachus or Odysseus is of a different nature than the authority of a poet like Demodocus. They may have in common a reliance on the urgings of a god through which they can at times produce sweet words, but the one context is the pragmatic one of human relations and political governance whereas the other has to do with the major forms of entertainment we and the Greeks possess. These two social sites remain more or less discrete to our way of thinking, and

Homer brings us back to a serious reconsideration of their very real linkages within aesthetic authority, that region in which neither subjective desire nor objective compulsion speaks but rather that which engenders subjectivity and objectivity in the first place.

We should also remember that the region of sight and wonder, of the appearances that engender astonishment, is not restricted exclusively to the political or the poetic world in Homer. Obviously the games of which the Greeks were fond, the contests to measure strengths of one kind or another, occupy the same region, and wonder can clearly be provoked in the ancient Greeks by the appearance of a body with beautiful characteristics. "Battle too may be an object of wonder" (p. 87), Prier reminds us, and so we shouldn't so easily reduce the experience to a few human locations. On the contrary, everywhere we find states with overpowering affective components to them, we are in the region of amazement that so governs the world as a whole for the Greeks, and that determines so much of what happens in our own world today, even if we remain far more oblivious of its effects because of our different ways of constituting these experiences and the lessened affectiveness to which we attend.

In order to understand better these states of wonder and the authority they provoke, we might think a bit more about what the poetic context and the political context we saw in Telemachus have in common. We could, for example, look at the moment in the *Odyssey* when Odysseus demonstrates through his remarks to Alcinous his appreciation of the value of song:

> "Alcinous, the king all men revere,
> it surely is a pleasant thing to hear
> a singer like Demodocus, a man
> whose voice is like the gods'. I say we reach
> the deepest of delights when, at a feast,

> beside the tables heaped with bread and meat,
> men, seated in due order, fill the hall
> and listen to a harper: joy takes all,
> and the cupbearer draws wine from the bowl
> and brings it round and brims the cups: my soul
> finds nothing on this earth more beautiful." (p. 173)

If Odysseus thinks that Demodocus is a singer "whose voice is like the gods'," that is because of the "style and truth" of what he has sung about the "fate of the Achaeans." Odysseus recognizes the truth in what Demodocus has sung because he himself was there, but what strikes him is that the poet "sang as if [he] had been there [himself] / or heard this tale from who shared those trials" (p. 166). The plausibility of the account is great, and that in combination with the beautiful style of Demodocus's words makes the song compelling indeed, sufficient to provoke both wonder and tears in Odysseus.

The wonder that a poet provokes, then, is unquestionably related to the style and truth through which his song is sung, and without the power of words and the discipline to speak truly, no wonder would be forthcoming. But Odysseus's remarks to Alcinous suggest that the context for wonder goes deeper still and depends on the rich and complex event of the feast itself. It is not simply that one needs first to fill one's belly full of food and wine before one can enjoy the tales of a singer; rather, the "deepest of delights" of a feast composed of "tables heaped with bread and meat," and men "seated in due order" and the brimming cups of wine and the sweet truths of the poet are all conceived of as part of the same experience. The delights of the one seep into the pleasures of the others, creating a rich experience of many senses that is designed thoroughly to sate one's desire for ease and satisfaction.

If "joy takes all" in such circumstances, and if the larger situation thus helps to engender the wonder provoked by a poet's song, it is clearly the product of a set of external events that have associated with them both tradition and the very real pleasures the senses can offer. Poetry's ability to astonish humans is seen as part of this larger experience of the feast and is not centralized in the words of the poet alone, not exclusively in either their style or their truth. The style and the truth are seen as partial functions of the context of the feast, song that comes through the poet as a result of the gift of voice given to him by a "gracious god." And if the event itself embraces everything to do with the feast and doesn't localize the astonishment in the words of the poet, then we must assume that the capacity for wonder within humans is also part of this larger context, or at the very least is more likely to come about as a part of such a rich situation.

We can readily enough provide some of the concomitant requirements for these deep delights to be found at the feast by assuming that such an event generally would occur only in circumstances that were thought to be *safe*. The measure of the guest would have been taken, and the possibilities for ease and delight could come about only when the potential threat of the visitor would have been overcome by some sort of assurance that he was truly "civilized" and thus feared the gods and obeyed the laws of hospitality. We can assume that a good bit of the delight of a feast comes from putting down one's wariness for a time. Even Odysseus, wiliest of men, must surely grow weary of warily assessing every move and utterance of the people around him, and delight is only possible, and is a direct result of, not having to worry every moment about what potential dangers might lurk in the immediate environment.

At the same time, it is worth noting that Odysseus doesn't emphasize the negative way of construing these aesthetic delights, as we might be more inclined to do in this century. He doesn't say that he loves a feast because it allows him to forget his cares and provides him with a context in which he doesn't have to think about the motives of those around him. He doesn't claim a great need to lay down the burdens of his self and give himself over to inebriation and stupor. On the contrary, he sees the experience in positive terms, as "the deepest of delights" would suggest; it is not *relief* he is after but rather an immersion into those experiences that allow one most fully to enjoy that which is capable of giving pleasure to humans. The abundance of the food and wine—as we see in the emphasis on "tables *heaped* with bread and meat" and cups that *brim* with wine—engenders delight in the straightforward way of providing one with more than enough to fulfill one's desires, but it also contributes to the experience by suggesting a world in which one's desires can *always* be met. The very abundance suggests that no lack is just around the corner, waiting for one after the completion of this final feast. The *idea* of abundance, and the way it too can provoke its own kind of wonder through images of perfect fulfillment, is as much a part of the complex experience of the feast as is the taste of the food and the drink.

These delights are capped by the singer whose chant of style and truth both entertains and provokes wonder, compels the audience to listen and moves them deeply. In the particular context at hand, Alcinous has had to stop the entertainment because the power of Demodocus's song has prompted Odysseus to tears and moaning. We know that the moaning has to do with Odysseus's identification with his own past trials, and so there is more than just cause for it, and he would obviously be moved by this tale more intensely than others simply because it is *his* tale. But we can assume that generally such audiences took delight in the accounts of war and bloodshed and final triumph and loss because they had the ring of truth to them, because they reflected the way the people saw their own history and construed the trials and delights of their own lives. Just as we today are given at times to saying how "true to life" this or that is, so too Demodocus's audience assesses his song in terms of the degree to which it is true to life. And just as surely, his great reputation as one who has learned his gift from the gods comes from his ability to evoke so completely a sense of reality through the style of his words. Their seeming reality engenders a reality in the audience that creates the astonishment they feel when they have been taken outside of themselves to that region of intermediation to which Prier refers.

We know how much more concrete and physical the lives

of the Homeric Greeks were than ours, and so we can understand easily enough how rich and deep a good poet's chant of life could be in the context of a feast full of various delights, but perhaps we are also incapable finally of appreciating that zone of intermediation through which these events manifested their wonder. Indeed, even Prier's account of this intermediation—even the very word "intermediation"—suggests that we have only the most obtuse and indirect ways of recovering what this sort of experience might have been. It took place, we might think, in a region in which the "this" of the "self" or proto-self came together with the "other" of the proto-object, and out of that event would come in turn the creation of the self and the hypostatization of the other. To think this way, however, is really to turn the Greek context on its head, to begin with what they ended with, the constitution of the self and the other. We try to imagine ourselves back from our subjectivities into the state that originally constituted them whereas the Greeks are originally in that state of intermediation out of which their constituted selves will come in time.

We, for instance, might be inclined to say that the feast "drew" the people out of "themselves" and thus produced the feeling we characterize as "wonder." But surely they had no self to be drawn out of in this sense, surely they were more a part of the intermediated realm than they were of any internal world. What differentiated their ordinary everyday state from the state of wonder was not a sense of self, which is how we would construe our own behavior, but rather a different kind of intermediated world, one that didn't produce the powerful feeling of wonder but one in which one was just as much "out there" somehow as one was when Demodocus's song captivated one. What distinguishes the state of wonder for the Greeks is *not* the escape from self into the world of intermediation, but rather the moment when the self first is recognized as a possibly separable entity. Wonder of both the fearful and the joyful varieties, and of the combination of the two, was that which brought the self most into the forefront of possibility for them, whereas we feel almost exactly the opposite about the experience, thinking of it as one that allows us momentarily to put off the burdens our selves have become for us.

Nevertheless, powerful as the wonder that is induced by the poet's song is, and compelling as the feast of which it is a part may be, there seems to be something to these deep delights that differentiates them from the other contexts in which wonder is to be found in the *Odyssey.* At the feast and in the poet's song we are recognizably in the midst of an aesthetic authority we all acknowledge, even if we might argue about the ways in which our tradition has interpreted its force. We all know the power of music even if at times we are inclined to argue that the power comes from the sociopolitical exercise of the self-interested will, and a term like "aesthetic authority" has a kind of credence here that it doesn't have so readily for us when we consider Telemachus's change of state or when we look at those moments of transformation in Odysseus's life, when he goes from tired old beggar or shipwrecked wanderer to one who is godlike in mien and stature.

Put another way, we grant a certain amount of credence to conceptions of poetic inspiration that make the presence of a god somewhat plausible to us in those contexts where a poet sings sweet truths, but in other places in the narrative the god's function seems excessive at best and incredible at worst. Telemachus couldn't have changed as much after the visit from Athena as Homer wants us to think; there is no way in fact that he could so quickly provoke astonishment in the suitors or the people of the town. So we can posit such astonishment as a poetic device, or we can think of it as a reflection of a change of state that occurred through the passage of more time than the text suggests, the passage of which Homer wouldn't mention because his sense of temporality was so different from ours. This would cover Telemachus's situation at least, for we could say that the astonishment he provokes in the suitors is a result of a period of, say, a month or two in which the suitors didn't actually see him, a span of time that could conceivably produce the final changes in the process of maturation that would provide the burnish that could be construed as a wonderful change of state. We would doubtless be doing a serious injustice to the text by so psychologizing the provocations of wonder that are clearly not construed in psychological terms by Homer, but we could at least "legitimize" these marvelous passages that do so much to make the poem the memorable piece that it is for us.

But what are we to do with scenes such as the one where Odysseus first meets Nausicaa, when he goes from being an object of horror to a godlike object of beauty? When Nausicaa first sees him, this is how he appears:

> And now he burst out of the underbrush;
> with his stout hand he tore a leafy branch
> from that thick wood, to hide his nakedness.
> He moved out as a mountain lion would
> when—sure of his own strength, his eyes ablaze—
> through driving wind and rain, he stalks his prey,
> wild deer or sheep or oxen; he'll attack
> a cattle-fold, however tight the fence
> that pens the herd—his hunger's so intense.
> So did Odysseus seem as he prepared
> to burst into the band of fair-haired girls,
> though he was naked; he was ravenous.
> But he—his form was filthy, fouled with brine—
> struck them as horrible; and terrified,
> they scattered on the shore, one here, one there,
> along the sandspits jutting out to sea.
> The daughter of Alcinous was left
> alone: her spirit had received the gift
> of courage from Athena, who had freed
> the limbs of the young girl from fear and trembling.
> (p. 121, 22)

We can certainly note a kind of continuity in Odysseus, for the blazing eyes he possesses are one of his distinguishing features; the only thing that differentiates those eyes here is that his appearance is such that they induce terror rather than a more positive form of astonishment. The metaphorical association of him with a mountain lion clearly suggests his animal nature, and the fire in the eyes is construed as the fierce force of one who could easily stalk his prey most anywhere. The threat to the young maidens here is real indeed, for not only does Odysseus strike them as one without civilizing attributes, thanks to his ferocity and his filthy, fouled form, but any strange male would be a potential threat to them. If that is so, how much more likely would it be for a man who looks as horrible as Odysseus does to be one who might well try to rape them all? Surely his nearly-naked state would only redouble such fears, and the women run off for good reason.

Nausicaa alone remains behind thanks to the gift of courage that Athena gives to her in order to help Odysseus out. Her limbs are freed of fright and do not tremble, and fear does not overtake her the way it does the other maidens. We could say that Nausicaa's presence is the exception that proves the rule, and the fact that even Athena is needed to keep her in place would suggest how truly horrible Odysseus does in fact look. Or it could be that there is something in spite of the brine and the ferocity that might strike one who has courage in a different way than it would one who saw every male as a potential threat. Whatever the reason, we are meant to think that those traits that normally make Odysseus a thing of wonder are easily enough construed as manifestations of potential horrors with little more than an application of sea brine. To be sure, it is difficult to imagine how brine would enhance anyone's visage, and also difficult to imagine how a nearly-naked man could be construed otherwise. More importantly, we can see how those traits that add most to Odysseus's stature can easily be interpreted in other ways with only a few shifts in external characteristics.

We realize how much this is so when we see Odysseus's quick transformation into an object of wonder once he has had a bath and a chance to present himself more in keeping with civilized company:

> Then in the waters of the river, bright
> Odysseus scrubbed his body free of brine
> that soiled his sturdy shoulders and his spine.
> And from his head he wiped away the crust

> left by the restless sea. When he had washed
> all of his body and smoothed down his flesh
> with ample olive oil, Odysseus dressed.
> And after he put on the clothing she—
> the unwed girl—had given him, Athena,
> the gray-eyed goddess, made him more robust
> and taller; and she gave him thicker hair,
> which flowed down from his head in curls and clusters
> that seemed much like the hyacinth in flower.
> Just as a craftsman who has learned his secrets
> from both the gray-eyed goddess and Hephaestus
> frames silver with fine gold and thus creates
> a work with greater plenitude and grace,
> so did the goddess now enhance with grace
> the head and shoulders of Odysseus. (p. 126)

Are we to believe that a human could be so radically changed with a good cleaning and a little olive oil? Or must we attribute such alterations to Athena, that master craftsperson who works in human flesh rather than silver and fine gold? Do we really need Athena here, or is it rather the case that we can't do without her, that even a good cleaning wouldn't begin to account for Odysseus's visage filled "with greater plenitude and grace"? In a way, of course, these questions are beside the point, for Homer clearly found Athena to be a necessary gesture to account for the transformations of Odysseus and others, and we can hardly doubt his need in this case. And given the fact that we are told that it is not simply a question of getting rid of the ill effects of sea water, that "the head and shoulders of Odysseus" were enhanced with "grace," we must assume that something nearly magical has occurred here. Only a god could work such wonders, though our own skepticism might encourage us to think of the situation in other ways.

I think that it is possible to assume, however, that the potentially revivifying force of a good cleaning up and some clothes and a bit of olive oil could go a long way toward reflecting the great change to be found in Odysseus. Without overly reducing the context, we could assume that the clothes alone would make him seem human rather than animal, that the washed face and body would eliminate the crusty and opaque surfaces that the brine would have given him, that the presence of beautiful humans and at least the momentary end of the need for wariness would lift Odysseus's spirits accordingly, and that that, combined with the shine on his skin from the oil and the already-present fire in the eyes, would make him truly a wonder. As his own self-confidence returned, his shoulders would straighten out and lift his head higher, and he would have the grace for which his godlike visage was known. This is not an altogether incredible scenario by any means, particularly if one assumes that the ancient Greeks had a much more mercurial vision of human beings. Probably the most striking thing to a modern reader of the text is the way that the characters within it surge from one state to another without apparent warning. Just as they perceive their own behavior as something that flows intensely one moment and with ease the next, with great ferocity on occasion and joyful bliss on another, so too did they imagine their fellow humans as "unpredictable" in this way. Lacking our sense of a stable and coherent self, they were inclined to recognize humans more for what they are than we do, construing their behavior in a variety of ways that depends on the context in which they are to be found.

We need only remember the great many different kinds of Odysseus we are faced with in the text to get a good sense of the flammability of temperament in the people of the time. Odysseus can be weeping and moaning at one moment about his terrible fate and everything that has happened to him, and the next he can be plotting stratagems of survival. He can be as ferocious and deadly as the mountain lion with whom he was associated on first meeting Nausicaa, and he can be the loving and sentimental husband who can't wait to return home. In some respects, we have no trouble imagining all these characteristics inhabiting the same human, for most of us feel many of these things over time. But we also live in a world in which most humans have smoothed out the edges between their various affective possibilities, where they don't run the gamut of emotions from complete rage to careful thought in quite the way Odysseus and the other people of the *Odyssey* do. Then, too, Odysseus would not be a likely candidate for a modern hero precisely because of his volatility: inasmuch as it is difficult for him to maintain continuity between states, he resembles more the kind of hero to be found in schlock horror movies and bad television shows. Perhaps his linkage to those more demotic forms of entertainment might give greater credibility to the fluid nature of Odysseus's character, though; perhaps his volatility is more reflective of the way humans really are than the ways we see them.

We need to remember that if Odysseus is highly dynamic and does not always demonstrate self-control, he truly is wise and disciplined, even if he seems to be less disciplined to us that Homer would have us think. After all, when he confronts Nausicaa—in the midst of a highly traumatic situation for him, for he doesn't know what will become of himself in this strange land—he manages very carefully to assess the situation in spite of his blazing eyes and his ferocious mode of being:

> Was he to clasp
> her knees, beseeching help from her, or keep
> his distance and, from there, present his plea
> with gentle words, entreating her to clothe
> his nakedness and guide him to the city?
> As he considered this, it seemed more seemly,
> more wise, to speak soft words but stay apart—
> and not to clasp her knees, lest her young heart
> be angry with him. (p. 122)

In a moment of calm, most anyone would come to the conclusion Odysseus reaches here, for it should be obvious to him that he might well be perceived as a threat or at the very least as an intrusive presence, particularly given the way he looks.

But this is a moment of high intensity for Odysseus, the kind of moment during which most people lose their composure and thus their ability carefully to evaluate how they should act. They might be inclined to do almost anything, grasping Nausicaa's knees or grabbing and threatening her; they would be least likely, though, to take the course Odysseus does, for it requires restraint, demands that he keep those blazing eyes and the blazing mind that goes with them in control. The ability so to discipline oneself, particularly in a human world where the surges of affective states are pretty much taken for granted and not really expected to be restrained, is in this respect unquestionably Odysseus's distinctive feature. He may be wily, but he is so only because he can usually carefully assess a situation and determine well what kind of stratagem will be required. He may be noble, but that is only because he is the equivalent in his age of a divine nature, one who can see things for what they are and act upon that basis. He may be strong, but he knows when to employ his strength and when not to. In short, he has cultivated his self and learned the necessary discipline that will allow him to manifest his intensity in ways that are usually fitting to the context.

❦

If we are considering the various forms of intensity to which the people of the *Odyssey* respond, we can conclude, I think, that they are extremely attentive to shifts in the flows of states because the flows are in some respects more "unpredictable" for them than they seem to be to us. One could in fact argue the case either way, stressing that indeed the ancient Greeks were more fluid and volatile precisely because they had no conception of a coherent self through which to discipline the various flows that surge through humans as a matter of course, or maintaining instead that it was their ability to understand humans as fluid creatures in the first place that made them such adept readers of the various flows and the potential they had for good or bad, wonder or horror. Either way, they clearly perceived human beings in a way that didn't rely upon the artificial imposition of an intellectual grid onto experience in order to determine its validity. They were trained to discern the nuances of what we call "body language" and the like because the truths of their lives manifested themselves in these ways.

What the poetic context of great delight finally has in common with these scenes in which Odysseus is first an object of horror and then an object of grace and wonder, after all, is that both of them manifest "truths" about the human world that are connected to the most obvious of aesthetic states, the ones in which the action produces the artifice of self and other rather than the ones where self and other produce interpretations of human action. The ancient Greeks might have been less intellectually sophisticated than we are in some respects, but their attentiveness to those moments of wonder, the horrifying ones and the beautiful ones, reflected their concrete understanding of the way that truth and authority manifest themselves in this world. The wisest of all humans, like Odysseus, also had a wariness about human actions that kept them from merely being swayed by any particular affective state—their skepticism thus keeping their own emotions in check well enough to allow them to interpret intelligently whether or not the wonder-provoking event was a ruse or an authentic experience.

But even the average humans were far from wrong in assuming that wonder and truth are two sides of the same context, that the fire in the eyes of Odysseus suggests something powerful and important about him—it could be the power of a maniac bent on murder or rape, or it could be the power of wisdom—and so the need for interpretation was always paramount. They were not wrong in thinking the fire of Odysseus's vision, the intensity of his focus, was the site of all important human events. Again, we need to remember that in this respect Odysseus is also a cautionary tale, for no one can tell lies better than he can, no one can more credibly weave a tale of deceit than him, and so the intensity itself is never enough, the wonder that he provokes by his fiery eyes and imposing mien is never sufficient. Nevertheless, it is also always the *only* place to begin. If we tend to prefer figures with charisma, there is good reason for that, even if such figures are always at least as potentially dangerous as any mere cultivator of bureaucratic authority. The true beauty and horror of our world resides in those simple facts today as much as they did in Odysseus's time; the only thing that has changed is that we are much less likely to recognize them than Odysseus was.

Wonder is the locus of the aesthetic event and thus the foundation of aesthetic authority, even though most often we find that authority deriving from less intense aesthetic contexts. The affective situation is almost always paramount for us, as exemplified in the *Odyssey* through gossip. The two most striking occasions in which gossip receives Homer's attention do little more in some respects than give us the sense of the community, though in both cases the poem makes it seem like something considerably more powerful than that. When Odysseus comes to the Phaeceans, Athena wants to make sure that his reception is a positive one, so she sets the tone by disseminating rumors about him:

> Meanwhile Athena, who was so intent
> on safe return for firm Odysseus, went
> throughout the town; she'd taken on the guise
> of wise Alcinous' herald; at the side
> of every man the goddess met, she cried:
>
> "Come now, Phaeacian lords and counselors:
> at the assembly ground you'll learn about
> the stranger newly come into the house
> of brave Alcinous—he sailed across
> wide seas, and he is like the deathless gods." (p. 149)

Athena's gossip reflects the interpretation of Odysseus that the Phaeacians are going to have on first seeing him, and by suggesting that he is "like the deathless gods," it prepares them for an individual who is almost more than mortal. In shaping the general perception of him in such a way, we might say, Athena has made the impressions of Odysseus incline favorably toward him and thus helps ease his way. But we might also say that gossip in general can be a crucial determinant in events and helps to evoke wonder or to suppress it depending on the context. If an aesthetic event always involves a context, that context always has something to do with a human language, and the language can add to or detract from the intensity of what is felt; in some cases, as with poetry, the language is the primary means through which the agent involved in the event gains authority, whereas in the case of gossip, there is no localizable authority for these remarks about Odysseus. And perhaps we would be less likely to make use of a goddess to account for the spread of gossip than we would to use her in the other contexts in which she appears. We would assume that gossip needs no origin, and even such useful remarks about Odysseus's godlike state hardly need a god to account for their presence.

In the case of the rumor that spreads the news about the deaths of the suitors, Athena plays no part in it, but rumor is turned into Rumor the messenger, and the anthropomorphization of the phenomenon places it in the same category as the divine attempt to evoke wonder in the presence of Odysseus:

> But even as they busied with their meal,
> Rumor, the messenger, was rushing through
> the city, telling everyone the news:
> the suitors' horrid death and doom. At once
> from here, from there, around Odysseus' house
> men swarmed. They wept. They mourned. And each
> one bore
> his own kin from the house and buried him.
> As for the dead who'd come from other towns,
> they were assigned to seamen; rapid ships
> then sailed each dead man back to his own kin.
> (p. 495)

Rumor here spreads as quickly as it possibly can, transforming an ordinary situation into one in which weeping and mourning are the order of the day. It is worth noting that the rumor in this case is true, just as what Athena spreads about Odysseus is more or less true too.

These scenes of the spreading fire of rumor or gossip are not counterbalanced by negative rumor or gossip, for those seem to be accounted for (quite properly) by specific human agents. When Odysseus's men turn on him and open up the bag of winds that Aeolus has given them, no rumor spreads across the ship. Instead, they all get together and discuss what might be in the bag:

> "Just see what love, what honor he commands
> from any man he meets in any land
> or town! Just see what booty, splendid spoils,
> he carries back from Troy, while we, who toiled
> beside him, must return with empty hands.
> To this, he now can add the friendly gift
> of Aeolus. Let's see what's in that sack—
> see how much gold and silver he has packed."
> (p. 196)

What we might call false gossip or untrue rumor seems always to be located within the self-interested conspiracies of particular humans. Odysseus's men are greedy for whatever booty there might be in the bag and are afraid that Odysseus will not share it with them, so they feed each other's weakness, convince themselves that it is their right to open the bag, and the result is unfavorable for all of them. The kin of the suitors are certainly not happy about what happened to the men, but the rumor of their death is still true, and it compels its own form of recognition and astonishment.

So we find in the *Odyssey* a hermeneutic in which gossip or rumor would seem to have the same affective potential and truth value that any scene of wonder, positive or negative, would have, whereas the negative rumors and the self-interested interpretations of events are contrived by those whose interests lie in distorting what is actually the case. And if we assume that wonder is always the site of truth in Homer, we can see why he must separate rumor and gossip that is aesthetic in nature, and thus true, by making it either the force of a god or an anthropomorphized version of Hermes, while he reduces rumor based on self-interested speculation to contexts of lesser intensity. We could say that this distinction exists as a retrospective reflection of the truth value of the rumor or the gossip, or we could argue that it is Homer's way of prejudging the situation so that he doesn't have to deal with the nettlesome problem inherent in all aesthetic authority. It compels our assent, but doesn't necessarily carry the truth we think it does as a result of its intensity. It is worth remembering that clothes do indeed contribute greatly to the making of the humans in the poem, as do considerably lesser things like a bath and some fine olive oil. The limitation of aesthetic authority is that any event that provokes it is inevitably filtered through the language that is part of the event, and the language can be the clothes that allow Odysseus to appear as he is in all his splendor, or the temporary rags that make him seem much less than he is.

The wondrous always bears the risk of being interpreted in self-interested ways. If we think back to Nausicaa for a moment, we can see how her courage in standing her ground and facing Odysseus when he first appears in all his brine-covered horror is a reflection of her ability to avoid construing events through self-interest or through a wariness that would prompt her too to run. Everything about this situation ought to move her to run as fast as she possibly can, for there is not likely to be anything that will forward her own interests in any way, and she has yet to be captivated by Odysseus's presence. Athena may be seen to give her courage, then, to inform us that Nausicaa is that rare kind of individual who can assess situations outside of self-interest, can see what happens outside of the envelope of her own particular needs and desires. Such abilities are rare indeed, though, at least when it comes to facing wondrous horrors rather than wondrous marvels of a positive kind.

The same question remains before us, though, and it is how can aesthetic authority inhere in the kind of events we have been looking at? What is there about them that places their effects in the realm where authority is based and evaluated in all its power and fragility? How are humans to be able to recognize aesthetic authority in all its dimensions, how do they develop ways of interpreting its effects, and how do the Greeks of the *Odyssey* help us to see these mechanisms in ways we aren't likely to find within our own social context? Prier's discussion of the act of seeing in the poem will again be helpful here, for he tells us quite specifically what he thinks characterizes the vision of the archaic Greeks: "The decidedly underdeveloped, inner place of the 'this' is characterized by a number of outward-projecting, tensioned, and intentioned terms and experiences of sight. The key phenomenological activity is one of projecting or assimilating the world at large on some kind of linear and geometrical intuition that is capable of coming to terms with the living being and his outwardly directed projections" (p. 41). What Prier is suggesting here is that inasmuch as the Greeks didn't have the internally-developed self that we have acquired in the intervening millennia, the "this" that was their location within a particular event was construed in terms of "outward-projecting, tensioned, and intentioned terms and experiences of sight." Sight, if you will, was that which drew the "this" away from its pure "thisness" and linked it to an "other" that was demonstrably outside of it. It metaphorically transported the "this" outside of itself to a region between it and the purely "other," that realm of intermediation where all important effects take place.

It is worth noting the ambiguity of Prier's statements here, for he refers to this activity as one of "projecting or assimilating the world" without arguing one way or the other for its projective or assimilative properties. The distinction between the two is important for us, for if the Greeks were merely projecting their own desires onto an external scene that they hoped to accommodate to their desires through their projections, then these moments of vision are more than highly suspect and can hardly be the locus of aesthetic authority. Instead they would be the location of an intersubjective space through which the Greek desires were able to cast an Apollonian tissue of illusions over the "other" of the world. Yet Prier is right to suggest both projective and assimilative possibilities here even as he implies that one or the other could be the case, for the projective is attached to the "this" of the experience and emphasizes its point of origin whereas the assimilative is attached to the "other," to that which needs to be assimilated, and emphasizes that the experience has its origin in the "outside" of the "other" that first catches the "this's" attention.

In effect, if the region of aesthetic authority is to have any conviction beyond that of mere self-interest or delusionary interpretation, it must be a scene in which the projective and the assimilative are both operative, or rather, when what is operative partakes of both the assimilative and the projective. Any location within the flows by definition projects its energies outward into the flows, and any location within the flows is also always in the midst of an assimilative process whereby it seeks to discern the patterns within the flows and its position within them. Given that, these moments of sight are necessarily both projective and assimilative and hence most obviously true. Without the blinders of pure self-interest to shape the "this's" sense of what is happening, the "other" can be assimilated in ways that more or less accord with its own nature, yet at the same time the "other" can always only be assimilated *for* a specific location within the flows, and that location always has projective tendencies that reflect its particular location—location, in this respect, is always a kind of interest in itself, though it is differentiated from pure self-interest by the fact that its interests are construed through the overall flows of the field and not merely through the centralizing desires of an isolated datum. The more rudimentary state of the early-Greek self allows us to see the way these two vectors of the assimilative and the projective always come together in a region that establishes the distance between them and brings them together at the same time.

Inasmuch as Odysseus and the other Greeks in the poem do not have to devote their energies to the maintenance and protection of a self—something that is different than seeking to keep alive and striving for the best that the world has to offer one—they are capable of a kind of attention to the world that we find much harder to achieve. For us the aesthetic event always has to be filtered through a more extreme discipline, one that works assiduously to keep our preoccupations with the self and its maintenance needs down to a minimum. And given the greater needs of the self and the great discipline necessary for us to get through those needs to the aesthetic events in the midst of which we always find ourselves, we are less adept at discerning different kinds of vision, of recognizing the difference between "seeming" and "appearance" as Prier defines them here: "The opposition between an intentional, sporadic seeming and an intense, all-pervasive appearing, an essential opposition in archaic experience, is probably best seen in the anthropo-etymological distinction between *thnetos* and *athanatos* where the alpha privative does indeed designate a world or position of the 'other/that.' These two places reflect the underlying opposition between the terminology of seeming and that of appearance. Generally speaking the one designates men and 'seeming'; the other, the gods and 'appearance.' The place of *phainesthai* yields sure proof of 'divine' or 'true' experience" (p. 41, 42). What Prier's remarks suggest is that Homer's gods are not mere devices through which he construes extraordinary events to humans so superstitious that they expect everything out of the ordinary to come from a god, nor are they merely metaphorical signs of profound sea changes in the events that unfold before humans; they are rather the archaic Greek way of marking out truly aesthetic events and their great authority from the more typical self-interested events that determine the make-up of the everyday social world.

If we might be inclined to condescend to the creaky machinery of gods and their dispensations within the human world that appear every time the going gets a little strange or every time Homer feels the need to justify something that seems implausible in the narrative, we might also realize that those gods covered a terrain and an aesthetic mode of evaluation that allowed the Greeks to determine the difference in value between seeming and appearance, that allowed them to distinguish, that is, that authority which stems from a purely self-interested expression of the will to power and the authority that comes from an aesthetic event where the "this" is truly only an agent in a much larger flow and derives its authority from the flow itself and not from the "self" that could be said to exist within it. We may have created a world in which the absurd business to do with the Greek gods has long been dispensed with, but in losing those gods, we also lost our sight in a real way, thereby increasing the difficulties inherent in distinguishing between seeming and appearing.

If it is possible that the early Greeks could better distinguish between that which merely seems—that which has its origin in an emerging self whose preoccupations are concerned with the interests of that self—and that which appears—that which has its origin outside of any particular self or "this" and rather brings that "this" into the region where its linkage to and difference from the "other" manifests itself—this pattern of evaluation in turn depends on the greater fluidity of self as well. If the shapes of humans can metaphorically expand and contract depending on the type of vision through which their actions are construed, then there is something to this less-constricted self that makes the difference between seeming and appearing easier to articulate. This is not to say that the very real problems of interpretation that are inherent in any aesthetic context were any "easier" for the Greeks; they did not live in an idyllic age in which it was always clear when the gods were speaking and when it was only a human who had designs on the space one occupied. The very fluidity of the gods, the way they could take on any shape and become any person at any given time, clearly demonstrates otherwise. If anything, the job of interpretation—or what passed for interpretation to the Greeks—was more difficult precisely because they were aware of a wider range of possibilities—gods could immediately and irrevocably alter the flow of a life in a moment, so one had to be aware of the prospect of their intrusion into one's life. There was always the possibility of another dimension of an event that one could miss altogether if one didn't attend properly to what was actually going on at the moment. But the very potential of that other dimension and the ability to perceive it in the first place depended on selves that took on various shapes and lacked the intellectual grid that we impose on our own locations within the flows.

It is somewhat artificial to suggest that there were essentially two dimensions to the Greek way of seeing, one based on seeming and the other based on appearance, the one connected almost exclusively to the world of humans and their actions and the other linked to the gods and aesthetic authority, for this too is to create grids that don't seem to fit the facts of a poem like the *Odyssey.* And Prier's assertions don't require us to see the difference between seeming and appearance strictly in terms of two dimensions, even if the realm of the gods is clearly different from the world of ordinary human activity. The realm of appearance as Prier describes it—the realm of aesthetic *truths,* we must emphasize, lest our conventional ways of construing the word attach it to human illusions—is not any more coherent that the self that perceives it. There is no overarching structure through which the events that appear could be said to make sense. There are, to be sure, the laws of the gods to which one must attend, and they have a kind of coherence to them, and the Greeks obviously ascribed certain characteristics to each of their gods and thus imposed continuities on them in that way. But there is no way to account for when a god will make an appearance, nor is there a way in which to construe the overall effects of a god on a person's life.

Odysseus, for example, obviously had Athena's help throughout his life, and both he and others recognize that a god has assisted him. But neither the others nor Odysseus can determine when Athena will appear and when she will not, nor do they strain after such interpretations. Things just happen in a lot of cases, and sometimes the gods are there to help one out and sometimes they are not. When they are not there, it could be because they didn't feel the need to intervene, or it could be because one offended them by not sacrificing enough to please them, or it could be that the particular god's interests in one are in conflict with the interests another god has in the same situation, as in the conflicts between Athena and Poseidon that are worked out through Odysseus's tortured fate. Odysseus at no point in his narrative looks back upon his life and recognizes a pattern to the appearances Athena makes, nor does he seek to impose such a pattern on his fate to give it greater sense. He simply accepts the fact that at times the gods appear to provide assistance, and at times they do not, even if he can also mightily lament his fate.

Odysseus's willingness more or less to let the gods come and go as they will—or rather his willingness to eschew the desire for a means whereby he can call Athena up on demand—is part of the greater volatility of the self to which the appearances are attached. Inasmuch as Odysseus himself has no way of accounting for just why or when his "self" will be moved in this direction or that, he has no way of knowing when an appearance will come forth to provoke wonder within him. Indeed, not surprisingly, the only regular human context through which the process of wonder is potentially available is to be found in the poetry that is chanted in the midst of a feast. *That* human event, albeit inspired by the gods, is the one location that, given the right singer, can call forth the appearances that are the mark of aesthetic authority. In the rest of the human world, those appearances seems pretty much to come and go as they will, dependent, from our perspective, on the way the flows of consciousness adapt to the larger flows of which they are in turn a part.

With *art* humans have found a means whereby they can produce a greater regularity of appearance. Even there, though, we should remember that Demodocus has to *wait* for the god to move him, so it is not that he is in control. But if he has a gift from the gods, if his poetic abilities come from the tutelage of the Muse, that is because his voice can make appearance appear, and no other human activity, except maybe the games, can make that claim. The appearances of poetry are linked to the gods precisely because they are a reflection of the aesthetic authority of a particular human event in a context that is more reproducible than any other. And if the original linkage of poetic appearance and the gods is something we have long disabused ourselves of, the original reason for that connection remains with us today as much as it ever did: poetry is the locus of aesthetic authority that we share with the early Greeks in a way that they themselves understood much better than we do, and it is our link to their gods, to their more fluid sense of self, and to their abilities to discern the difference between seeming and appearance. Keats was surely right in saying that beauty was truth and truth was beauty, and the archaic Greeks knew this full well. It is *we* who have forgotten this most fundamental site of authority, and *we* who so regularly pay the consequences for our ignorance.

Odysseus has many snares he must face during the

course of his long journey, but when he is in the midst of an aesthetic event, he knows full well the truths of the appearance. That is one snare he doesn't worry about. We in turn face fewer life-threatening snares than Odysseus, but we have paid the price of a much more mediated connection to aesthetic authority, making the small, everyday events we find ourselves in the midst of to be an endless thicket of snares in their own right. Odysseus's more fluid "self" allows him more fully to respond to whatever situation he finds himself in the midst of at any given moment, for he doesn't need to filter the context through the mediations of the intellectual grid of the self, and thus he is capable of recognizing more often those moments of great importance and distinguishing them from the insignificant ones. We who have distanced ourselves from the fluidity and volatility of the self by imposing an artificial coherence upon it so that we may be better protected from its uncertainties have made it almost impossible to distinguish a significant event from a moment of little import to us. And even if we are willing at some level to concede the gain and the loss involved in the artificial constructs and constraints of the self we have created and seek to perpetuate, we want to console ourselves with the fact that we are more civilized and hence have traded a lesser good for a greater good.

❦

When we think of the consequences of the greater volatility of individuals we find in the *Odyssey*—even if we are willing to concede that the more fluid "self" they possessed also provided them with the ability to discern between seeming and appearance in a way that we cannot—we are likely eventually to assert that they purchased their strengths as humans at the cost of a greater barbarity. After all, Odysseus is clearly something of a savage himself, a man whose great volatility is not to be trifled with because there is no telling when his "more fluid self" will lose its grip on things and flow forth into a rage or an act of violence of one sort or another. Anyone who passes through the scenes at the end of the *Odyssey* when the suitors are slaughtered cannot help but feel great disgust in the face of the powers that Athena gives to Odysseus and Telemachus. We may be glad that they have them, and we may also recognize that they could only live in peace if they killed off all the suitors, but we still can't help but be filled with loathing for these bloody events, unquestionably the most awful in the entire poem.

And whereas such violence is still possible today, we would cautiously like to think that we are not as barbaric as Odysseus and Telemachus are. Whether or not this is true is finally irrelevant when it comes to the "barbarity" of a figure like Odysseus, though, for even if he can fight as furiously as any human he must face, he is also every bit as civilized as we are. What distinguishes his barbarity more than anything else is not his inherent savagery, and it is certainly not that more fluid and volatile "self" that might erupt into almost anything at any given moment, but rather the cultural values through which that fluidity manifests itself. And even if one backs up a step further and argues that the fluid self is irretrievably linked to a set of cultural values that construes human activities in such a way in the first place, something that is indeed true, the larger question is whether Odysseus's fluid self is *inevitably* tied to a savage and violent culture. If we could imagine a world in which our admittedly artificial mediations of self were eliminated for the greater fluidity of the archaic Greek context; if, that is, we were willing to let our "selves" feel and express the full range of affects they are capable of on a regular basis; would we find ourselves back in a world in which brute savagery and violent brutality were the rule? Or are there other possibilities as well? Can one imagine that more fluid self and the aesthetic authority to which it is attached in a context that would not be *less* "civilized" but rather *more* "civilized"?

Odysseus himself would suggest, I think, that we can indeed imagine the greater fluidity of self in a context that is more rather than less violent, and that the greater ability to discern aesthetic authority in the contexts of our lives would more than compensate for any loss that would come from giving up the larger continuities we have sought to impose on our selves. Odysseus truly was a product of his own culture, and that culture was unquestionably a violent and vengeful one, but the genius of Odysseus does not inhere in vengeance per se any more than it necessarily requires violence. In Odysseus's day, violence was a prerequisite for "greatness" because one had to be able to defend oneself in the midst of the very real violence of the world around one; and in Odysseus's day that violence was exacerbated by a set of human values that placed a high priority on *ressentiment.* Vengeance was not only a necessity in the sense that one had to partake of it in order to preserve oneself; it was a *sacred duty,* something one was compelled to do in order to preserve the essential links to kin and clan upon which the order and authority of the times were based. And so Odysseus is unquestionably violent and vengeful, bloodily so in all respects, and hardly a model of perfect human behavior.

If I suggested earlier that in some crucial respects Odysseus still comes close to being a model of the Confucian divine nature in spite of his very real attachments to violence and *ressentiment,* that was not because either Confucius's divine nature or Nietzsche's overman would have anything to do with the physical violence or the seething desire for revenge that Odysseus possesses. Rather, it is because I see Odysseus as a truly great human exemplar whose worst characteristics are chiefly a function of his culture and not of him. If that does not exculpate Odysseus in terms of the values we possess today, it does allow him the measure of his own time, something he surely deserves as much as we do.

In arguing that Odysseus's greater fluidity and volatility are not inherently connected to an "unstable" self that is always potentially violent and destructive, I would suggest that the most compelling reason for this is to be found in his equally great self-discipline. He *is* human, and he *does* have lapses like any other human, and those lapses *do* cause deaths and great misadventure; even more, the famous "sacker of cities" takes pride in the results of his violent surges. But overall there can be little doubt that Odysseus is a man possessed of incredible self-discipline, and that that self-discipline provides him with the two gifts he needs most to complete the arduous journey fate gives him: he is capable of monstrous feats of *attention*—he more than anyone else in the poem knows how to attend to that which is, knows how to investigate things when circumstances require it—and he knows how to control his fluidity when his "self" tells him that self-control is necessary.

The most compelling examples of Odysseus's self-discipline come toward the end of the *Odyssey* when the necessity of dealing with the suitors prompts him to confront situations he would rather not deal with, situations that range from the degrading to the near-bestial. Witness the moment within his own halls when he decides to beg from the suitors:

> Athena
> stood by Laertes' son; she urged him on
> to beg for bits of bread among the suitors,
> to learn which men were just and which were wanton,
> though she was hardly set on saving any—
> not even those who gave. (p. 357)

One might think that it wouldn't require much of Odysseus to undertake the act of begging, given the stratagem to which he is committed and the ultimate aim of eliminating the suitors from his life. But the very need for Athena to urge him on shows how difficult it is for him to do this, how degrading it is for him to stoop to such a level, particularly in the face of the depraved suitors who have been doing everything they can to ruin his house. But if Odysseus is "to learn which men were just and which were wanton," he must go about and test the generosity of each by begging, even if the result should be that all of them will be killed anyway. Against his own well-honed instincts, then, Odysseus responds to Athena's urging and takes up the degrading activity.

In the midst of his rounds, Odysseus encounters just what he expects to find, degrading behavior from people who have no proper sense of the laws that pertain to the relations between host and guest, and one of the manifestations of this godlessness comes when he is struck by a stool thrown at him by Antinous:

> That said, [Antinous] grabbed the stool and threw it at
> Odysseus; and it hit him in the back,
> just under his right shoulder blade. When struck,
> he did not budge; he stood, firm as a rock;
> he only shook his head; within his heart,
> in silence, he devised a deadly plot. (p. 361)

Again, we might think the self-restraint that Odysseus displays here is relatively insignificant, that the indignity of having things thrown at him by Antinous is relatively small given the fact that he knows that Antinous will shortly pay for his brutality. But in the context, it clearly requires a great deal of Odysseus to keep still. The restraint is emphasized by the total stillness he presents to us. If "he did not budge," if he "stood, firm as a rock," that in itself reflects how much will power he is exerting to keep from reciprocating the violence. That "he only shook his head" reflects the degree to which he has agreed, in effect, to stay in his "role" as beggar, for only one who was truly powerless would do no more than this. And if the self-restraint leads also to the deadly plot wherein Antinous is the first to be killed, that is only to be expected in the context of Odysseus's life.

Given our own sense of values, it is easy enough for us to assume that Odysseus's restraint is in effect really only a reflection of his relative barbarity. After all, we learn to mediate our desires for revenge much better than he and are much more accustomed to suffering abuse and degradation in silence, so we might think that the very fact that it takes great self-discipline for Odysseus to keep from strangling Antinous or throwing chairs at the suitors or hurling verbal insults shows how poorly civilized he is and how much he is a victim of the flows of his own person. But the man of many wiles lives in a more perilous world than ours, a world in which the appearance one puts forth has much more at stake in it than in our own. In each case it may be the status of the individual that is reflected by the pose one adopts, but in

Odysseus's world, one's status has a much greater effect on the outcome of one's life.

We should rather recognize that the man of many wiles has such great stratagems because, given his circumstances, he manifests repeated examples of incredible *patience*, a virtue not always to be found among those who so willingly follow the surges of their mind the way the archaic Greeks do. And we find that Odysseus too recognizes the relationship between his power and his self-restraint, as seen here when he wrestles sleeplessly with himself about how to eliminate the suitors on the following morning:

> "Be still, my heart. You've suffered greater shame:
> the Cyclops' ruthless frenzy when he ate
> your sturdy friends; you found the strength to wait—
> although you thought you'd die—within his cave
> until your cunning led to your escape."
>
> He held in check the heart within his breast;
> obedient now, his pride submitted; yet
> Odysseus' own self thrashed this way and that.
> Just as a man before a blazing fire
> who's skewered a paunch that's stuffed with blood
>   and fat
> will swiftly turn the spit this way and that,
> eager to have it roasted fast, so did
> Odysseus toss from side to side; he thought
> of traps in which the suitors could be caught,
> though he was one alone and they a crowd. (p. 411, 12)

When Odysseus says to himself that he has in the past "found the strength to wait" in the face of even more shameful situations—as when the Cyclops was eating his men, a situation he feels shame about because he was the one who wanted to stay and see if the Cyclops feared the gods—he acknowledges that his mastery of stratagems and wiles comes more from the strength to hold himself in than from an ability to exert great force in the world. The surges of his mind tell him to lash out and perform an outrageous act that will show the suitors that he is more powerful than them, as he is, but he knows that this will not further his goals, that he must keep his heart in check if he is going to succeed with his stratagem.

So, Homer tells us, "obedient now, his pride submitted; yet / Odysseus' own self thrashed this way and that." We are not told to what Odysseus is obedient, so we might wonder to what his pride submitted. There is no reference to Athena here until *after* Odysseus holds his pride in check and restrains his anger, so we cannot assume that he is obedient to her or to any of the other gods. Rather, he is obedient to *himself*, that is, to his own self-discipline, to his sense of what is appropriate to his needs. He simply *must* curtail the normal effects of his injured pride if he is to survive, if his "cunning" is to have an opportunity to work its wiles on the following day.

Even at that Odysseus has a hard time stilling his mind, and so his "own self" thrashes about rather than finding restful sleep, a problem only overcome because Athena intervenes at that point to quiet his mind. But the distinction between his "own self" that thrashes about and the fact that "obedient now, his pride submitted," suggests that Odysseus himself doesn't see his obedience or his self-discipline as located within his "self," a fragile enough construct, we know, in any case. Even though Athena has not yet made herself known, Odysseus seems to find his strength in a region that is not encompassed by the "this" of his self so much as by the demands of the events in the midst of which he finds himself. He forces himself to submit to the necessities of the moment, and if we think it is easy enough so thoroughly to address the moment and its necessities in the midst of the indignities he has faced, we have not ourselves been forced to confront a crisis of the same magnitude.

So Homer tells us that Odysseus's "own self" is only partially encompassed by the discipline that prompts Odysseus to stem his pride and maintain his silence in the face of great outrage, that rather there is an "out there" to which he submits himself, on the basis of which he subordinates his pride to restraint, and there is no better way of accounting for such moments of self-discipline in Odysseus's life or our own, for it is always an "out there"—the circumstances that inevitably prompt our need for patience or self-restraint—that imposes the necessity for obedience upon us, that sways us away from the demands that our pride is also imposing on us. There is something of a battle between the "self" whose pride goads one to strike out and the circumstances of the "out there" that tell one to check one's pride, to chain one's dogs given the necessities of the moment.

The patience that is required for significant deeds, then, is located by Odysseus somewhere outside of himself, even if he also realizes that it is his own strength that allows him to respond to it. And we should emphasize once more that it is this great strength of restraint that makes Odysseus the striking figure he is rather than his equally powerful physical prowess and courage. Those in themselves would never have gotten him through his ordeals. As he suggests here, physical strength is not sufficient to cover all the situations one's life throws one's way, for there is a Cyclops in everyone's fate, an event where muscle-power will fail without the mental strength to wait, to have patience, to discipline one's various strengths to provide a common front.

The great courage of patience we see here, then, is a triumph of the will over the will to power, at least for the moment, a self-discipline that knows how to engender restraint even in the midst of one's own considerable shame. Odysseus's sense of shame calls forth from within him for some redress—shame can, it would seem, only be expunged by a reciprocal act of degradation of some sort, precisely the sensibility one would expect to find in a culture driven by *ressentiment*—and both his rudimentary self and the social situation know full well that *others* see his shame as a mark of weakness that lowers his potential power in their eyes. In a culture whose dynamics depend so much on how one is perceived, how one's eyes and physical mien strike the other, it can be fatal to allow such shame to be attached to the other's interpretation of one. So there is risk in restraint, and reason enough for Odysseus to act before the stain becomes a permanent part of the way he is seen by others.

In this way we get at least some sense of the stakes involved in his restraint, and we can also recognize that Odysseus doesn't see his situation quite the way we would. It is worth remembering, as Jean-Pierre Vernant and Pierre Vidal-Naquet point out, that the idea of an autonomous will had not yet come about and was not to take place until the age of the great tragedies, and even then only in halting and incomplete form: "This experimentation, still wavering and indecisive, of what was subsequently in the psychological history of Western man to become the category of the will—as is well known, in ancient Greece there was no true vocabulary to cover willing—is expressed in tragedy in the form of an anxious questioning concerning the relation of the agent to his actions. . . ."[3] Odysseus has no sense of himself *willing* himself to be patient, to wait until the right moment to act, so he submits his pride to something, but as far as he is concerned it is not he who has forced it to capitulate. Rather, the circumstances themselves dictate to him that his pride should be held in check, that, as he has seen on earlier occasions, only such restraint will allow him to put into effect the strategies through which he can change those circumstances.

Without the vocabulary of *willing* to guide him through this thicket, Odysseus may seem at a loss to account for a fairly commonplace act of the will, but in some respects his way of thinking about his situation is more accurate than ours. For the circumstances themselves are the chief actor here, and his own agency is dependent on how well he attends to them. In that sense, to say that he "wills" this or that he "wills" that would be to misconstrue the vectors of force in the situation. The events themselves prompt him to hold his pride in check, and if there is "will" involved in restraint, in a willingness to do nothing when every cell in one's body wants to strike out, then Odysseus does in a manner of speaking will self-restraint. But the word *will* makes sense only to the extent that we argue that Odysseus could just as easily not have restrained himself, could have ruined his strategy by striking back at one or more of the suitors, and even then the word clearly covers a purely negative "act," a choice that reflects the patience *not* to do *anything*. Odysseus's way of seeing the manner in which his situation forces his pride into a mode of obedience that is not characteristic of it once again helps us to see the way that this kind of event, like most other human events, takes place in a region between Prier's "this" (our modern sense of subjectivity) and the "other/that" (our modern sense of the objective world). And it is the "other/that" to which Odysseus's pride submits, not to his own self-determination, and not to Athena's wise advice.

Yet another compelling manifestation of Odysseus's great self-discipline comes when he shapes the responses of other people's reactions to the carnage he and Telemachus unleashed on the suitors. After the great triumph, feelings of exultation would naturally follow, and joy would be the immediate reaction, if for no other reason than as a result of a sense of relief at having overcome great obstacles. But Odysseus neither exudes such joy nor allows it in others, as we find when he cautionsly reins in his old nurse Eurycleia:

> "Old woman, check yourself; you must restrain
> your joy—don't shout aloud. It is profane
> to let your voice exult when men are slain.
> These men were struck down by a god-sent fate
> and by their wanton acts; for they, in truth,
> had no respect for any man on earth—
> not only evil men, but even those
> we deem most good and fair, whoever was
> unfortunate enough to cross their path.
> Their insolence has earned this squalid end." (p. 459)

Odysseus has just completed an entirely merciless war of vengeance of the bloodiest sort, and yet to him his acts fall within the domain of the given: this is what must be done to submit to the will of the gods. Now that the acts are done, however, "It is profane / to let [one's] voice exult when men are slain," even if that is also one of the most "natural" of human reactions.

Odysseus sees the need for restraint *after* the battle in the same way he saw the need for it *before* the carnage: events—the "god-sent fate"—have dictated both his actions and his patience, and nothing has changed once that god-sent fate has been meted out. The deaths of the suitors were "earned" by their evil acts, and Odysseus has done nothing more than respond to the situation they themselves had created. This way of thinking about the patience of restraint that curbs the pride and allows one to choose the proper time for action and the patience of restraint afterward that constrains one from exulting in the face of profane death may indeed seem strange to us, but whatever else can be said about it, there can be no denying that Odysseus is guided through these events by a carefully calibrated sense of what is fitting to the situation. Restraint is nothing more than that, the careful personal cultivation that lets one gauge one's actions on the basis of the prevailing conditions. One attends to what is and acts on the basis of what it presents one with. Confucius would ask no more.

It is again significant that the cultural values Odysseus expresses are to us incredibly wanton in their violence, just as the general basis of the culture in *ressentiment* is no more something we can admire than Nietzsche or Confucius could. But Odysseus himself, as consummate expression of those values, is at the same time the perfect reflection of one who sees his actions and his agency in the context of a larger series of flows to which he is responding even as he initiates new acts. Restraint, patience, self-discipline and courage have no value outside of this context, regardless of the cultural values that shape it, and if Odysseus continues to be such an exemplary hero, it is because of his ability to focus so intensely on the nature of what is and to engender actions that are thoroughly in accord with it, at least in the best of circumstances.

Perhaps the most telling measure of Odysseus's self-restraint and his willingness to respond to the aesthetic authority of the event that might in one case require restraint, in another great patience, and in still another bloody, mad fury, comes at the very end of the *Odyssey* when the suitors have been routed and the question of violent reciprocation is at stake, when the kin of the suitors ready themselves for a battle to the death and Odysseus pursues them with the same seeming abandon as he used on the suitors. We know that Athena has asked Zeus for permission to intervene in these events and keep them from turning into an endless series of vengeful reciprocation, and we know that she manages to turn the townsmen back "toward the city, keen to live" (p. 500). We also know that it is she who finally restrains Odysseus as well through her words of admonition:

> "Laertes' son, Odysseus, sprung from Zeus,
> o man of many wiles, this is too much.
> Halt now; have done with this relentless war,
> lest you provoke the wrath of Zeus, the lord
> of thunder, he whose voice is carried far."
>
> He heard Athena's words and, glad at heart,
> obeyed. A pact was sworn between the parts,
> a treaty for all time: Athena's work
> when she, the daughter of aegis-bearing Zeus,
> had taken on lord Mentor's form and voice. (p. 500)

Homer has Athena perform the final acts here that lead to lasting peace for good reason inasmuch as the more likely human outcome would indeed be endless strife. It must surely seem the act of a god that after so much bloodshed peace can actually be achieved. Given the cultural values that *demand* vengeance for the murder of a kinsman, there truly is no way for the carnage to end, for the suitors' kinfolk must avenge their dead, just as in turn any deaths they cause would need to be avenged. Only a miracle or a god could stop the bloodletting in such circumstances, so it is fitting that Athena return one more time in the guise of wise, old Mentor to bring order to the world and ensure a happy old age for Odysseus.

In spite of the incredible nature of the tale, though, we can also see that Homer provides us with sufficient psychological plausibility in the last events of the poem to account for the magic ending without the direct intervention of a god. The kinfolk of the suitors obviously know full well how completely overwhelmed the many suitors were in the face of the onslaught Odysseus and Telemachus engineered, so they must have that in mind even as they are committed to avenging those deaths. And when it becomes clear that Odysseus's furies have not abated a bit but if anything seem stronger, it is possible that their fear comes from the belief that he will be able to slay all of them as well. At least Homer would have us believe that this would be the likely outcome:

> Odysseus and his stout son fell upon
> the forward ranks; with swords and two-edged
> spears,
> they thrust and would have killed them all, cut off
> all chance of their returning home, had not
> Athena, daughter of aegis-bearing Zeus,
> cried out. (p. 500)

It is easy enough to imagine that when the townsmen see the incredible fury of Odysseus and Telemachus, they come to the conclusion that mere numbers will not be enough in their case either. The horribly striking visages of father and son combine with the terrors they already know about to convince them, "pale with fear," to drop their weapons and run back to town. Athena simply provides an added measure of authority, accounting for the rout in ways that are not necessary from our current perspective.

Given the fact that the townsmen have been so completely routed, though, we might find it less than magnificent that Odysseus too finally achieves restraint and decides that he will not pursue them. After all, they are clearly not a threat to him at the moment once they break ranks and flee in terror. He has won, we might think, so stilling his own fury would hardly confer great virtue on Odysseus. Strategically, however, it would probably indeed be best for Odysseus to deal with the townsmen while they are in flight and thoroughly at chaos within themselves, for they, like other forces, might well regather and mount another assault on him at a later date. War strategy would suggest that Odysseus and Telemachus should kill them while they have the chance, while their own madness is sufficiently upon them to unleash its full fury on relatively easy prey.

From this perspective, Odysseus does indeed reflect yet again the perfect measure of the situation. He knows when the relentless war has gone too far; he can determine when the point of excess has been reached and bring his irrational furies back within the bounds of normality. That Homer also thinks Athena is required in this case suggests again that the more plausible reaction would be for Odysseus to pursue the townsmen until they were all dead. If so, then the courage of restraint calls back Odysseus's most violent furies, and if he properly construes that restraint in terms of a force outside of his "this"—in this case Athena again—he is also right in discerning that that which prompted his sense of excess was the larger context of the carnage already unleashed and the potential for more and more bloodshed to come. The flows of which he is a part suggest to him that restraint is called for at this point when the townsmen have demonstrated their lack of willingness to confront him and when there are not still more deaths for them to feel the need to avenge.

One could argue that whatever restraint Odysseus manifests throughout the poem and particularly in these last events comes far too late in the day to qualify as any manifestation of virtue or divine nature. Odysseus is surely no overman, even if he does abjure the desire for revenge at the end, and he is surely not civilized in our sense of the term. But if we assume that his acts and the management of his own flows and furies take on the shape they have in the poem as a result of the circumstances of his world more than as an inevitable function of a world in which the flows of an individual are recognizably "unstable" and fluid, then we can see how powerfully in control Odysseus's acts really were, and we can then also recognize that those tendencies within him we find most appalling at our distance from him—the rapes and pillage and murders—are not a necessary function of the sense of the human world he establishes.

There is, I think, one further reflection of the fact that Odysseus is indeed a character whose courage is to be found in his restraint, whose genius is to be located in his ability to recognize the way his agency always depends on the flows of a field of which he is but a part, and whose value is to be perceived in the way he is able to discern the perfect fit between the authority of the field in which his action must take place and the action he chooses on that basis, and that is the humility he has in the face of all that has happened to him during the long adventures of his life. He reflects that humility most fully when he explains to Amphinomus his understanding of human life after Amphinomus has toasted his health:

> "Of all the things that move and breathe on earth,
> earth nurtures nothing frailer than a man.
> As long as gods bestow prosperity
> and he can move about with agile knees,
> he thinks the future holds no misery;
> but when, against his will, the blessed gods
> allot his share of griefs, he yields to these
> with patient heart. And so indeed it shifts—
> the mind of man on earth: it changes with
> the changes in the days sent by the father
> of men and gods. I, too, might once have ruled,
> but stupidly beguiled by power and pride,
> misused my strength—I acted wantonly;
> I trusted in my father and my brothers.
> Thus, let no man—and at no time—be lawless;
> whatever gifts the gods have given him,
> let him guard these in silence." (p. 373, 74)

It is possible to construe this statement as part of Odysseus's wiliness, another stratagem designed to snare the suitors in his net, but to do so is to lose sight of the great power of what the mighty Odysseus has to say here. He is pretending to be someone else in order to preserve his disguise as a beggar, but his remarks nevertheless bear the ring of truth and suggest how his own experiences have not engendered hubris but humility, have not prompted him to think better of himself but to realize how much the shifts of fate that happen to anyone are beyond the knowledge or control of that individual.

"And so indeed," as he says, the "mind of man on earth"

shifts and "changes with / the changes in the days sent by the father / of men and gods"; the changes reflect the need to adjust to the circumstances that fate has meted out to one and also the modifications within one that come from suffering or experiencing the joys of life, both of which prompt alterations in the way one addresses one's existence. And if Odysseus here has not really lost power in his own region because he was "stupidly beguiled by power and pride," this is not because he hasn't suffered as a result of his own past acts—the pride and curiosity that kept him too long at the cave of the Cyclops is only one of several key examples—but rather simply the fate that he has had. Odysseus has made his own mistakes and has been carried away by pride, by power, and by his own strength, but he has also learned from those mistakes and recognized the great frailty of humans. No power beside the gods' is eternal, he knows, and no strength is sufficient in itself to overcome all the obstacles a human is called upon to face during the course of a lifetime, so pride is hardly warranted given the fragility of our hold on good fortune and the life of ease.

Our prosperity is bestowed upon us by the gods and doesn't come from our own abilities, though to be sure Odysseus is liked by Athena because he is such an exceptional human being and can come up with stratagems and outwit those who would steal his life from him. And if the gods are something of an obstacle to our understanding of Odysseus's viewpoint here, they really shouldn't be, for we need to remember that they do not provide the human world with the kinds of continuities and coherence we would expect from them: they do not give each life a particular shape that it deserves on the basis of the relative goodness or badness of the individual, nor do they necessarily guarantee that a good person's life will turn out good in the end. Odysseus ended up with a happy life after more than twenty years of struggle, but the poem is not a model that suggests how its hearers too can end up with such greatness and happiness, for no one knows what misery or prosperity will come one's way, and Odysseus can no more suggest how to effect positive outcomes in one's life than any other human can.

The operative word in Odysseus's assessment of human life is "change," a word we toss around today as though it too is the defining characteristic of our age. Certainly Odysseus recognized the most important fact of human existence: that one can never know what will come next, and that the only thing one can be sure of is that as long as one is alive one will be called upon to deal with changes in one's way of living and in oneself. One never knows just what those changes will be and can only arrive at the wisdom to acknowledge that they will come, whatever their form, and that thus one will have to address the altered circumstances on their own terms rather than assume they can be met on the basis of what one has already learned. Odysseus was always ready to investigate things, was always eager to cultivate his own personal discipline on the basis of what fate threw his way, and even if he has a little help in the consolation that Athena may be there to assist him when his challenges become too great, he also knows that he can always offend another god by stepping over the borders allotted to the acts of humans. Like any person who has learned from his experiences, Odysseus has discovered over time how far he can and should go in any particular context, has disciplined himself to attend to the circumstances at hand and determine his behavior on that basis. Simple though this ongoing discovery within a human life is, it is the process that Odysseus's own life measures out most clearly through his wiliness and his carefully calibrated sense of what is fitting to the context.

In the case of his assessment of life as a whole, Odysseus concludes from his own experiences that "no man—and at no time—[should] be lawless," for only grief can result from an offense against the borders that have been established for human action. Odysseus has worked those borders out for himself well enough to have survived a difficult life, whereas the people he is directly and indirectly speaking to at this moment, the suitors, have failed to learn them and will suffer accordingly. But the laws themselves are that which, according to Odysseus, determine the course of one's life. It is not Odysseus who takes it upon himself to assess what laws the suitors have broken and then to punish them accordingly; he is simply responding to the laws of hospitality and seeking to preserve what is left of his own fortune. And in concluding that "whatever gifts the gods have given him," an individual should "guard these in silence," Odysseus has moved away from his prideful declaration of his name to the Cyclops and come to see that the value of his gifts resides not in his ability to make them known to others but rather in his chances of surviving the hazards that come his way. If one should guard one's gifts in silence, that is only because doing otherwise can only prompt envy that will in turn create further difficulties in one's life, which always already has more than enough turbulence in it.

❦

Odysseus's assertion that one should recognize the frailty and uncertainty of life and guard one's gifts from the gods in silence is the statement of a "victor," of one who has survived his own excesses well enough to recognize both the nature of the excesses and the divine way through which one's life can come to one with ease, and it is worth placing his statement against the conclusions of the chorus in *Oedipus Rex* that are a reflection of another possible outcome in life, the one Oedipus meets:

> O citizens of Thebes, this is Oedipus,
> who solved the famous riddle, who held more power
>   than any mortal.
> See what he is: all men gazed on his fortunate life,
> all men envied him, but look at him, look.
> All he had, all this man was,
> pulled down and swallowed by the storm of his own
>   life,
> and by the god.
> Keep your eyes on that last day, on your dying.
> Happiness and peace, they were not yours
> unless at death you can look back on your life and say
> I lived, I did not suffer.[4]

The same circumspection about the good and bad fortune of life is present here with full force, and the measure of a life is clearly only to be found at its end—only then can one determine whether or not the life itself was indeed one of happiness and peace or one of grief and woe. If Oedipus himself reflects the need to guard one's gifts in silence, to recognize the frailty of humans in the face of an always-unpredictable fate, that is because he has been "swallowed by the storm of his own life," overwhelmed by the woes that have come to him as a result of the mere accident of being who he was. Neither Oedipus nor Odysseus could determine his own fate in spite of their very great gifts, and neither one of them is fool enough to take all the credit for the good fortune that has come his way. Oedipus seemed to have had more trouble remembering that future misery is always possible, perhaps because he lived a good number of years with relative peace and prosperity and thus forgot what could happen in any life. But both Greek figures live the fates they are fated to lead, and both are willing to accept those fates once they recognize them for what they are. Likewise, both have in the end the necessary humility in the face of their lives to have gauged the possibilities for humans in general.

The truths of the lives of both Oedipus and Odysseus are caught within the tangled chain of circumstances and the fluidity of their own beings, and the ability they have to attend to the authority of the circumstances with which life presents them is that which distinguishes them—it accounts for Oedipus's fierce insistence on seeing the course of his investigation into Laius's murder through to the end, and it covers Odysseus's long struggles and his recognition that there was always an "other/that" to which he had to attend, a context of which his own orientation was only a part. The "self" of these two great figures plays a small role in the outcome of events in some crucial respects, and that which is called "fate" or the "will of the gods" is by far the greater element in the way things unfold. In recognizing this, Odysseus and Oedipus also give up "control" of their lives in important ways and thereby acknowledge that their role in their future really comes down to their ability thoroughly to attend to that in the midst of which they always find themselves, the aesthetic authority of the context through which they measure the flows of their lives. Their "genius" is this sense is to have acknowledged that "other," that field of circumstances out of which their lives are constantly being evolved; they literally *see* how their own fate's course can be swayed by their own doings only to the extent that it is ever-mindful of the flows of the fields through which the "fates" measure out their lives, and so they develop the gift of attending to that which is. Even then, though, their genius is not sufficient to determine the outcome of their lives, for Odysseus finally "succeeds" whereas Oedipus "fails" and his life turns to great misery.

But the lives of Odysseus and Oedipus also thereby suggest the misguided direction of our own assessments of things, and it is worth noting that both the chorus in Oedipus and Odysseus himself focus on the role of envy in human life. Although neither text asserts specifically that envy is the most uncalled for of human emotions because it focusses erroneously on the agent rather than the event and thus totally misconstrues the flows of aesthetic authority through the event itself and not the agent, in effect that is the gist of both statements about the need for humility and for the proper gauge of life to be one that is applied only after the individual has died. If *our* concern with Odysseus's life and being is that its very fluidity and volatility, its lack of a coherent self through which to construe his actions, can cause the kind of violence to which our own culture is presumably so greatly opposed, Odysseus's concern with our culture would surely be the same one he would have about his own: that *envy* determines the artificial locations through which we attribute good and bad fortune in life when more often than not it is *circumstances and our failure to attend properly to them* that prompts the "good" and "bad" outcomes of life.

Envy focusses exclusively on the agent and thereby is that through which the specific self to which we are heirs begins to develop, and both Odysseus and Oedipus suffer from that artificial localization of the self or the "this" outside of the flows in which it is always embedded. Odysseus and Oedipus implicitly suggest, then, that the violence of the human world is much more likely to come from the tendency to localize truth and power in an agent rather than a context, and to determine authority therefore on the basis of people rather than on the flows in the midst of which they find themselves. The results of this false method of construing things are almost always negative in the long run because such a way of seeing the world misinterprets its lines of action and the flows of its forces and thereby loses sight of that into which it must play if it is to be successful. Yet most often it is precisely the larger context that is lost, out of envy toward one who seems to be in a superior position or out of self-pity over that which one lacks, or out of a short-term self-interest that loses sight of the larger flows.

When one considers Odysseus's powerful ability to attend to the moment and to derive his authority from it, and when one recognizes what self-discipline is necessary to get the mind to attend exclusively to what is, one loses sight of the great rigors that are to be found in such straightforward sentences. As is always the case in the human world, people tend to think that the good fortune of a life is somehow easily purchased if only the "secret" of the life is to be found; and as always, such people fail to note that the life they envy is based upon a kind of discipline they themselves are unwilling to effect in their own lives. If Odysseus's self-discipline allows him to attend fully to the moment and thus to assess its aesthetic truths, that is why he is a leader, why his crew depends on him for direction. Yet when they lose sight of their need for direction, they allow their self-interest to overwhelm their sense of the context in a way that Odysseus himself seldom does.

The most striking example of this is when Odysseus's men are chafing under his declaration that they cannot stop at the land of Helios because disaster was predicted for them if they did. These predictions didn't come from Oedipus himself, so it could hardly be said that he was furthering his own self-interests by holding to them, yet as the rigors of the journey and the unkind winds make life on board the ship increasingly intolerable, Odysseus's men begin to turn on him, and Eurolochus, the one who always seems most ready to work against Odysseus's leadership, turns with fury to Odysseus and exclaims:

> "Odysseus, your demands are merciless;
> no man can match your courage, and your strength
> will not relent. You surely must be made
> of iron if you do not let your friends—
> worn-out, in need of sleep—set foot ashore,
> where, on this seagirt land, we might once more
> prepare a proper meal. . . ." (p. 252, 53)

Eurolochus has obviously lost sight of the fact that Odysseus's "demands" were hardly demands at all but rather his response to the situation. He has been told what he needs to do if he and his men are to arrive at their destination, and he is willing to measure up to the necessities the context places on him in order to survive.

Once the rigors of the journey grow difficult, though, Eurolochus loses sight of the larger context out of which the demand arose, and he reduces it to a specific agent, Odysseus. Having done that, he accuses Odysseus of being merciless, when, of course, the merciless nature of the circumstances is hardly his fault but is rather something he is trying his best to overcome. And having done that, Eurolochus proceeds to take those characteristics that make Odysseus the wise man he is and gives them a negative twist: Odysseus's courage is so great that he forgets how weak other people are; his strength becomes something harsh and unfair to his crew whose abilities are much lesser; he is, in short, cruel precisely as a result of his good characteristics and thus no friend to his friends. Unrelenting in his demands, merciless in their execution, Odysseus stands accused as the agent of the crew's agony, and of course eventually they succumb to their own misreading of the situation and to their own lack of self-discipline and destroy their lives in the process. Odysseus's self-discipline, his ability to assess the truths of a larger context and recognize the limited role of his agency within it, makes him the *object* of envy when things are going well and the *object* of hatred when those in his midst suffer because in both cases the people are looking for an agent of their own relative disadvantage, and Odysseus and his great courage are the most likely location for that disadvantage.

Odysseus's strength comes from his ability to see his life in a larger context than one that is merely self-interested, or rather, to see that his own self-interest is best furthered through a careful investigation of the way things are, through the personal cultivation that engenders the sincere will that allows him to arrive at the aesthetic truths his context always is capable of providing him with if only he attends to its authority and his limited role as agent within it. This strength in turn is that which allows Odysseus to recognize the limits of what he or any other agent can do, even as his assessments of the fields of which he is a part make him aware of the fluidity of the "this" he always is within the "other/that" of the flows around him. His ability to assess the flows is contingent upon his facility for being most fully what the circumstances demand of him, drawing out of his nature that which is most fitting to the context rather than seeking to impose upon it that which he as agent might think most useful. The fluid self is not restricted to a kind of coherence and logic that would necessitate "predictable" responses; instead, its continuities are to be found in the way in which it returns with regularity to the various possibilities to be located within it as the circumstances in which it finds itself change and require new responses.

The regularities of the fluid self are thus not linear but recurrent, not predictable unless the contexts are themselves mere repetitions, but understandable over time simply because contexts eventually present themselves to us in ways that allow us to gauge their regularities and thus discern equivalent regularities within ourselves. This mode of being may be fluid, but that is its strength and not its weakness; and it may be unpredictable and hence potentially volatile, but as long as its assessments of the flows of the field remain based on the aesthetic authority of the context and don't attempt to reduce that authority to its own agency, the potential violence to be found in any human is perhaps less likely to force its way onto the scene than it would be if it were construed through an endless round of agents of envy, hatred, success and failure, good fortune and bad.

These would seem to be the conclusions to be derived from the nature of Odysseus's journey and his own assessment of it, and if we are not quite accustomed to seeing his courage and wisdom in these ways, that is because we live in the reductive world of agents of authority and truth rather than in the world wherein truth and authority are always determined through a context and then measured through the agents who are part of that context. It is perhaps difficult for us to construe such a violent person as an exemplary one in our own age of great violence, perhaps harder still for us to see his genius as inherent in precisely that which we lack, the personal cultivation that allows one most fully to live within and address with attentiveness the world one finds oneself in, but this is where Odysseus's agency is to be found, this is the region from which his authority flows. And if his cultural circumstances determine for him a life much different than the one either Confucius or Nietzsche would imagine for a wholly human person, that is nevertheless precisely what Odysseus presents us with and precisely where his life comes closest to the measure of the divine nature and the potential of the overman.

# Conclusion

## Beauty and Truth

If aesthetic authority represents that elusive category of understanding we all seek throughout our lives and perhaps come close to comprehending on occasion, and if its truths are those to which we need to attend if we are to engender the personal cultivation that leads to wisdom and to a better world, we can find no more fitting place for its articulation than in the work of Foucault, Weber, Nietzsche, Confucius, and Homer, texts as diverse and seemingly unrelated as one could imagine from cultural contexts that are equally diverse. In looking at them, we can certainly see that Homer's world is far different from Confucius's, and that both of their worlds are much different than the ones to be found in Nietzsche, Weber, and Foucault. But we can also see how the aspiration toward a kind of human wisdom does reflect some of the same features in each of these works even as it is mediated through the particular circumstances that generated them, circumstances that, in each case, we might well wish to dissociate ourselves from.

We are perhaps disinclined to admire the conservative, rigid, and hierarchical views to which Confucius attaches his ideas of personal cultivation and the divine nature; we do not wish to live in the violent and rapacious world of Homer either and certainly don't want to countenance much of what passes for civilized behavior in his poem; and we are not inclined to support Nietzsche's madness or his self-aggrandizing tendencies any more than we want to uphold his misogyny, his elitism, or his very considerable *ressentiment*. If some of us may have less to quarrel about with

Weber or Foucault, that is no doubt because of their relative nearness to us in time and thus is a reflection of the degree to which we still see the world through their eyes.

One way or the other, though, the aesthetic authority of Homer, Confucius, Nietzsche, Weber and Foucault is dependent on circumstances we might well wish to strip them of in order to imagine an ideal world in which human wisdom purges itself of the poisons of local contexts and avoids thereby the limitations of the cultural circumstances through which all human utterances take place. As our debt to Nietzsche, we have conceded that local circumstances can never be eliminated from cultural productions, and so we have learned that one of the "laws" of the human world is that the peculiarities of any culture's vision of the wisdom and potential of humanity are such that over time they will become curiosities at best and fall into great disfavor at worst. Indeed, the genius of our epoch is to be found in the ability we have developed to critique the forms of traditional and rational authority to which aesthetic authority is always linked, and it is these other forms of authority to which the aesthetic is joined that make its expression always something that is bounded by rules that seem to be laws only to the culture whose expression it is.

If we have learned no more than that over the past century, though, we have failed to profit from our experience, for our critical abilities at present do little more than make us smug spectators at a never-ending inquisition into the inevitable limitations of human discourse. We need always to remind ourselves of those limitations, to be sure, but we should also recognize that those limitations do not constitute the entire nature of the flows of discourse, that there is something else to be found within them that I have characterized as aesthetic authority. *That* is the authority to which we most often attend when we are committed to an investigation of things, and it is the authority to which all memorable human productions attend in their making. Some of those productions may be obviously aesthetic in nature, as the *Odyssey* is, and some may come to us under different rubrics, as the "scientific" approach of Weber would suggest or the ethical framework of Confucius demonstrates. But all productions are generated out of an aesthetic authority that comes not from the "self" whose name is attached to the text but to a situation that produces the "this" of the self and the "other/that" through which the "this" construes its uniqueness. Our awareness of who we are is bounded by these limits and doubtless always will be, but those limits also just as obviously make our awareness possible in the first place.

If the aesthetic has the authority I have ascribed to it, though, we have yet to see either it or the world in quite that way, and with so many texts in so many different cultures pointing in much the same direction, one has to wonder why humans have such a difficult time recognizing the force of the authority through which the flows of life are always constituted. Perhaps this problem is best understood by returning to a context that is far from our own, Homer's world, to look once more at Zeus's remarks about humans at the very beginning of the *Odyssey:*

> "Men are so quick to blame the gods: they say
> that we devise their misery. But they
> themselves—in their depravity—design
> grief greater than the griefs that fate assigns." (p. 6)

One of the continuities that is shared by most cultures would indeed be that humans are always looking for an agent of their misery. As Zeus says, they are "quick to blame the gods" for anything that goes wrong in their lives and unwilling to recognize the degree to which their own contributions to the miseries they suffer is greater. Proportion is important here, for Homer doesn't deny that "fate assigns" griefs to individuals too. The implication is that whereas the human situation inevitably involves misery as a matter of course, the tendency to find the origin of all one's misery in the gods or the fates is an excessive gesture through which humans seek to displace their own responsibility for their plight onto another.

One who is quick to blame the gods for one's misery is also one who has an insufficient understanding of agency within the flows of life, first because the individual improperly recognizes the degree to which his own choices within those flows determines in many respects the degree of misery that will come his or her way, and second because such a person fails to understand the seemingly contradictory fact that one is more likely to avoid making misery for oneself if one recognizes how far one's powers actually extend within any given field. Both misperceptions stem from the same mistake, a purely self-interested perspective of things that artificially extends the lines of a "this" that is a marker within a field into a "self" of essential importance, complete with autonomy, continuity, and coherence. In failing to note how the "this" is that which is produced by the flows rather than the other way around, the individual who endlessly looks for agents of his own misery creates the largest agency of misery of all, the artificial boundaries of a self that will make the aesthetic authority of the fields harder and harder to discern, thereby increasing the chances for misery that stems from poor choices within the flows.

It is true that we have a more fully developed sense of self than the people of Homer's day did, and there is no way we could return to the rudimentary selves of that time even if we wanted to. If we were able to, though, nothing would change, for we know that the rudimentary self of the archaic Greek world is equally quick to blame the gods for misery that stems from a failure to assess properly the flows of the field. This suggests that it is not so much the degree to which one's self-conception is developed that is important but rather the *orientation* one gives to that self-conception. We need to remember that Confucius characterized his own discipline in terms of "personal cultivation," a phrase that unquestionably refers to a kind of intense cultivation of the self. In his case, though, personal cultivation was contrary to the mere pursuit of self-interest in the world, even if one could put the point the opposite way as well and argue that true self-interest from a Confucian point of view is so thoroughly aware of the way that the self's interests are dependent on the flows of larger fields that it simply cultivates that interest from a different vantage point. This too makes perfect sense, but it also calls forth the danger found in the region we are dealing with, the danger that begins with a different form of self-interest and ends with futile quests for the origins of one's misery.

The problem with all aesthetic authority is, we have seen, that it always depends on the context in which it is found and on the assessment that is made of that context. Thus, most basically, what is indeed self-interest in one situation might seem to be self-denying in another. The problems humans face in this respect concern the ever-shifting borders between perspectives. Confucius's perspective is undeniably self-interested in a way, as is Nietzsche's, but it is less obviously so than Nietzsche's, and so it seems to us to be part of an ascetic regime that is greatly different from what Nietzsche had in mind. And a good bit of the apparent difference comes from Nietzsche's endless expostulations about the necessity and virtue of what he calls *selfishness,* the ground of his perspective. That the selfishness to which he refers is also the road to the overman, that it is dependent on a discipline through which one seeks to purge oneself of *ressentiment* rather than spread its effects further and further, is something that alters one's understanding of the word "selfishness," just as to argue that Confucius's "personal cultivation" is also a form of heightened self-interest would change our conception of an interested self. We often seem to lack the capacity for distinguishing between forms of self-interest, and this lack leads to the self-justifying kinds of activity that engender further misery in our (and others') lives.

What, then, distinguishes the self-interest of Confucius from ordinary self-interest? What separates Nietzsche's selfishness from the usual variety with which we are so familiar? And how are these distinctions essential for an understanding of aesthetic authority? Confucius bases his sense of personal cultivation on the need to investigate things, and from that investigation comes knowledge, through which in turn we can develop the sincerity of the will and order the heart and thereby achieve the cultivated state wherein we are in harmony with ourselves. This in turn provides the possibility for order within the family, the nation, and the world as a whole. There is no doubt that such personal cultivation is self-interested, for it is based on the development of a world in which the self is pleased by what is and contributes to it. But such self-interest is construed through an intense self-discipline that requires steady attention to the circumstances in which one always finds oneself, and thus it displaces the "this" the self is from central consideration.

Confucius's self is cultivated through such a displacement and thus moves in the opposite direction of the kinds of self-interest with which we are all too familiar that are based on nothing more than a very local and banal expression of the immediate needs of the self that is thoroughly lacking in the discipline that would lead to an order that would be useful to the larger fields of family, nation, and world. One's life cannot help but be improved through personal cultivation, then, yet the object of that cultivation, the self, is displaced into a larger conception of order that is based on what is rather than on the desires and illusions of a self that is unwilling to concede its relationship to flows that are much larger and more important than it will ever be.

Likewise, Nietzsche found himself using the phrase "will to power" in two different ways, the one way expressing conventional assertions of pure self-interest, the other referring to a self-interest that is based upon an assessment and exuberant expression of the overabundance of life itself. One denies the world by reducing everything exclusively to the concerns of a single agent, oneself, whereas the other expands the self and its interests by diminishing and displacing it, by seeing it as only one of the locations through which the energy of the world plays itself out. What is more clearly visible from Nietzsche's perspective is that both forms of self-interest can be based on great self-discipline. Confucius's work suggests in some respects that without the discipline of personal cultivation he has in mind, chaos is the only result, and this is true in the larger sense. But in the smaller frame of vision, a self can devote incredible self-discipline to the goals of a purely self-centered conception of value, a perspective that creates its own kind of local order, even if that order is sufficiently in conflict with the flows of the world to engender eventually chaos of its own.

Nietzsche's will to power emphasizes that both forms of self-interest are dependent on a *willing* on the part of the individual, who can put that will to work on behalf of the resentments that have become markers of the self's history of misery or who can will an affirmation of what is that puts to the side the resentments that inevitably accumulate in any human life. The one form of self-discipline is based on a cultivation of resentment and the centering effects that such a form of cultivation would have, whereas the other form is based on a self-discipline that displaces both the resentments and the centered self that is dependent on them for its definition. In this respect, it is difficult to argue that the one perspective is less or more self-interested than the other, nor should we want to in any case, for those who would assert that all forms of self-interest are inimical are themselves part of a framework that is designed to persuade people to discipline themselves for the wrong reasons, out of *guilt* rather than out of a desire more fully to express the great value of what is.

Unless one is interested in cultivating self-discipline through guilt, a term like "self-interested" can only make sense on the basis of the context through which it is interpreted, and at that point, having lost its necessary pejorative connotations, it becomes a different word altogether. The virtue of Confucius's path to self-cultivation, after all, like Nietzsche's, is that it is *not* predicated on guilt or on the imposition of some external discipline onto the self; rather, it depends on a discipline that is to be found within the self that is cultivated out of a desire to express more fully the nature of what is. It is not a graft from an "other/that" onto a "this" but rather a manifestation of the way the "other/that" and the "this" are always produced out of the aesthetic context through which their relations are measured. So too with Nietzsche's "selfishness": it depends on a discipline that is not imposed from an external source upon an unruly self that will engender only evil in the world if it doesn't submit to the larger force of God. Instead it is based upon an ongoing assessment of the way the location one *is* is capable of expressing most fully the flows of the world and affirming their great value.

At the same time, Nietzsche recognizes full well why the external discipline of guilt and the negative regime of life-denying activities have developed as alternatives to the discipline of the self that he favors: they are at once responses to the perils of *ressentiment* and yet further expressions of it. No one understood more thoroughly than Nietzsche the inevitable double-bind to be found at the heart of any discipline that seeks to impose something from the outside onto a self, for he saw that the traditional form of authority in the West was based on an awareness of the highly destructive effects personal resentment has on the world, yet in seeking to put those effects out of play, it instead *institutionalized* them by the guilty imposition of an artificial and life-denying discipline. Instead of cultivating the self in order to overcome one's resentments, one should deny that one has such impulses at all. And to deny that one has such inclinations, one has to reject the realm of the body, the historical and cultural context through which one lives one's life, and anything else to do with the temporal world—one must, in other words, become *selfless* to achieve the ideal vision of the traditional forms of the West. At the same time, as we well know, no civilization has been *more* committed to expressions of the self than the West, so clearly its externally-imposed discipline failed at every level. Far from putting that nasty self out of play by denying it and cultivating a state of pure good, the self became the paramount enterprise in the world, and everything became filtered through its localized interests. The failure of this traditional system of authority is written into the great mania for localized self-interest it unleashed on the world through its presumed discipline of selflessness.

Nietzsche's response to the selfishness of the traditional forms of life-denying authority in the West was to announce his selfishness, to declare that the discipline of the human world must not be predicated on a denial of one's resentments but rather on a full awareness of the degree to which *ressentiment* has been the defining characteristic of human action in the world. Instead of guaranteeing the return of the repressed resentment through the guilty discipline of hiding the interests of the self, Nietzsche's version of self-interest asserts that there are forms of self-interest that are also in *others'* interests, and that as joyful expressions of what is, they manage therefore also to do justice to the nature of the world. From the traditional perspective, however—a vantage point that refuses to make a distinction between forms of self-interest—Nietzsche's assertions (or Confucius's for that matter) can only be the expression of a truly evil man, one who is willing to unleash all the nasty forces of ego onto a world without any guilt at having done so. The result, traditional authority would conclude, will be terrors worse than any we have yet to see. Hence, traditional authority will refuse to countenance any idea of an aesthetic authority that is dependent on context, for to do so would be to recognize the basic point underlying Nietzsche's argument.

It is worth noting that both the traditional religious viewpoint and the liberal vision of a distinction-free series of disciplines and ways of life are predicated on the same form of traditional authority and rely upon the same arguments. If Nietzsche is an object of revulsion for the religious world, that is because his viewpoint is indeed perspectival and thus without ground. And inasmuch as a groundless perspective can only lead to a world in which everyone merely devotes him- or herself to expressions of personal need, chaos and destruction can be the only result. If there is no external power to discipline the forces within humans, the argument runs, then the negative form of will to power as expression of the essential greediness of humans can be the only result.

So too the liberal vision would have us understand that our impulses can only be disciplined properly once we recognize the lack of essential distinctions between the various groups that exist in the world and can see that our own self-interests must be put aside in order to further this larger world of undifferentiated humanity. It too would impose an external discipline onto humans in order to deal with the same problem: we need through guilt to convince people to give up their self-interests for the greater good. It is difficult in the end to distinguish how this form of traditional authority differs from that to be found within the religious conception of human behavior, for the only thing that separates the two visions is that the one posits the ground of human discipline within a God whereas the other posits the ground of human discipline within those who argue for the particular vision they themselves advocate.

The liberals simply reflect a secular response to the same problem the religious world tried but failed to deal with. They seek to address the inequities that have come about in the world through the resentful expressions of self that have produced the flows of the social fields by reversing the flows of resentment and guilt, and they do so because, as with the religious view, they recognize that a world based solely on resentful will to power can only be horrific. Yet from foundation to ultimate effect, their own vision is driven by *ressentiment* and by the false imposition of their own self-interested authority upon others. It is hard to escape the conclusion that they have simply sought to take over the role that God plays in the religious world, harder still to escape the inference that all too often their own vision is driven by the resentments that God too was supposed to be able to discipline.

All this is not to say that it is wrong or foolish to wish (and *work*) for a world in which the flows are distributed more evenly, in which discrimination and unfair barriers to the conduct of life are eliminated. Confucius's personal cultivation is based on the ideal of a harmonious world in which the discipline of the self engenders the fair regulation of orders in the social world as well. And if Nietzsche himself was inclined in all too many respects to be against any egalitarian goals, the overman is a conception that leads to the same goals as those that are found within the liberal vision of things and, at least in some respects, in the religious viewpoint as well: a social order in which *ressentiment* is no longer the determining force. Through the personal cultivation of the self that abjures the grounds of resentment, humans inevitably aspire to a life in which the social world is not defined by the expressions of resentment, and in seeking to effect such an attitude in one's own life, one couldn't help but contribute to the betterment of the species as a whole.

The chief virtue of the Nietzschean and Confucian perspectives is that neither one of them is predicated on the hopeless contradiction to be found in the Western religious and liberal perspectives. Both Nietzsche and Confucius realize that the betterment of humankind depends on *personal* cultivation within an aesthetic context without ground, and both realize that this means the need to discipline the self in order to abjure resentment. Instead of arguing for a better world on the basis of a denial of the very real resentment that is to be found within every human being, Nietzsche and Confucius insist that we investigate the way things are and derive our sense of self and our discipline from what we find. Instead of using resentment to get rid of resentment (for guilt is nothing more than resentment turned inside out), Confucius and Nietzsche begin with Zeus's viewpoint that the greatest share of human misery comes from humans themselves and not from some external agent, and that indeed more misery has come from the various expressions of resentment and its self-centering effects than any other human phenomenon.

❦

Aesthetic authority is the location through which the alternative visions of Nietzsche and Confucius emerge, and it is the only locus through which we can escape the double-binds of resentment that are built into every human culture. If there is a problem with the work of Nietzsche and Confucius, it doesn't reside in their understanding of the possibilities available to us and the two attitudes toward self-interest upon which they are predicated; on the contrary, their genius is to be found in the way they frame for us our inevitable choice: self-interest via *ressentiment* and the chaos it breeds, or self-interest via the cultivation and affirmation of life that can be achieved only through the discipline which allows us to abjure our resentments. No, the difficulty of their thought has to do with the perpetual problem the species has always faced: the effectuality of a self-interest predicated on an affirmation of the world in the face of a socius based upon resentful self-interest.

What possible positive effects could Nietzsche's overman have, we might ask, unless *everyone* adopted that perspective? What conceivable good can come from Confucius's divine nature if the world itself remains populated by humans whose nature is anything but divine? The religious viewpoint, after all, like the liberal viewpoint, is based on the assumption that *others* are basically driven by *ressentiment* whereas those who share the religious or liberal vision are the few on the planet who have managed to get past their own resentments (or are at least putatively willing to acknowledge them). They in turn therefore seek to impose a regime on those others who inevitably are too self-interested to do so. Nietzsche's overman gets trampled in such a regime, as does Confucius's divine nature.

So we have two essentially theological frameworks—the traditional religious viewpoint and the liberal perspective—that assume humans are degraded and need to be disciplined from the outside for their own good, and the Confucian or Nietzschean perspective that argues that any such attempt to discipline humans will only lead to further degradation and thereby defeat its own purpose, and which asserts in opposition to these regimes the goal of disciplining the self on the basis of the aesthetic authority in the midst of which that self is always to be found. If humans are to improve their lot from this perspective, the discipline cannot come from without, for that is nothing more than another form of traditional authority arbitrarily imposing its will on others "for their own good." Yet the Nietzschean and Confucian perspectives—in spite of what Nietzsche himself might have thought—depend on the ability of *all* humans to master themselves and overcome their resentments, and they thus seem hopelessly unreal given the way the world works, and thus hopelessly ineffectual when it comes to engendering meaningful changes within the flows of the social fields.

Is there any way to mediate between these two visions of human existence, or are they inevitably mutually exclusive choices for human conduct that cannot seriously coexist because of their different orientations? The one thing both seem to have in common is their attitude toward the socius itself, which is a skeptical orientation that would agree with much of the intellectual critique of Western culture since Nietzsche. The liberal position has derived its points of attack from Nietzsche, even if Nietzsche himself was hardly a liberal, and a good number of today's religious perspectives are informed by a "liberation theology" that is based on the critique of the West. Beyond the critique itself, though, there is the attitude toward authority and the way to deal with it, and here there would seem to be no way of bridging the gap between an essentially religious viewpoint and the one embraced by Confucius or Nietzsche, for if the authority must come from the outside, if humans are not in themselves capable of the discipline that is required for them to discern the truths of the aesthetic and thus learn how to establish their lives on the basis of its authority, then neither Confucius's vision of the divine nature nor Nietzsche's conception of the overman can find a point of agreement with either traditional religion or the liberal politics of the day.

This is not to say that one with a Nietzschean inclination would necessarily be opposed to the goals of current liberal politics, even if Nietzsche himself maintained his elitism to the end. Surely the goal of Nietzsche's work was to imagine a human species that could deal with what it is and thus would be capable of instituting social structures that were based on affirmative rather than negative principles of discipline. And no one reviled the resentment-driven nature of the current socius more than Nietzsche; indeed, his overman is inconceivable without such seething resentment as is to be found in modern Western societies. But if the Nietzschean perspective is at least as committed to change as is the liberal viewpoint, the means of effecting that change are incompatible because of the curious reversal that takes place: Nietzsche the elitist will only embrace a discipline that comes from *within* the individual whereas the liberal egalitarian willingly accepts a discipline that is imposed in hierarchical ways on those who resist the egalitarian viewpoint that is promulgated—the elitist turns into an egalitarian in his means and ideals, the egalitarian turns into an elitist in his means, if not his ideals. There is no way around this impasse.

Aesthetic authority, dependent on contexts as it always is, cannot make use of a strategy that imposes unilateral assertions on the world because the world it construes is too complex to be measured by unequivocal judgments. Each situation requires its own assessment, and the thicket of relations that exists within each context provides in turn its own way of determining the value of the flows of the fields. The difficulty inherent in this framework, though, becomes its chief obstacle. First, because aesthetic authority cannot be easily translated from one context to another, it requires the perpetual assessment of the humans who perceive its value. Second, because the perspective through which aesthetic authority is perceived is one that we are disciplined away from as we grow up, we must learn again to submit ourselves to its discipline and to commit ourselves to seeing what is in the face of much we should prefer to will away.

Third, the discipline of the aesthetic itself is indeed in opposition to the traditional means through which our societies have constituted value, so it leads one inevitably into conflict with the prevailing ways of measuring the worth of human events. Fourth, because the positive values through which aesthetic authority is constituted inevitably lead to opposition of the givens of one's culture, it is quite easy over time to lose sight of the positive values with which one started and begin to construe one's sense of things on the basis of one's opposition to the flows of discourse to which one is opposed. At that point, one's own values become negative, simple markers of opposition to that which is rather than assertions of the need for personal cultivation and a sincere will. And fifth, because the rigors of individual discipline alone are such as to provide great challenge, it is easy to assume the hopelessness of the larger venture, to conclude that it is impossible to take seriously the notion that societies can be constituted on the basis of aesthetic authority. Given that, personal cultivation does not expand to the larger orders to which it must also be attached.

The virtue of the Confucian or Nietzschean perspective is that it acknowledges the great difficulty in achieving a nation that is well ordered, yet the individual discipline upon which that goal is based is sufficient in itself. Surely Confucius hoped to help make his own social system better, just as Nietzsche very much wanted to turn the European societies away from their decadence and nihilistic tendencies. But the divine nature and the overman do not depend on the emergence of such transformations, for they recognize that if the change doesn't come from within, the authoritarian means of the socius—the central problem inherent in it—has not really been dispensed with at all but only been displaced onto another illusionary system that purports to give all people the rights they have coming to them.

It is not an accident in this respect that both Confucius and Nietzsche articulate exemplary perspectives; that is, in Weber's sense they were both based upon the charisma of the "leader," and their value for the socius as a whole is dependent on the way in which the ideas within them can form a fitting model for the discipline they seek to embody. If Nietzsche himself was not exemplary in precisely the way that Confucius was, falling short of the model of the "divine nature," in some respects he was even more exemplary, for he demonstrated the necessity of his vision of the overman even as he embodied the inevitable traps in which one becomes ensnared when one fails to escape one's resentments. But an exemplary perspective has no particular agenda beyond the discipline that is necessary to perceive the aesthetic and thus to respond to the authority of the flows of fields, and its goals "end" in a sense when the individual finally understands the role of his or her agency within a field whose authority is always larger than the particular effects of any agent within it. More authoritarian perspectives only begin at such a point as they seek to implement a plan of action to force others to submit to their will.

As the work of Foucault, Weber, Nietzsche, Confucius and Homer demonstrates, the great virtue and necessity of aesthetic authority is that it provides for us the lines of action that connect one thing to another, relate a "this" to an "other/that" even as they show the ways in which the "this" constitutes itself in terms of the "other/that" that is also extruded through the ways the flows of the field resolve themselves first this way and then that way. Through the aesthetic each agent within the flows learns the ways in which it is affected and effective within its own regions and thus comes to understand the degree to which its agency furthers or diminishes the overall flows of the fields. The agent comes to understand that the value of its "this" is thus dependent on the location it is within the field itself rather than something that exists independent of all contexts, and in so doing, the "this" becomes a different kind of "self," one that recognizes the ways in which that self is "made" out of those events that come its way through the actions of the fields and their interplay with the ever-changing roles one has within them.

From the aesthetic perspective, one first begins to see the ways in which the ruse of origin has artificially constituted our world in all the ways that Nietzsche, Heidegger, Derrida and Foucault have demonstrated. One sees, for example, that any discussion of whether the agent in a field is "active" or "passive" misses the point from the very beginning, for one is always to be found in the midst of flows that are ongoing, and thus it is impossible to determine the origin of any action or effect. How, then, could one figure out whether this or that act was a passive response to events or an "original" act that had nothing to do with what had already happened? All actions are inevitably "passive" because the flows into which we fit ourselves and through which we constitute our sense of things are always already flowing before we are placed within them. In this sense it could be argued that all our actions are in fact reactions.

But such a gross oversimplification of the network of relations that establishes itself through the play of the fields and the agents within them could only have plausibility within a system that reduces everything to subjects and objects, for even the most casual observation of any network of effects would demonstrate that if all agents within the network—whether they are humans or electrons—are essentially "passive," that is, dependent on the flows of the field for the basis of their own actions, yet at the same time all the agents must necessarily be "active" as well, for their responses to the forces of the fields effect changes within them that could not come about if each particular agent didn't have its own uniqueness, its own particular way of acting within the forces that help to constitute it and are constituted through it. Within such an aesthetic viewpoint, one cannot help but see the absurdity of seeking to determine activity or passivity even as one recognizes the futility to be found in arguments that attempt to establish the degree to which humans are determined or free in their choices. One sees that the best assessment we can make of such things is to state that whatever the relative degree of freedom and determinism might be within our species, one is always relatively more free to the extent that one recognizes those constraints upon one's actions that are unavoidable, and those constraints—and the vectors for action they provide us with—can only be adequately determined from an aesthetic viewpoint. Its authority resides precisely in the way it allows us to discern the constraints through which we can understand our position within a field and thus act intelligently within it. The ease of the divine nature that hits upon what is right without effort is nothing more than the full recognition of the authority of the context in which one finds oneself.

❦

In the end, though, there is still the problem that inheres in the relationship between Weber's charismatic authority and the traditional forms of authority, in the fact that in some respects charismatic authority must always be routinized. Perpetual revolution is not possible within the human community even if in some respects that is precisely what is going on all the time. Weber insisted that bureaucratic structures are finally necessary for the implementation of charismatic authority, and thus the original force is displaced into regimes that become traditional and thus lose the authority with which they began. He also argued that aesthetic authority is antithetical to economic activity as we know it, and inasmuch as the world today is almost exclusively constituted through economic mediations, one has to consider the usefulness of the aesthetic in the face of the attempts to define human activity entirely on the basis of the economic model. Again, there seems to be another conflict between unreconcilable viewpoints here that has yet to be addressed.

Aesthetic authority compels us to see ourselves as both more and less than an economic marker within the celebration of market dynamics, first by putting the economic flows themselves into a context that construes them as only one kind of flow among many, second by demonstrating that our more fundamental linkages to the flows of the world are constituted through a Confucian kind of sincerity whose goal is not greater appropriation but rather greater understanding and order, personal cultivation. The economic model of human behavior, regardless of whether it posits rational or irrational choices within the economic flows, inevitably assumes that the choices made reflect enlightened or some other kind of self-interest that is centralizing, that removes from the flows a greater and greater proportion of the goods purely for one's own benefit. The focus on the self in this narrow way cannot be reconciled with the orientation toward the self's activities that is found in an aesthetic perspective. It is not that humans do not consider their own interests from the aesthetic viewpoint, for we have found that they do; nor is it that they no longer consider the self-interests of the traditional modes of authority, for they do that too; it is rather that the displaced self of the aesthetic is paramount, and the other ways of construing the self are always subordinate and collateral conceptions. From the economic or the traditional perspective, the centered self must inevitably be the "ground" through which one conceives one's activities.

Nevertheless, one who has an aesthetic perspective is fully capable of acting properly within the economic flows, just as such an individual can avoid taking vows of poverty, for aesthetic authority allows one an understanding of the dynamics of economic activity as well and should as a result allow one the means through which to make sense of one's position within it. But it is true that aesthetic authority is irreconcilable with economic power, that the kinds of self-interest the two perspectives provide are incompatible in the vectors of force and energy they articulate. One sees this most obviously in the current world by the lengths to which people must go to convince the socioeconomic apparatus that not everything on the planet should be destroyed for the purpose of a few jobs or for a greater gross national product. Instead of being able to argue that old stands of forest, for example, should be left alone, regardless of the economic consequences, one has to "discover" rare species of birds or plants that would be endangered if the forest were to be cut down, and then one can argue that the forests should remain standing. Indeed, perhaps the majority of individuals in the United States would be unwilling to agree that our moral vision is dependent on more than our own economic self-interest, that the very notion that there are ethical reasons why old stands of timber ought to be left alone is an absurd one.

The thought that in some cases trees might be more important than humans strikes most people in the United States as a delusionary perspective, yet that is precisely what aesthetic authority would suggest to us. The overall view of the planet and what it is and does compels us—again, from one angle purely out of self-interest—to leave some areas of the world alone, and large enough areas so they can more or less maintain their flows rather than fall into decrepitude. The overall aesthetics of the planet as we understand it today depends on the existence of original-growth forests, and that is paramount, regardless of other interests. If we are incapable of recognizing other interests than our own on the planet, we are truly doomed as a species, and certainly our actions of the past few hundred years in particular would suggest that we are indeed doomed precisely because we cannot escape from the self-centered, self-interested viewpoint that today is driven almost exclusively by the economic engines of our social systems.

One could add that of course it is also in our self-interest to preserve what's left of the original-growth forests because they provide us with locations through which we can study the activities of the planet without the heavy intrusiveness of our own interests, something that might be of profound use to us if ever some kind of environmental crisis should appear. And we know it is in our self-interest to allow enough trees to live to deal with the potential problems of the greenhouse effect and its consequences. We recognize further that it is in our interests to leave old stands to work as they do because of the potential benefits to be found within some of the more obscure species of plants that might exist within them, plants whose properties we remain unaware of and yet might find the need for at some future date.

These purely self-centered reasons for maintaining old-growth forests ought to be more than enough to keep us from mowing down what is left, but the more compelling reasons for leaving them alone are based exclusively on aesthetic authority, most profoundly that there is something seriously wrong with a species given the self-awareness we have that cannot at the same time see it as a positive—indeed an *essential*—virtue to imagine many places in the world that remain relatively unaffected by our interests. The very idea of the planet as a large resource-bed for our own exclusive interests is so repulsive that it should prompt people to rebel at the way everything is exploited for economic and localized interests with no regard for the overall flow of the fields that constitute the activity on the earth. Even the idea that we have the right to destroy members of species that are far older than we will ever be, and that we have the right to do so for the lowest of reasons—to gain cheap pulp, say, that could be acquired by "harvesting" much younger trees that we have planted especially for such uses—should strike us as dreadfully appalling, and yet in the world we live in it seems on the contrary ridiculous to even suggest such alternative ways of construing things.

Aesthetic and economic authority are mutually exclusive in nature, at least as they are presently constituted, and of all the forms of traditional authority that are at odds with aesthetic authority, it is the economic variety that is most likely thoroughly to overrun the aesthetic in any domain it declares itself interested in. But it remains possible for us to imagine an economic system that is based upon aesthetic authority, and I would argue that it is not only possible for us to do so but ultimately necessary for our survival. The very fact that in small ways our current system considers the effects of choices and seeks to rectify the negative consequences suggests that there have at least been minor alterations in the economic flows that reflect an aesthetic awareness. Lumber companies, for example, might create tree farms to placate public outrage over their clear-cutting destruction of large stands of trees, but they might also start such farms out of an awareness of the "renewable resource" upon which their activity is based. They extend the temporal horizon of their economic considerations sufficiently in order to be able to see that finally it is in their self-interest to keep the growth of trees going, that eventually there will be no trees left to "harvest" if they themselves do not plant them.

Planting new trees hardly makes up for mowing down vast stretches of old forest, but it does reflect a growing awareness that long-term economic stability depends on an aesthetic awareness of the flows of the planet itself and not simply on the localized extrusion of a product for a market. The invisible hand is not looking out for the trees, and our own awareness of the circularity of the flows of the planet might well come too late and too slowly to keep us from devouring precisely that upon which our future possibilities depend, but even within the economic world we have arrived at the point where in some cases we at least pay lip service to this aesthetic way of thinking, recognizing that in displacing our localized self-interest into the flows of the fields in general we end up with an enhanced series of possibilities, to say nothing for a much better sense of the way the world is.

Confucius saw no reason why economic activity should be incompatible with the aesthetic authority on the basis of which personal cultivation is possible, and even if he himself became disillusioned about such prospects over his lifetime, there is every reason to think at the moment that we have no choice but to imagine an economic system that reflects the knowledge of aesthetic authority throughout. We are told by cultural anthropologists that in the gift-giving systems that preceded the complex economic networks we presently have, gifts were always proffered with a sense of obligation: one gave something in the expectation of getting something even "better" in return. But one also gave to establish linkages between locations, relations between people and communities that would make human collaboration more likely and that would eliminate social discord.

This "primitive" act was a kind of magic that performed all sorts of essential functions for the local community. It was an attempt to control the economic flows through mysterious means, giving something now in the hopes of receiving something more later. It was a way of measuring the dynamics of human interchange, a means of managing the distribution of goods, a method for assessing the limits of human exchange, a strategy whereby it was at least possible that the eventual linkages that were established through gift-exchange could lead to a system in which not everything was construed purely through economic self-interest. This is not to say that gift-giving didn't involve serious self-interest but rather to argue that nonetheless such exchanges had something of an aesthetic authority to them, had built into them an awareness of the very real magic of exchange itself, a giving that can also be a getting, a flow that inevitably goes but that might also return, a process that was not marked by the accumulation of goods but rather by their endless circulation. We certainly do not inhabit this kind of economic system today, and there is no way that we can return to such a naively-predicated order given the sheer number of humans that need to be supported. But there is no reason to think that the flows of our economy cannot one day be made more commensurate with our knowledge of the aesthetic authority that is the basis of our understanding of all the flows of which we are a part, and there is every reason to think that we should make such a system our highest priority.

In the end, though, the virtues and limitations of aesthetic authority are constituted through the acts of the individual working in consort with the flows of which he or she is a part, and no amount of theoretical speculation about new economic or social systems will be of any use unless we come to understand the ways through which to cultivate that which we are. In order to do that, we must first recognize that it does indeed matter who's speaking, though not in the ways we have previously thought. The agent is not a fitting locus of fetishization, for his activity can no more be separated from the field in which it takes place than his authority can be carried across the borders of one field into another. Truth and authority always inhere in the context of their production, and within that context there are agents who are linked to that authority and truth, but their value can always only be measured in terms of their relationship to the field of which they are a part and through which their authority is established.

Given this set of circumstances, it is impossible for us to measure the authority of agents in terms of their unique essences because we must assume that they themselves are the products of the fields of which they are a part and cannot be separated from them any more than any other creature can be separated from its habitat. In establishing the agent in a displaced position of authority, and in stripping him of the characteristics that would allow us to fetishize him in one way or another, we have in some respects indeed acknowledged the end of man, as the post-structuralists have asserted for decades now. But contrary to what the post-structuralists have said, we have *not* reduced the agent to his roles within the social discourse and the production and regulation of its flows. Humans are not merely markers in a power game of endless self-interest, though they are always in the midst of such a situation; nor are they divine agents of God come down to establish His kingdom on earth or to prepare for His kingdom in heaven.

Rather, humans are residents in multiple locations who produce their lives and allow their lives to be produced through the fields in which they discern their locatedness, and over time they come to understand the ways in which their authority in the world depends upon the sincerity to be found in Confucius's personal cultivation, in the manner in which they assess the flows in the midst of which they find themselves, and in the degree to which they fully occupy their positions within the fields. Their authority is derived from their understanding and assessment of the authority of the aesthetic context itself, and its displaced form of self-interest allows them to recognize the limits of the authority they obtain by virtue of acknowledging the effects of the field, just as the way they make use of that authority in turn affects the manner in which the field produces effects through its flows.

In this way, it may not matter what names are attached to the agents whose authority is derived from the flows of the field, but it is important for us to acknowledge the locations within the flows through which the forces of a field are regulated, both to know the way things are and to be able to assess the value of that which is produced. The values through which we live our lives are determined in this fashion, and we have no other way of discerning what can and cannot be done in the future without recognizing both the agents and the context of authority. The difficulty comes in figuring out what is and is not effective, in finding what is and is not consonant with the field itself, assuming that in most contexts what is appropriate for the field is the determining criterion of production and not simply what is useful to us. What is suitable for us ought to be established through an understanding of what is fitting for the flows of the field and not the other way around, and unless we are willing to adopt that viewpoint, aesthetic authority gives way to the arbitrariness of other forms of authority that depend exclusively on tradition or brute assertions of the will to power as self-interest.

Within the human world there is no way we can escape the endless assertions of self-interest, so we need constantly to be evaluating the flows of the fields and our understanding of our location within them. But if we truly desire to investigate things, and if we establish a fitting measure for the course of our lives—whether it be something akin to Confucius's divine nature, Nietzsche's overman, or Odysseus's sense of excellence—the sincerity of our will can engender the aesthetic authority that will provide us with the discernment we need in order to know our place in the world, to better direct our actions within the always-complex events in the midst of which we find ourselves, and to celebrate the life we share with the multifarious flows around us.

# Notes

## *Introduction*

1. Michel Foucault, "What Is an Author?" in *Language, Counter-Memory, Practice,* ed. Donald F. Bouchard (Ithaca, NY: Cornell University Press, 1977), p. 121. Subsequent quotations from this essay will be from this translation and will be noted parenthetically with page numbers in the text.

2. See especially *The Origins of the Gods* (Albany: State University of New York Press, 1991).

3. I will have more to say about other kinds of authority in the next chapter when I discuss Max Weber's breakdown of authority into legal, traditional, and charismatic varieties.

## *Chapter One*

1. Max Weber, *The Theory of Social and Economic Organization,* trans. A. M. Henderson and Talcott Parsons, New York, The Free Press, 1947, p. 328. Subsequent quotations from this volume will be noted parenthetically with page numbers in the text.

## *Chapter Two*

1. Friedrich Nietzsche, *On the Genealogy of Morals* and *Ecce Homo,* trans. Walter Kaufmann, New York, Vintage Books, 1967, p. 201. Subsequent quotations from this work will be from this translation and will be noted parenthetically with page numbers in the text.

2. For a fuller discussion of the consequences of Nietzsche's *ressentiment,* see my *The Question of Value: Thinking through Nietzsche, Heidegger, and Freud* (Carbondale, IL: Southern Illinois University Press, 1989).

## Chapter Three

1. *The Wisdom of Confucius,* trans. Lin Yutang (New York: Modern Library, 1966), pp. 138, 39. Subsequent quotations from Confucius's work will be from this translation and will be noted parenthetically with page numbers in the text. Strictly speaking, of course, this quotation and others I will be using are not Confucius's own remarks. I refer to them as though they are the words of Confucius both for the sake of convenience and because in a general way he does indeed remain the chief agent of their authority, regardless of whether or not they are his words, his grandson's, or someone else's.

2. Friedrich Nietzsche, *The Gay Science,* trans. Walter Kaufmann (New York: Vintage Books, 1974), p. 329.

3. See *The Origin of the Gods* (Albany, NY: State University of New York Press, 1991).

## Chapter Four

1. *The Odyssey of Homer,* trans. Allen Mandelbaum (Berkeley: University of California Press, 1990), p. 6. Subsequent quotations from the poem will be from this translation and will be noted parenthetically in the text with page numbers.

2. Raymond Adolph Prier, *Thauma Idesthai: The Phenomenology of Sight and Appearance in Archaic Greek* (Tallahassee: The Florida State University Press, 1989), p. 79. Subsequent quotations from this volume will be noted parenthetically with page numbers in the text.

3. Jean-Pierre Vernant and Pierre Vidal-Naquet, *Myth and Tragedy in Ancient Greece,* trans. Janet Lloyd (New York: Zone Books, 1988), p. 46.

4. Sophocles, *Oedipus the King,* trans. Stephen Berg and Diskin Clay (New York: Oxford University Press, 1978), p. 94.